Rev. Richard Hermann
114 Burgundy Circle
West Seneca, NY 14224
716-821-9526

LOVE, HENRI

LOVE, HENRI

LETTERS ON THE SPIRITUAL LIFE

HENRI J. M. NOUWEN

Edited and with a preface by Gabrielle Earnshaw
Foreword by Brené Brown

CONVERGENT
NEW YORK

All rights reserved.
Published in the United States by Convergent Books,
an imprint of the Crown Publishing Group,
a division of Penguin Random House LLC, New York.
crownpublishing.com

CONVERGENT BOOKS is a registered trademark and its
C colophon is a trademark of Penguin Random House LLC.

Library of Congress Cataloging-in-Publication Data is available upon request.

ISBN 978-1-101-90635-4
Ebook ISBN 978-1-101-90636-1

Printed in the United States of America

Book design: Andrea Lau
Jacket design: Jessie Sayward Bright
Jacket photographs: (Nouwen) photo provided by The Topeka Capital-Journal; *(letters)*
courtesy of the Henri Nouwen Legacy Trust

10 9 8 7 6 5 4 3 2 1

First Edition

FOR SUE MOSTELLER

CONTENTS

PREFACE

When Henri Nouwen died in 1996, he left us thirty-nine books and hundreds of articles on the spiritual life and what he called his "adventures with God."* He also bequeathed a treasury of personal papers. The largest part of the cache was correspondence. Over his lifetime Henri received more than 16,000 letters. He kept every postcard, piece of paper, fax and greeting card that arrived in his mail. And he responded to each of them. Managing his correspondence was an integral part of his working day. The sheer volume of mail made it necessary to employ an administrative assistant to sort, preread, and highlight what needed an immediate response. Henri would then read them himself and reply into a Dictaphone for transcription. Letters to close friends were usually handwritten, often on postcards from his large collection of art cards. His penmanship was neat and flowing. He never wrote drafts and rarely made corrections.

Shortly after I started as Henri's archivist in the summer of 2000, I was taken to the attic of a house at L'Arche Daybreak, the community near Toronto where Henri had made his last home. After climbing a steep staircase into an overheated attic, I confronted a dozen or more filing cabinets—tall, short, in a variety of

---

* Letter to Jurjen Beumer, September 5, 1989.

colors—lined up in the middle of the room. Along the walls and in every corner were stacks of boxes. All were filled with letters.

For the next fifteen years, I identified, numbered and catalogued each page in this remarkable collection. It was a daunting task, but one that evolved into a labor of love. The letters now form part of the Henri J. M. Nouwen Archives and Research Collection at the University of St. Michael's College, University of Toronto. Housed in their new acid-free folders and boxes, they extend to sixty-five linear feet!

It has been slow work, but the time has come to share them. This first volume is being released to commemorate the twentieth anniversary of Henri's death in 1996. It celebrates his lasting legacy both to original readers and to a new generation of spiritual seekers. It is a testament to his deep need to connect with others, knowing that in any genuine encounter we are reaching out to the Divine.

Though some of the letters are drawn from his personal archive, most come from the original recipients. In the twenty years since his death, over three thousand letters have been collected from the homes, offices, basements and attics of his correspondents. Although the letters began as an intimate exchange between two people, their power today speaks to Henri's belief that what is most personal—our brokenness, our insecurities, our jagged edges—is most universal.

For Henri, letter writing was an integral part of friendship. In 1996, just months before his death, he recorded in his journal:

This afternoon I wrote many postcards. While writing I experienced a deep love for all the friends I was writing to. My heart was full of gratitude and affection, and I wish I could embrace each of my friends and let them know how much they mean to me and how much I miss them.[*]

---

[*] *Sabbatical Journey: The Diary of His Final Year* (New York: Crossroad, 1998), 73.

He attached great importance to words to reach out across soli-
tudes of experience. "I can't tell you how healing and consoling
your gentle and loving words are to me," he wrote to his friend
Jim.* Words, he felt, had the power to give life and when offered in
friendship could be a source of grace. "Your letter is a real oasis in
my desert," he confided.†

Henri wrote generous and intimate letters. In response to
people seeking his advice he never condemned or judged but instead used stories from his own experience to inspire or teach.
At the same time, he could be challenging, even demanding. He
called his readers to be faithful to choices they had made and
to practice the spiritual disciplines of prayer, community and
solidarity with the poor. He cautioned against the temptations
that pulled people off the "narrow path" and emphasized the
importance of making choices that took the needs of others into
account.

He had a gift for deep listening. After reading a pain-filled letter, he identified the struggle with precision and responded with
compassion. "You have been heard. You are loved. You are not
alone" was the implicit message.

After receiving a letter from Henri on how to care for her dying
mother, a woman wrote back:

> I am so grateful to you for helping me to find and make meaning
> of my journey on earth. . . . My heart is bursting with gratitude for
> the comfort you have provided me during my mother's illness and
> death last month. . . . You gave me insight and courage to stay with
> the pain and wait with her for God. I feel transformed by my expe-
> rience and I want to thank you for helping me to endure her suffer-
> ing, and therefore be with her, really be with her. . . . So you see why
> I feel such community with you? You have helped me to hope in

---

* Letter to Jim Antal, October 30, 1982.

† Ibid.

and not wish for, and I feel I have really learned to be present in the lives of my mother and father, from who I first learned about God.[*]

Henri created a safe place for vulnerabilities because he was honest with his own. "You probably realize," he wrote to a woman struggling with a chronic illness, "that I have no answers for all your questions, but I receive your questions more as an invitation for a relationship between two searching Christians than as a request to be taught."[†]

As I considered what letters to include in this volume, my guiding question was: What do people need to hear right now? The times we live in have changed—there are now email and text messages—fleeting forms of communication; few people put pen to paper anymore—but our human challenges remain the same: loss, sickness, injustice, finding and losing love, discerning a career path, handling conflict, managing our emotions and coping with self-doubt. Yet Henri believed that it is precisely in those struggles that we ultimately find God. It is in the big questions—who is God, and what is the meaning of our life?—that we are drawn to know ourselves better.

Henri's responses to readers are powerful because he drew from his own lived experience. He wrote to a friend:

> *Jesus' invitation to "lay down my life for others" has always meant more to me than physical martyrdom. I have always heard these words as an invitation to make my own life struggles, my doubt, my hopes, my fear and my joys, my pains and my moments of ecstasy available to others as source of consolation and healing. To witness*

---

* Letter from Marca v. O. Piehuta, August 8, 1991 (Henri Nouwen Fonds, Henri J. M. Nouwen Archives and Research Collection, University of St. Michael's College, General Files, 7549).

† Letter to Dr. B.M. Dineke van Kooten, September 6, 1995.

*for Christ means to me to witness for Him what I have seen with my
own eyes, heard with my own ears and touched with my own hands.**

Whereas others hid their vulnerabilities and weakness, Henri
drew on them to form a community of solidarity with his friends
and readers.

The letters in this volume trace twenty-two years in Henri's life
journey—from his time as a teacher to an interlude as a visiting
Trappist monk to his time as a Latin American missionary and
finally to pastor of a community with people with disabilities.
We see that in spite of outward success and popularity, he suffered from what he called "his demons"—loneliness, restlessness,
falls into depression and feelings of rejection. Yet it is how he lived
those lifelong struggles that makes him an inspiring guide for
our own lives. He lived with courage and self-awareness, gradually
learning to befriend his pain and ultimately being redeemed by it.
He knew that the only way out of suffering is through it.

Where did his "demons" come from? His early life was filled
with opportunity and privilege. Even the German wartime occu-
pation of Holland left his family relatively unscathed. He received
his academic education—in theology, philosophy and psychology—
from some of the most eminent teachers in his home country and
the United States. He had a curious mind and an artist's eye.

What troubled him was an inner contradiction on how he was
meant to live his life. As a young man he heard two voices in his
head:

*One voice said, "Henri, be sure you make it on your own, be sure
you can do it yourself, be sure you become an independent person.
Be sure that I can be proud of you." And another voice said, "Henri,
whatever you are going to do, even if you don't do anything very*

---

* Letter to Mark, September 4, 1982.

interesting in the eyes of the world, be sure you stay close to the heart of Jesus, be sure you stay close to the love of God."*

He was torn between the two imperatives of upward and downward mobility. As a Catholic, he experienced it as a struggle between the priorities of his earthly father and his heavenly father. Could he please both? Did he deserve to be loved? His feelings of inadequacy were exacerbated by an unusual degree of emotional sensitivity that left him with little insulation from the abrasions of life. A close friend, Sue Mosteller, CSJ, observed:

He is truly a man whose heart is so open and so vulnerable, so receptive and so giving that our own little hearts feel solidarity and safety when he speaks to us and calls us to grow in like manner. It is the authenticity of his own heart which we recognize, identify with, and hope to imitate.†

He also struggled with intimacy and conflicting feelings about his sexuality. The vocation of celibate priest exacted a heavy price. His desire for a "unique friendship"‡ conflicted with his vow to give his heart only to Jesus. He never publicly acknowledged his homosexuality, deciding that coming out in public would eclipse his larger mission of connecting people with God.§ Nor did he leave the Church, as many of his generation of Catholic clergy

---

* Excerpt from "Journey to L'Arche," *30 Good Minutes,* Chicago Sunday Evening Club, program 3301, first air date October 1, 1989.

† Letter from Sue Mosteller to Annice Callahan, RSCJ, October 16, 1990 (Henri J. M. Nouwen Archives and Research Collection, University of St. Michael's College, accession 2002 33[1]).

‡ *The Road to Daybreak: A Spiritual Journey* (Garden City, NY: Doubleday, 1988), 223.

§ Henri's sexual orientation was made public in 1999 by Michael Ford, a British journalist, in his biography *Wounded Prophet: A Portrait of Henri J. M. Nouwen* (New York: Doubleday).

did. His letters document the painful effort to live out this choice. Toward the end of his life he wrote:

> *My sexuality will remain a great source of suffering to me until I die. I don't think there is any "solution." The pain is truly "mine" and I have to own it. Any "relational solution" will be a disaster. I feel deeply called by God to live my vows well even when it means a lot of pain. But I trust that the pain will be fruitful.*[*]

He never entirely transcended his struggles. In spite of his insights into solitude and silence, busyness dogged him throughout his life. Though often fatigued, he rarely took proper care of himself. For all his ability to listen deeply to people in crisis, he could be impatient with those around him. His longing for human affection and frequent slides into self-rejection made him a needy and demanding friend. However, by the end of his life, he had grown to accept his "unresolvable struggle":[†]

> *I know that I do not need to be ashamed of my needs, that my demons are not really demons but angels in disguise, allowing me to love generously, to be faithful to my friends, to be sensitive to the many forms of human suffering and to live my priesthood with courage and confidence.*[‡]

In his final years, his letters became shorter and lighter. We sense his increasing capacity for "childlike" wonder. To a friend struggling with aging, he wrote:

> *Personally I believe that being an elder can be a real grace. After having seen so much of life and having "made it" in so many ways*

---

[*] Letter to a friend, July 1996 (not included in this volume).

[†] Letter to a friend, July 1996 (not included in this volume).

[‡] Letter to a friend, 1993 (not included in this volume).

*there is still that possibility of growing into a second childhood, a
second naiveté. I think that is quite an exciting possibility and I
pray that God will allow you to be reborn in such a new way of
being.*[*]

Each letter in this volume tells a story. Together they serve as
an inspiration that peace and inner freedom are attainable. Henri
saw our struggles not as "problems" to be overcome but as gateways through which we can learn generosity and tenderness. By
living our struggles well, we move beyond a life of constriction to
a life that is expansive and generative.

Our goal, Henri felt, is to move from the house of fear to the
house of love:

*Hardly a day passes in our lives without our experience of inner
and outer fear, anxieties, apprehensions and preoccupations.
These dark powers have pervaded every part of our world to such
a degree that we can never fully escape them. Still it is possible not
to belong to these powers, not to build our dwelling place among
them, but to choose the house of love as our home. This choice
is made not just once and for all but by living a spiritual life,
praying at all times and thus breathing God's breath. Through
the spiritual life we gradually move from the house of fear to the
house of love.*[†]

As a trained psychologist in the complexities of the human
psyche, Henri unmasks our hidden motives. As a pastor, he calls
us to reach for a higher level that acknowledges the spiritual dimension of life. As a fellow pilgrim, he honors our flawed lives

---

* Letter to Ron, February 20, 1995.

† *Behold the Beauty of the Lord: Praying with Icons* (Notre Dame, IN: Ave Maria Press,
1987), 30–31.

and allows space for our failures and bad choices. His letters have transformed the way I live my own struggles. My hope is that they will do the same for you.

Gabrielle Earnshaw
February 29, 2016
Toronto, Ontario, Canada

FOREWORD

BY BRENÉ BROWN

Dear Henri,

I'll start my letter as you start all of yours—with a note of thanks. I'm deeply grateful for the courageous and vulnerable way you lived, for your ability to show us the sacred in the ordinary, and for your commitment to making holy the irreducible human need for connection.

When asked to write the foreword for this book, I agreed without hesitation. I wish I could say that I did so for generous reasons, but that would be untrue. I've been experiencing a crisis of faith for the past year and when I read the request, I hit reply and responded out of selfish desperation. My offer wasn't about how I could honor you, but how you could help me find my way out of what you might call the spiritual desert.

The irony is that once I had this book in my hands, I couldn't open the manuscript for weeks. In fact, it got to the point where a mere glimpse of the cover would make me anxious. The combination of your words and my need felt too vulnerable to take on. Finally, with the publication clock ticking and the "final-final deadline" looming I began to read your letters.

I have to say that my fear was a bit warranted. Like love itself, your letters are demanding and generous, fierce and tender, and a call for both radical forgiveness and disciplined accountability. My fear slowly melted into hope as I found God and my own struggles with faithfulness alive in every single letter.

I wrestled with how I'd approach writing this piece. The first draft was very much an academic piece written by my "vulnerability researcher" self. This felt safe especially as I started questioning my ability to craft something that would be worthy of this collection. But I didn't want to study you—I wanted to be in connection with you. I don't think you would have liked a removed, disconnected analysis. I think you would have seen right through my fear. Like you, I want to "live vulnerable with the vulnerable."

My truth is that, like most people, I am tired. I struggle with feeling alone and overwhelmed, and I spend an excruciating amount of time analyzing my demons and overcompensating for them rather than simply listening to God, loving God, and loving those around me as God has called me to do. You explain many times and in many ways that the latter is simpler but far more difficult and requires two commitments—listening and time.

I wasn't conducting a covert thematic analysis on these letters but I'm a researcher at heart and if you asked me what major patterns emerged across all of these letters, I would say there are two: 1. Loving and listening to God and, 2. Carving out God-centered time in our lives. In almost every letter—despite the diverse topics and subjects—you call us to make time for listening, prayer, solitude, contemplation and thought.

I understand what you're suggesting, but here's the thing—we have no time. No time for prayer. No time to write letters. No time to be still. No time for connectedness with God. You've only been gone for twenty years, but it's been a really tough two decades when it comes to time. We have email now. And smartphones. And texting. We multitask and schedule quality time with the people we love using calendaring apps.

Listening has also become a challenge. I tell myself that you lived in a quieter place than we do, and I'm not just talking about your time in the monastery. The world is so much louder than it used to be. There's so much yelling. To survive the constant barrage of noise, we've stopped listening. I know it's dangerous but it's also self-protection. The idea of quiet contemplation has become a source of anxiety for many of us. It would require a vigil of discernment—something most of us haven't learned how to do.

The combination of time scarcity and not listening has made being present with God, ourselves, and each other almost impossible.

You wrote, *"We should live in the present where love can touch us."*

When I read this advice in one of your letters, I started crying. That's what I want. That's what we all want and need, every one of us across all of the false divisions of religion, race, gender, orientation, class and country—we all crave the ability to touch love and be touched by love. And now, through these letters, you have reminded us exactly what it's going to take to "live beyond the familiar and to follow Jesus more radically." It's going to mean uncomfortable, messy, wholehearted courage. We must make time and we must listen.

You have asked me if I'm willing to give to God, the people I love, and even the experience of suffering the most precious, unrenewable resource we have—time. My answer is yes. I will make time. For God. For love. For contemplation. For mystery. For justice. And, for the wisdom that pain brings.

You have asked me if I will develop a practice of listening for the wisdom that only silence and prayer can bring. I know I will need help and it will be imperfect, but I'm willing to make the commitment.

I will close my letter the way you close yours, with a promise to pray for you and our shared faithfulness, and a request that you pray for me and continue to lift me up to the presence of God. And, Henri, there's no need to write back. Your timeless words and loving spirit are quiet prayers that will forever live in my heart.

Love,

Brené

A NOTE FROM THE EDITOR

The letters in this volume span a twenty-two-year period from December 29, 1973, to August 4, 1996, just six weeks before Henri died. They are ordered chronologically and have been divided into three parts based on significant themes in his life:

Part I: December 1973–1985
Part II: 1986–1989
Part III: 1990–1996

The majority of letters in this volume were chosen from more than three thousand donated to the Nouwen Archives through the Henri Nouwen Letter Project. Others were selected from Henri's correspondence files. Letters in Dutch and letters to his family were not available for inclusion.

There has been minor editing for clarity and cogency. Some errors of grammar and spelling were corrected while other charming Dutchisms were retained for flavor.

Unless otherwise indicated, quotes from letters in the preface and chapter introductions are from letters included in this volume.

All references to Henri Nouwen works are to first editions.

Most letters in this volume were donated to the Nouwen Archives with permission to publish. Every attempt has been made to contact all people whose letters appear in the book to inform them of its publication. In some cases, as requested, names and other details have been changed to protect privacy.

PERMISSIONS

The publisher gratefully acknowledges the cooperation of the following sources, who provided copies of letters in their collections.

The Fred Rogers Company

Lilly Library, Dan Wakefield papers, Indiana University

Madonna House Archives

Maryknoll Mission Archives

Swarthmore College Peace Collection, Swarthmore College

Special Collections Research Center, James Luther Adams papers, Syracuse University Libraries

LOVE, HENRI

PART I

December 1973–1985

THE LETTERS BEGIN IN late 1973, just weeks before Henri's forty-second birthday. By that time Henri had been a priest for sixteen years. He was teaching at Yale Divinity School, and beginning to emerge as a widely read writer on spirituality. The chapter concludes more than a decade later, in 1985, when—now at Harvard Divinity School—he experienced his first stirrings of attraction to L'Arche and the path he would follow for the rest of his life.

Henri's early life had been one of privilege and opportunity. He had grown up in the Netherlands within a loving and cultured family, traveled extensively, and circulated easily within Holland's important social and intellectual circles. After his ordination in 1957, he was sent to the University of Nijmegen to study psychology. This was followed by a two-year graduate training program in theology and psychiatric theory at the Menninger Foundation in Topeka, Kansas, where he distinguished himself among the leading minds in the emerging disciplines of pastoral psychology and clinical pastoral education.

The time spent at the Menninger Foundation was Henri's first extensive stay in the United States and, as he describes it, the place where he grew up:

It was here that my life came into focus. For the first time I was dealt with as someone who also had something to say. For the first time I

*had to think for myself, and people took what I said critically. There
I came in touch with myself as a separate human being.*[*]

He also became aware of wider political events. He learned of
the civil rights movement and the work of Dr. Martin Luther King,
Jr. He participated in the march from Selma to Montgomery, Alabama, in 1965 and was introduced to the voices of conscientious
objectors to the Vietnam War and anti-nuclear war protestors in
the US peace movement.

His emerging confidence and bold integration of psychology
with pastoral care began to draw attention. After completing the
certificate program in 1966, he was offered a teaching position
in the newly established psychology department at the University
of Notre Dame, Indiana. He accepted, and for two years taught
courses there including "Psychology of Religion," "The Psychology
of Personality," and "Abnormal Psychology."

Henri's ambitions, however, didn't lie in the United States. He
assumed that he would return to Holland and find his place in
Dutch society. He left Notre Dame in 1968, returned home and
taught first at the Amsterdam Joint Pastoral Institute and then
at the Catholic Theological Institute in Utrecht, two new Catholic schools set up to integrate psychology into pastoral education.

Henri became popular with the students, but his "American"
teaching style and focus on the methodologies he had learned at
the Menninger Foundation put him into conflict with colleagues.[†]
It was the first indication that his home was not in fact, to be in

---

* From unpublished interview with Gene Knudsen Hoffman, "Concertmaster of
Souls," The Compassionate Listening Project, 1982, 5, in Gene K. Hoffman Fonds,
Henri J. M. Nouwen Archives and Research Collection, University of St. Michael's
College.

† Author's conversation with Petrus George (Piet) van Hooijdonk, October 10, 2011.
Van Hooijdonk was Henri's supervisor and a fellow priest.

Holland.* He decided to earn a doctorate in theology at the University of Nijmegen, hoping it might add to his credibility, but the tensions only increased.

For his thesis, Henri expanded on research from his time at Menninger. However, his dissertation was found insufficiently theological and he was told to rework it. He tried to submit it for a doctorate in psychology instead, but in that department it was deemed not empirical enough. He became frustrated and restless. An associate from that time describes him as "running out of patience" and feeling like "all was going on in a slow way."†

Meanwhile, American interest in Henri's academic approach was growing. In 1969, he had published his first book, *Intimacy: Pastoral Psychological Essays* (Notre Dame, IN: Fides, 1969), based on a series of lectures he gave at Notre Dame on pastoral care. In it, Henri explored a question that would become central to his life: "How can I find a creative and fulfilling intimacy with God and my fellow human beings?" The book resonated with American readers, who saw his question as their own.

As Henri considered his options for the doctorate, he received an invitation from Yale Divinity School in New Haven, Connecticut, to teach pastoral theology. Impatient with the Dutch academic system, he accepted and by August 1971 was on his way back to the United States. He would never live in Holland again.

When Henri arrived at the Protestant, nondenominational Yale, he was one of only two Catholics on the faculty. But he

---

* This sentiment that he was too American for a European audience was still prevalent in 1996. In his final journal he recorded the words of a friend after a talk to Czech students: "Some students felt you were too American—too much walking around, gesturing and dramatic expression. We are not used to that here. We are more quiet and sedate." He continued, "It is interesting for me, a Dutch man living in Canada, to be considered 'too American.' They should have said, 'You are too Henri Nouwen!'" (Henri J. M. Nouwen, *Sabbatical Journey: The Diary of His Final Year* [New York: Crossroad, 1998], 92).

† Author's conversation with Piet van Hooijdonk, October 10, 2011.

quickly became a popular lecturer, teaching a range of courses on the spiritual life including "Christian Spirituality," "Pastoral Care and Counseling," "Prison Ministry," "Ministry to the Elderly" and "The Life and Works of Thomas Merton." His writing continued apace. By 1974, he had published three more books, including his best seller *The Wounded Healer: Ministry in Contemporary Society* (Garden City, NY: Doubleday, 1972).

He enjoyed the vibrant community life at Yale but soon became restless about his vocational path. He was drawn to the contemplative tradition of the fourth-century Desert Mothers and Fathers and was inspired by the monk and writer Thomas Merton. Over the next few years he made two extended stays in a Trappist monastery in upstate New York to explore that calling.

He also considered a life of action in service to the poor. At the time, Latin America was exploding in violence. Henri was drawn to the plight of the people there and made regular visits to the region. In 1981, after ten good years at Yale, he left his tenured position to become a missionary with the Maryknoll Fathers in a barrio in Lima, Peru.

But neither missionary work nor the life of contemplation proved a good fit. Though he didn't have the temperament for missionary work, he was an impassioned speaker about the spirituality of peacemaking, and in 1983 he went on a ten-week tour of the United States to speak about the injustice he had witnessed in Nicaragua. And though he didn't have the aptitude for the cloistered life, his book *The Genesee Diary: Report from a Trappist Monastery* (Garden City, NY: Doubleday, 1976) was enthusiastically received by many wanting to learn about life in a contemporary monastery.

What was beginning to emerge was that, at his core, Henri was a pastor. Wherever he went, people were drawn to his gifts for ministry and counseling. He began to receive more and more letters asking for help. They came from students, some long graduated, in times of vocational discernment or life-crisis. They came from ministers who had heard him speak and needed support and en-

couragement. Hundreds of requests for advice came from his rap-
idly growing reading audience.

In 1983, after being courted by the Harvard Divinity School to
rejoin academia, Henri decided to continue with his teaching career on a part-time basis. He would teach one semester a year and
continue his work in Latin America for the remaining months.
However, Harvard was another bad fit. His personal, pastoral style
ran up against the competitive culture of the Divinity School. He
wrote of the time: "I had a feeling that Harvard was not where God
wanted me to be. It's too much podium, too much publicity, too
public. Too many people came to listen.... It's not an intimate
place. It's a place of intellectual battle."* He became increasingly
lonely and depressed.

In this time of doubt, Henri received an invitation from Jean
Vanier, a Canadian who in 1964 had started a community for people with physical and mental disabilities. Vanier invited Henri to
visit L'Arche in Trosly-Breuil, a small village north of Paris. Henri
visited L'Arche several times between 1982 and 1985, staying for
longer intervals each time.

Vanier saw Henri as a deeply spiritual man with many gifts,
but also one who needed a home. L'Arche became that home. In
July 1985, Henri resigned from Harvard and took up a one-year
residency at L'Arche à Trosly beginning in August. He had finally
found his vocational path.

*In this first letter, Henri writes from Holland, where he is visiting his fam-
ily before beginning a sabbatical. It is four days after Christmas, 1973. He
is still unclear about where he will work and live in the coming years. He*

---

* *The Road to Peace: Writings on Peace and Justice*, ed. John Dear (Maryknoll, NY: Orbis,
1998), 153.

*has received permission from his bishop to remain in the United States, but
as he does not have tenure, he is keeping his options open to returning to
Holland.*

*Henri plans to use his sabbatical to explore a monastic vocation in the
Abbey of the Genesee in upstate New York. His interest in monasticism
began in the 1960s with his discovery of the life and work of Thomas Merton (1915–1968), a Trappist monk and writer.**

*Henri writes to his friends Claude Pomerleau and Don McNeill, two
American Holy Cross priests who attended his class on "Pastoral Care" at
Notre Dame University in 1967. Pomerleau and McNeill would remain
lifelong friends.*

DECEMBER 29, 1973

Dear Don and Claude,

Happy times, Blessed Christmas and a very good new year. I hope
that all the misery in the country and the world in general will
deepen your hope for the kingdom of God, will strengthen your
eschatological perspective, will make you more interested in the
last book of the Bible, will make you more critical toward psychology and political sciences, will make you simple of mind and
heart, make you pray more and love more and make your heart
and mind open toward Him who is the Lord of life and who calls
us to transcend all human endeavors.

In Holland the mood is sentimental, romantic, nostalgic and
full of tears. T.V., books and entertainment make us think back
to the happy years gone by and students who were sarcastic and
distant do not hesitate to cry in your arms and show their great
need for affection. Quite a challenge again for theology! In general, the Church is still in the "critical mood" and therefore does

---

* Henri's second book, published in 1970 after *Intimacy: Pastoral Psychological Essays*
(Notre Dame, IN: Fides, 1969), was a biography of Merton, *Bidden om het Leven: Het
Contemplatief Engagement van Thomas Merton* (Bilthoven, Netherlands: Ambo, 1970). It
was published in English as *Pray to Live: Thomas Merton: A Contemplative Critic* (Notre
Dame, IN: Fides, 1972).

not seem to realize the great need for home, for candles, for statues, for incense and for all the things which helped us in the past to feel close to God and to each other. I do not say that we should go back to the early days but we definitively should respond to this enormous need and show God again as a loving, caring, gentle God under whose wings we can find refuge. I am less and less clear what is good or bad religion, what is regressive or progressive, but I am more and more convinced how important it is to respond to real needs and to prevent ourselves from narrowing God to one or two images. I also feel that there is not too much difference between Holland and the States and that we would do well to think what pastoral care for nostalgic people means. After all, don't we all desire to return to paradise? The good old times when we could play naked in the garden?

Dear friends, my thoughts are with you a lot and we should deepen, strengthen and broaden our friendship in the future. I love you very much and we need to do everything to stay together while the moods of the time change and we see the world turn and lead us to our graves slowly but surely. I often desire to die since that seems so quiet and restful and without busy things. But then again, I know that I am not ready yet, too attached, too concerned, too pre-occupied and too serious about the knowledge of God, as if I ever could know him.

My plans? Well, I talked to the Cardinal [Bernardus Alfrink, archbishop of Utrecht, Nouwen's bishop], with my friends in the priesthood, with students, etc. etc. and I feel that I should return to the States and not to Holland. It is quite possible that I will be invited to stay at Yale and at this moment that seems a good invitation to accept.* I have my doubts but they are not strong enough. I very much look forward to my stay in [the Abbey of the] Genesee and I have no idea where that will lead me. I am wondering now if half a year is long enough and I have to think about maybe a

---

* Henri would receive tenure later in the year.

longer stay. But Colin Williams [the dean of Yale Divinity School] wants me back in 1975. But maybe I have to convince him that it is better for me to stay longer there or somewhere else. At this moment everything is still up in the air. I first need to be reappointed and then I will be ready to make definitive plans with John Eudes [Bamberger, abbot of the Abbey of the Genesee]. So consider it as a confidential for the time being.

I hope you had a good Christmas and will have a very good time coming up. I have to see you both soon again and I hope that I can make it to South Bend [the location of Notre Dame University] soon.

I will fly back to New York on the 7th of January. I need to prepare courses ("On Care" and "On Prisoners"), and I want to write more in the coming months.

Please send my best wishes to friends, family and all the good people you and I know.

Love,
Henri

Henri offers two letters of consolation to the parents of Beth Canning, a twenty-three-year-old jockey who died in a horse-racing accident in Idaho.

Both letters are written from the Abbey of the Genesee, where less than two weeks earlier Henri started a seven-month stay as a temporary monk.

JUNE 9, 1974

Dear Mr. and Mrs. Healey,

Your visit in New Haven meant very much to me. I cannot express how glad I was that you came to see me and how happy I am that I got to know you. I regretted it very much that I was not able to come to Topsfield [Massachusetts] after Bob had called me and therefore it was like a special blessing that you came to see me just a few hours before I left to this monastery.

As I already told you, Beth meant very much to me. We had some very meaningful conversations when she was in Holland, and ever since we felt close.* I regretted it very much that Beth could only come once to the divinity school and that her many travels prevented her from coming more often. But even without much writing or visiting Beth was often in my thoughts and I had a great sympathy for her independent, original and very sensitive personality. It often seems to me that she had a sixth sense which enabled her to "feel" people and animals in a very special way.

I remember very well how she told me about the world of horses and horseracing and I became growingly aware how courageous she was to find her own way in this tough and very competitive world.

Beth also had a great sensitivity for the deeper questions in life, and although she didn't feel at home in church she was a very religious woman with a deep sense of the mysteriousness of life. I personally feel a deep loss by her death. She gave me much, just by her kindness and by opening aspects of life to me which were new for me, and I feel very sad and pained that I can no longer listen to her and share ideas with her.

I am very much aware how hard these days, weeks and months must be for you. She is gone from you and you will miss her painfully. But I hope that you can find comfort and consolation in the awareness that she has meant so much to her friends. The value of life is not in the amount of years but in the intensity and fullness with which it is lived. Beth lived a very intense and full life.

Personally I have a strong belief that there is much more to life than we can see and that, although Beth has died, she also has entered into a new life in which her best self continues to exist in

---

* Henri may have met Beth through his brother Paul, who had a keen interest in horse racing.

the love of God. Sometimes it even seems to me that a special deep
and even grateful communication can exist between us and those
we loved so much and left us. Jesus said: "It is good for you that
I leave, so that I can send my Spirit." I think that anyone who we
love send us his or her spirit when they die. I am convinced that
in a very deep sense Beth remains with us, not just in our memory
but also in our life with each other.

When I celebrate Mass I pray for Beth every day and all the
Trappist Monks pray with me for her. I hope that in these hours
of grief and mourning, you can also have a moment of gratefulness, that this beautiful woman was such an intimate part of your
life. Even those who are most close to us are only like guests who
enter into our homes but leave it again to follow their own often
mysterious way. Even children are guests who have to let go when
the time has come. This is very hard and painful, but don't forget
to be grateful for the moments they were with us.

I have not yet been able to find the best words to engrave on
the communion plate, but I will write you soon about it. I am very
grateful for this beautiful gesture. With this plate Beth will always
be very close to all I do as a priest.

With many thanks again for your kindness and precious visit.

Sincerely yours,
Henri J. M. Nouwen

AUGUST 2, 1974

Dear Mrs. Healey,

Many thanks for your very kind letter. I was very happy to hear
from you again. I realize that Beth's death will remain a source of
deep grief and much pain for you. Few people will probably fully

understand what it means to lose your own child. It is a very deep and very intimate pain and in a certain sense you have to die with her to find new life and new hope for yourself.

Jesus said: "If the grain of wheat dies, it produces much fruit." I think that you are realizing this too, that you feel the death of Beth hurting you deeply but also that her death can bring many fruits to you and other people. We have to go through the pain and the grief to realize this, but this is the mystery of our life and of our faith. When Jesus spoke about his own death he said to his disciples: "Did not the Messiah have to undergo all this, so as to enter into his glory?" I think that he tells us that this is also true for us. We have to suffer to enter into glory. I believe that Beth's death has made us suffer but also can make us already now sense some of the glory that is promised to them who accept their pain.

This is also the meaning of the Eucharist, the Holy Communion. We eat bread made from crushed grain to realize that we enter into new life by participating in the suffering and death of Jesus.

Maybe you would like to use these words for the communion plate:

> *"If the grain of wheat dies*
> *It produces much fruit."*

In memory of Beth Canning, September 16, 1950–May 25, 1974

The text is from the Gospel of St. John (Chapter 12, verse 24).

I think this is a beautiful text since it brings Beth's life in deep contact with the life of Christ and with our lives, and it also expresses the deep meaning of the Holy Communion. But if you have other ideas or feelings about this just feel free to let me know.

We pray here often for Beth and she is often in my thoughts. I also pray for you and your family that Beth's death will not only bring you grief but also new hope.

Meanwhile my life here goes well. I am grateful for the

opportunity to live a contemplative life with the Trappists for a few months and so deepen my own life and vocation.

With many greetings to your husband and all the members of your family, especially to Beth's sisters Carol and Jane.

> Wishing you much hope, courage and confidence,
> Yours,
> Henri

❀

The letter is written to his friend Richard, an American historian and human rights activist in Central and Latin America. Henri writes from the Abbey of the Genesee.

SEPTEMBER 1, 1974

Dear Richard,

Months go fast here and I can hardly believe that the summer is already coming to an end. I often thought about you and wondered how you are doing, how your back is, how your dissertation is going and how the summer has been for you. I hope that you are in good health and good spirits and that you have some good plans for the coming year.

My life here has been very good. Better than I even expected. So many things have happened to me interiorly that it would take a book to write about. But the distance from my little world (no horse to ride upon!) and the continuing silence of the monastic life have opened deep feelings in me and have given me a renewed sense of life. The early hours, the manual work (in the bakery and in the fields), the many hours for prayer and meditation, the chance to read, study and write without interruptions and the very good spiritual guidance by a strict but very competent guide (John

Eudes Bamberger) have made the stay a unique experience. I do not think it would have had the same meaning for me if I had done this twenty years ago, but after my life in Holland and the U.S.A. this retreat really offers a chance to stop and ask, "What did I do until now and where do I want to go?" I read much early Christian literature from the 2nd-3rd century and also much from the 12th century, the time in which the Cistercians (Trappists) developed their life style. It all has been very revealing to me and made me aware that being a priest is what I really want to be in an authentic way and that in the deepening and strengthening of that vocation I find real power and joy. I have had a chance to read the Bible better and deeper than before and am constantly overwhelmed by its revealing nature. The continuing silence brought me back to very basic convictions and ideas and made me experience the presence of God in my life much more directly than before.

Meanwhile I feel that it is good for me to get physically exhausted once in a while. Collecting granite rocks in the riverbed is hard and backbreaking work, but it is a side of life that most people feel daily but what for me had never been very close.

Originally I had no plans to write, but the many experiences urge me to write in order to sort out many feelings and I feel that it is good to express as well as I can the ideas and feelings as they come and go.*

Because of the distance from my little New Haven world I feel more in touch with things going on in Chile, Cyprus, North Africa and many other areas of conflict, oppression and famine. Claude [Pomerleau] and Don [McNeill] were in Chile and wrote me about their impressions and had some first-hand information about the oppression there, and the White Fathers who work in the Sahel area send news about the relief work there. The monks here do a lot

---

* His notes were eventually published as *Genesee Diary: Report from a Trappist Monastery* (Garden City, NY: Doubleday, 1976).

to help within their limitations. Also the situation of the Buddhist monks in South Vietnam is very much on people's minds here.

Merton keeps fascinating me and I read new things by him which are truly remarkable. I think I will teach another Merton course when I am back at Yale.[*]

Well, there are so many things I could write about, that it seems hopeless to give it a start. Just know that you are a lot in my thoughts and prayer and that I very much hope to hear from you.

Yours with love,
Henri

Jim Antal, a United Church of Christ minister, had been Henri's student and teaching assistant at Yale. He and his wife Cindy Shannon became good friends of Henri, and their vibrant and close friendship over two decades was marked by many visits and a regular exchange of letters about ministry, social action, and quotidian details of their lives.

In this first letter of many letters in this volume to Jim (and later to Jim and Cindy), Henri responds to his younger friend's struggles with busyness as a Divinity School student.

Henri is in his six month as a temporary Trappist at the Abbey of the Genessee.

NOVEMBER 7, 1974

Dear Jim,

Many thanks for your very good letter. I was happy to hear from you and read about the "too much," which is a joy and a burden at the same time. I know what you are talking about!

Be sure to keep your priorities straight. You are in school

---

[*] Henri taught three courses on Merton at Yale.

to study and to have a chance for a real concentration on "no-emergency" issues. That is what school is all about. In order to live a hospitable life—not just a hospitable year—you need a lot of time for yourself to read, to write, to study, to meditate, to pray, to just be alone. If you do not claim that for yourself, you are not hospitable enough because you do not create the quiet restful place where people can find healing.

Sometimes this requires that you are very clear-cut in your decision, the way you spend time, the parties you go to, etc. etc. But never forget that the majority of your time—during this period of your life—should be for reflection. If you can't get it at Y.D.S. [Yale Divinity School] take off for a few days regularly to be just by yourself.

Go to the Mercy Center (Madison, Connecticut) or a similar place alone or with a friend and just read, study, meditate and pray. An exhausted, irritable host will never be able to give what the guest is looking for!

And don't forget the early hours. Between 5 and 9 a.m. people tend to leave you alone! Somewhere you have to make a few clear-cut decisions; let your friends know about it and stick to it. In that way you mean a lot for them simply by showing that you try to live from the center and so encourage others to try the same.

Meanwhile I keep enjoying my life here very much. Many good experiences. Time for prayer, for study, for reading, for writing and a real atmosphere of brotherly love. It is indeed as the fathers say: Life is like a wheel. God is the hub. By focusing on the hub of life you come closer to God. The closer you come to the center, the closer you also come to each other. Everyone travels on a different spoke, but as long as we travel to God we travel to each other. What about that image for a bike specialist?!

> Wishing you many blessings,
> Love,
> Henri

✢

In January 1975, after seven months at the Abbey of the Genesee, Henri
returned to Yale Divinity School to teach.

In the fall of 1975, at the invitation of Reverend Edwin Beers, Henri
spoke in Madison, Wisconsin. Beers wrote to thank Henri for his talk and
asked if his schedule had been too much.

OCTOBER 8, 1975

Dear Ed,

Many thanks for your very kind letter. I really appreciated the time
you took to write me and to let me know that something good had
happened.

I have good memories of my stay. I very much appreciated your
kind hospitality and the gentleness and kindness of all the people
on the staff.

Was the schedule too much? Yes it was. I felt that you all had
been able to squeeze out of me in a few hours all that was in me
at the time. I felt totally exhausted, very tired and absolutely emptied out. I think that very few people realize what happens inside
of a person when he tries to speak in a creative way to 500 people.
Something happens in a dialogue between one and 500! Next
morning I was in Kansas City talking to 1700. I tried very hard
to overcome my fatigue and did it, unconsciously, with my body.
The interesting result you can read in the *National Catholic Reporter*,
where I was described as a dancer!

But don't feel guilty about any of this. I just tell you this as a
friend. It was a good fatigue, a good emptiness and a good exhaustion. I did not feel angry or anything like that. In fact I felt grateful to you and all the kind people. But I also realized that this
should not happen too often and that I am responsible to indicate
my own limits.

Meanwhile many other things took place in my little life. I

went to Cincinnati for the religious conference and gave a retreat at Union Theological Seminary and spoke at Mount Clair. Next week I have to go to Spokane, Washington. As you see, I have to keep struggling to stay home more and be more of a quiet person. But it is a good struggle to have.

Yours,
Henri

Mary Ellen Neill met Henri through a mutual friend, Fr. Don McNeill, shortly after moving to New Haven. She and her husband, Dr. Thomas Kerby Neill, maintained a friendship with Henri for many years after moving from New Haven to Kentucky in 1974.

Henri writes to them after the death of Mary Ellen's father.

FEBRUARY 15, 1976

Dear Mary Ellen and Kerby,

Daphne wrote me about the death of your father. She wrote me about your great care for your father and about the requiem Mass in which you both participated so personally. My parents are still both alive and I find it even hard to imagine that one day I might have to bury my father too. I realize how deep the death of a parent touches us. We suddenly realize that some of the most intimate ties are broken and that we are called to let our parents move away from us and take their place in history.

And still I also believe that your father's absence might lead to the awareness of a new presence. Lately I have found much comfort in the words of Jesus: "It is for your good that I leave, because unless I leave my Spirit cannot come." Jesus' leaving meant that he would become more intimately present to us, that he would unite himself in a new way with us. Because of his death we can say:

"Not I live but Christ lives in me." I have a feeling that this is not just true of Jesus, but in and through Jesus of all people who leave us. In their absence we can develop a new intimacy with them and grow. We even can become more like them and fulfill their mission in life until the day comes that we too have to leave so that our spirit can stay with those we love. In this way mourning can slowly turn into joy, and grief into rebirth. I hope and pray that the Lord will strengthen you in this time of pain and will bring you closer to each other. I also pray for your mother in this difficult time. Tonight in the liturgy I will especially pray for your father and all he left behind but not alone.

In love,
Henri

Henri responds to his friend Jim Antal's struggles with faithfulness, questions of where to put his energies and spiritual dryness.
He writes from his family's vacation home in Losone, Switzerland.

MAY 30, 1976

Dear Jim,

Many thanks for your very kind letter. I was very glad that you wrote and I read and reread your letter with much gratitude. Thanks for all you write about yourself, me and both of us.

Let me start with disagreeing with you! I do not think that the life of Faithfulness in response to God is a very complex affair. I believe that it is very simple affair and therefore so very hard! Maybe this is not much more than a play with words, but still it can help me express myself better to you. A simple-minded, simple-eyed commitment to God is all that counts. Maybe we have become—especially in academics—so addicted to analysis, to sorting out the many elements of the problems we and others have, that we lose sight of the "Unum Necessarium." Therefore I also enjoy disagreeing with you when you say: "Naming the demons is the initial and greatest chore." I don't think so. The first and most important task we have is to keep our eyes on God and Him alone. We will never overcome the demons by analyzing them, but only by forgetting them in an all-consuming love for God. God is simple, demons are complex. Demons like to be analyzed, because that keeps our attention directed to them. God wants to be loved. I am more and more convinced that the first commandment indeed needs to be the first: to love God with all our heart, all our soul and our entire mind. Our heart, soul and mind can never be divided between God and neighbor or anything else. God is a jealous God who wants our love without any reservations. But in our total undivided commitment to God we will find that God is the God of our neighbor and of all our concerns and that in him we can embrace all the complexities of the world. This, as you and I know, is very simple but very hard.

I write you all this because your letter told me that you are spiritually tired, feel a certain loss of vitality and spontaneity and suffer from a narrowing down of perspective. Well I share a lot of that with you. My Genesee diary might have given you a glimpse of that. My only fear is that you will fight your fight on the wrong front. Don't spend too much energy fighting demons, but give all you have to God. There is no other way in finding where to go, what to do, and how to understand your pains.

My personal feeling is that you are at the right place doing the right things and that it would be a temptation to quit. I might be wrong but this is my personal feeling. Your intuitions are so right and your basic orientation so valuable that a PhD might in the long run offer you the best frame to put your own painting in.

But you need a spiritual discipline. You need a lot of time to pray, to spend time in solitude and to speak regularly about your love for God, and God's love for you. Once you take this route life will certainly not become easier but it will be a lot more real and a lot more vital. Nurture your contemplative side, be in a constant conversation (conversatio) with Him, who loves you most intimately, and let yourself be swept off your feet in that great encounter. Don't worry too much about Yoga or fasting. They might be helpful, they might not. They might even prove to be somewhat of a distraction. You will soon know.

I wished that you could spend a good amount of time in a place where you can do nothing else than pray. Pray with words, songs, silence, or just pray by being here and now. Maybe you can go to an abbey or a monastery for that purpose. I love to help you find a good place. But it seems important that at some point you take time out for God and God alone so that after that you will have an inner sensitivity to the spiritual life which will also help you a lot in your studies.

Well, I hope some of this makes any sense to you and can give you some hope and confidence. Meanwhile I am spending time in Switzerland with my parents and I enjoy the time for reading, writing and prayer. No phone calls, no running around, no big religious gestures to anyone. Just long beautiful days in which I am trying to make reading, writing and prayer just one thing.

Please send my best wishes to all common friends and be sure that you are in my prayers and thoughts. I very much am grateful for your warm friendship and I will do anything and everything to deepen and sustain it. Your friendship means a lot to me.

With love,
Henri

This is the first letter of several in this volume to Reverend C. Leland Udell, an Episcopal priest, clinical pastoral education supervisor and hospital chaplain. Henri was Udell's spiritual director for fifteen years, beginning

*in 1981. In this letter Henri responds to Udell on a number of pastoral sub-
jects, including the supervision of chaplains of differing faiths and questions
about the charismatic movement.*

*Henri is writing from the Institute for Ecumenical and Cultural Re-
search in Collegeville, Minnesota, where he is teaching during the fall semester. This is a center of scholarly research for Protestant, Catholic and
Orthodox theology, grounded in a Benedictine rhythm of worship and
work in community.*

SEPTEMBER 27, 1976

Dear Lee,

Many thanks for your good letter. I was very happy to hear from
you again. I appreciate your taking the time to write. I look forward
to meeting you again in Detroit. I am struggling hard with the lectures which I have to give in Detroit. Your remarks were, therefore,
especially important for me. I am more and more convinced that
there is not such a thing as an uncommitted ministry. As Christian ministers we are called to speak and act in the name of Jesus
Christ. If we do not do that and become neutral enablers, I think
that we betray our vocation. I feel that this is true for supervisors
as well as for parish ministers and hospital chaplains. Therefore,
I think that we can only help a Buddhist and a Jew when they (the
Buddhist and the Jew) accept us as Christian ministers and allow
us to speak to them from this perspective with the expectation
that we respect and fully acknowledge their point of view. I do not
know if this can work out in practice. My first inclination is to say
that real in-depth supervision asks for a mutual sharing of our
faith and that we should wonder if we really can supervise people
from a tradition in which Christ does not play a central role. If the
student can no longer discuss his personal relationship with Jesus
Christ with his supervisor, I think that no pastoral supervision
can take place. Witness is and remains the central mode of ministry (1 John 1:1-3). If you have any more ideas about this, please let
me know. It would be a great help in the preparation of my talks.

I am happy that you find strength in the charismatic movement. I am also happy that you remain critical toward it. I believe that we all need the baptism of the Holy Spirit, but I do not believe that the charismatic way is the only way. In fact, I feel that God sends his Spirit to us in just as many ways as there are people, and I feel that any exclusive claim on God's way to send his Spirit is dangerous and sectarian. I appreciate many aspects of the charismatic movement, especially with its renewed emphasis on prayer and its deep faith in the strength of God's Spirit. But any form of elitism or exclusivism I find questionable. It is the Incarnate Christ who sends his Spirit. Therefore, it remains true that the Spirit of God reveals itself in the continuing incarnation of God in human history. Doctors, psychologists, therapists, all can be part of this continuing incarnation and so the instrument of God's Spirit. I also believe that God does not depend on doctors, etc. to do his healing work and that, therefore, a certain direct experience of God's healing is quite possible although exceptional. I find it very dangerous to look at the healing professions as competitors of God. From your letter I gather that you think about the same as I do.

I hope you keep some quiet time every day to be with God and him alone. A daily time for silent prayer will do you a lot of good. Sometimes the reading of a few psalms or another biblical reading is the best preparation for the quiet time. Always end with a personal prayer and an Our Father. I hope you can keep faithful to some type of discipline in this way.

Best wishes,
Yours,
Henri

In September 1978, Henri's parents visited him at Yale. Almost immediately, the trip was cut short when his mother fell ill. Upon return to Holland, it was discovered she had pancreatic cancer. Henri's mother died on October 9, 1978. This letter is written within weeks of her death and captures Henri's raw feelings of grief. Although he shares that he is not ready to write about his mother's death, he did eventually publish two short books on the subject, In Memoriam *(Notre Dame, IN: Ave Maria Press, 1980)* and A Letter of Consolation *(San Francisco: Harper and Row, 1982).*

The letter is written to Jim Forest, a cofounder of the Catholic Peace Fellowship, and at this time general secretary of the International Fellowship of Reconciliation. Their friendship began after Henri invited Jim as a guest lecturer to one of his classes.

OCTOBER 25, 1978

Dear Jim,

A few days ago I returned from Holland, where I buried my mother. Only five weeks ago she was with me in New Haven. She returned four days afterwards with my Father after the internist had discovered a tumor which caused the jaundice. Two weeks later she was operated on, a week after that she died. I am still in a daze. Everything seems different to me and I am slowly rediscovering the world which she loved so much. She has been so much part of my life that I have to do some real relearning. I am spending a still week at a retreat center trying to let my mother's death reform me and lead me to new fields. It is all very intimate and very deep, very sad and very joyful, very beautiful and very painful. I am trying to write a little bit about these last few weeks, but I am still too close to all that has happened to do it well and with the necessary peace of mind. But I keep trying. It seems at this moment my way of letting her spirit come to me. I am still somewhere between Easter and Pentecost not knowing what really has happened. Keep me in your prayers and pray for her. Nobody has ever been as close to me as she was and never did I lose anyone whom I loved so deeply. Somewhere life needs to be rediscovered. But I am sure that her death will mean many new births for me.

Best wishes,

Love,

Henri

John Garvey, who converted from Catholicism to the Orthodox Church and was ordained as a priest in the Orthodox Church of America in 1992, was a longtime friend of Henri. They met in 1966 at the University of Notre Dame and exchanged letters, ideas and experiences for the next thirty years. Garvey, a regular columnist for Commonweal, *wrote on many aspects of the Orthodox tradition, including celibacy and married priests. In 1988, Garvey edited the first anthology of Nouwen's writings, entitled* Circles of Love: Daily Readings with Henri J. M. Nouwen *(Springfield, IL: Templegate, 1988).*

DECEMBER 20, 1978

Dear John,

Your article on Celibacy is excellent. I very much feel on your wavelength. You say very important things and I believe that your approach is necessary to express the meaning of this life choice. If I have any remarks it is that I hope that you keep working on the positive side of it. I felt that your treatment of Celibacy as an affirmation that God alone is enough could have been worked on a little more. You are very good in "unmasking" the false or weak arguments for celibacy. And that needs to be done, but I hope that you will keep working on the Love which celibacy reveals. I am more and more overwhelmed by the degree to which our "religious" world has been psychologized. It seems as if we have forgotten to raise spiritual questions and go beyond worldly justification. This also is true for marriage. It is no surprise that the crisis in marriage and the crisis in celibacy go hand in hand. I therefore am very "excited" (what a worldly term!) about your interest in the Eastern Churches. Anthony Bloom and Timothy Ware have a lot to offer and they are pointing us in very important directions. I hope we will have more opportunity to share ideas about this.

Many good wishes for Christmas to you, to Regina and the little one.

Peace,
Henri

Peter G. Ladley was a student in Henri's class on Thomas Merton in the spring semester of 1976. Henri first connected with Ladley in April 1975 during a Catholic Worker meeting, at which Henri was speaking.

At the time of this letter, Ladley was working as campus minister at various campuses and wondering if he should put his energies in the front lines of peace and social justice movements.

Henri writes to Peter and his wife, Pat, cautioning Peter against making a decision to quit his work.

AUGUST 29, 1978

Dear Peter and Pat,

Many thanks for your very good letter. It was good to hear from you again. Many thanks for the lovely pictures which you sent me, and also many congratulations on the new expectation in your life. It must be great to look forward to this guest in the family.

I appreciate very much your sharing your experiences and feelings about your work. It is hard for me to respond helpfully from such a distance, but my first inclination is to encourage you in your work which you have started. It seems you are in a spot which is hard, but which has many, many opportunities, and there are indeed people there who need your presence, your encouragement, your insights, and most of all, your deep religious commitment.

I have a feeling that in the future you will be called to other places and to other types of work, but it seems that a few years in this desert might in fact be a good preparation for the more involved type of ministry. I realize that the loneliness and the lack of creative relationships that you are experiencing are difficult, but I have the sense that together you can make your life and work in Wheeling an important experience, and also one that will deepen your own spiritual life.

Be sure to be very faithful to a regular prayer life, to spend a lot of time in reading and to stay in good contact with friends whom you trust. I am sure that after a while it will become clear where God is calling you, but my first response to your letter is that right now he calls you to be just where you are. While this is just a first response and might not be all that you might want, always feel free to give me a call, collect, to my home, after September 4th, and maybe we can have a chance to talk a little more about it.

Be sure of my constant prayers and love for you. I am looking forward very much to the opportunity to see you in October. Best wishes to you both.

Yours,
Henri

John Mogabgab was Henri's teaching and research assistant for five years during the 1970s while Henri taught at Yale. During that time he edited several of Henri's books and they forged a lifelong friendship. At Yale they

cotaught a course on Hesychasm and the spirituality of the early Desert
Mothers and Fathers.† This was the subject of Henri's book* The Way of
the Heart: Desert Spirituality and Contemporary Ministry *(New
York: Seabury Press, 1981), which he dedicated to Mogabgab. In this letter, written while on his second extended stay in the Abbey of the Genesee,
Henri describes his inner state as he moves from a life of action as a university professor to a monastic life of contemplation. Even in the monastery,
concerns about his outside commitments continue to distract him.*

FEBRUARY 27, 1979

Dear John,

My first week in the Abbey is already past. It has been a good time,
but not easy. It has been a time to try to adapt myself to the new
life and to deal creatively with the silence and the daily rhythm.
The life is very beautiful but my mind was still so loaded with old
stuff and old concerns that it was not always easy to fully enter
into the new world. I guess it will take me a while to fully enter
into the world of prayer and contemplation. I very much desire to
do so and I realize how my life during the last years has been filled
with many things which do not lead to contemplation. After all
the talk and writing about spirituality it is time for me to try to
live a spiritual life. And as you know this is quite demanding.

I have been reading the book of Bouyer [Louis Bouyer, *A History
of Christian Spirituality* (New York: Desclee Co., c1963)] which you
gave me for my birthday. It is really excellent. I am reading every
day a chapter and try to summarize it as well as I can. It gives the
ideal background for our course on hesychasm. The next two volumes I also plan to read since they contain large parts on Orthodox Spirituality in the Middle Ages and in modern times.

---

* Hesychasm is a mystical prayer tradition in the Eastern Orthodox Church.

† The Desert Mothers and Fathers were early Christian hermits, ascetics and monks
who lived mainly in the Scetes Desert of Egypt beginning around the third century
AD. The model of Christian monasticism grew out of the informal gathering of
monks into desert communities.

I hope things are going well at the office. I wrote a list with little things for Jane [Bouvier, one of Henri's assistants] which I kept thinking about. A few things you might be willing to take care of. Meanwhile I hope that you can give *In Memoriam* [Henri's book of reflections about his mother's death, published by Ave Maria Press in 1980] a priority. I very much would like to work on it soon. I hope you can have it retyped and then send to me. I still do not feel ready to work on the compassion manuscript.* That probably has to wait a while. I feel strongly that I have to really feel ready for it and not just force myself to finish it. Especially since I want to write about Christ, I want to be able to write from "within." And in order to do so I feel I need more time and rest and more "inner readiness." I hope that I will get there. Meanwhile you might be able to collect all the notes on the manuscript. I forgot to take them with me. But there must be a letter by John Breslin about the manuscript with concrete suggestions. Also there must be notes you and I made during our discussions in September. Please send them to me so I have all I need to start when I am ready.

I am planning to make a list of literature for the hesychasm course. But that will take a while. I first want to read the Bouyer books since they give me a better grasp on what is important and what is not.

I hope and pray that this is going to be a good semester for you with much quiet time for study and writing and also a little more tranquil than last semester. The more I think about it the more I realize what a restless hectic and unnatural life we live at Y.D.S. [Yale Divinity School]. I hope that in some way or another we can make the coming year less restless and more contemplative. Certainly when we want to teach on hesychasm!

Thanks again for all the help you have given me in the last se-

---

* Henri was working on a book about compassion with Donald P. McNeill and Douglas A. Morrison. It would be published as *Compassion: A Reflection on the Christian Life* (Garden City, NY: Doubleday, 1982).

mester. Your constant friendship and support mean very much to
me and fill me with immense gratitude.

> May God bless you and give you peace,
> Yours,
> Henri

In a letter to his friends Lee and Sue Udell, Henri writes from the Abbey of
the Genesee, offering advice on how to live in the midst of suffering. Udell is
having eye problems as his wife struggles with a serious illness.

JUNE 2, 1979

Dear Lee and Sue,

Many thanks for your letter. It was really good to hear from you
again even though you had to tell me many painful things. I often
had been thinking about you and wondering about many things—
spiritual and mental and physical!—so your letter was indeed a
happy surprise.

Can I say anything helpful? I don't know. What came to my
mind when I prayed for both of you was that I should advise you to
pray for others more than for yourself. In some way I had the sense
that many things will become clear to you when you direct your
prayers to the needs of your friends, the needs of your enemies,
the needs of the city, the country and the world. It might be possible that the Lord will give you new insights and feelings which
you will not be able to receive when you concentrate primarily on
your own healing. On the other hand ask others to pray for you. I
will pray especially for both of you in the coming weeks and will
ask the monks to join me in this prayer. It is important for you to
have a real sense of being held up to the Lord by others. We here
in the monastery think about you, pray for you and ask the Lord

that he will bring you healing insight and most of all, hope and confidence.

We all want to be of service, but it is very hard to be a servant when we realize that that implies that we cannot determine the nature of our service ourselves. It seems very important for both of you to keep holding on to the conviction that the Lord loves you, that He is active in your lives here and now and that the many pains you are struggling with are not outside of His knowledge or care. Somewhere He is doing something lovingly to you, even when what you experience is only hurt. Is He carving out a cave to dwell in? If so, the cutting away of rocks might hurt very much and you might not be aware of the space He is creating for Himself.

Finally, think about compassion. Compassion with the Lord. St. Francis of Assisi saw compassion as a suffering with the Lord. Only in a secondary sense he considered compassion as a suffering with other people. That explains why he was given the stigmata. That was a sign of the intimate way he was united with the suffering of Christ and a sign of his call to fill up what is lacking in the suffering of Christ for the sake of His body the Church (Col. 1, 24). Just reflect on this in your quiet time of meditation. The Lord will not leave you without understanding. But keep taking time for Him and Him alone.

I very much hope that we can meet again. I am sure that we will see each other in the near future. It would be good to stay in touch, so that we can be of support to each other in these hard times.

> Many good wishes and many prayers,
> Yours,
> Wishing you hope, courage and confidence.
> Henri

Henri's friend Mary Ellen Neill has written after reading Pray to Live: Thomas Merton: A Contemplative Critic *(Fides, 1972). She is at Pendle Hill, a Quaker spirituality center in Wallingford, Pennsylvania, directed by Parker Palmer, and is asking big questions, including how to keep centered in her faith.*

Parker Palmer was dean of studies at Pendle Hill during the 1970s and formed a close collaborative relationship with Henri. Palmer guest-lectured many of Henri's courses at Yale Divinity School. Henri spent considerable amounts of time at Pendle Hill from 1976 to 1982, attending and teaching at the center's summer institutes.

JUNE 3, 1979

Dear Mary Ellen,

Many thanks for your lovely and good letter. Be sure to make the Eucharist the center of your life. Attend Mass as often as you can and read about it and think about it. In the Eucharist we become most intimately united with Christ. It gives you a whole new space to "Stretch, turn, look, listen and move." God becomes our boundless space.

I keep you in my prayers. Keep your eyes on Him and He will guide you even "there where you would rather not go"! But God is always holding you in the palm of His hand.

So keep courage and trust in Him. I keep you in my prayers and the monks join me.

Peace,
Yours,
Henri

This is the first of several letters published in this volume to Walter J. Gaffney and his first wife, Jet. Henri met Gaffney at Yale Divinity School in his first year there. At the time Gaffney was a Roman Catholic priest, studying for his Master of Sacred Theology. They formed an immediate friendship. While at Yale, Gaffney served as Henri's teaching assistant and later they co-taught two courses—a seminar on "Hospitality" and another on "Ministry in Nonreligious Institutions." Gaffney coauthored Aging: The Fulfillment of Life *(Garden City, NY: Doubleday, 1974) with Henri based on a course they taught together on "Ministry to the Elderly." Gaffney left the priesthood to marry Jet in 1973. Henri was the officiant at the wedding.*

Henri is writing in response to a letter from the young couple, who are struggling against society's expectation for them to get "settled with title, salary and prestige."

JULY 8, 1979

Dear Walt and Jet,

Many thanks for your very good letter. It was good to hear from you. I was excited to read that you have moved to a better place and that you feel good about the new house. I can't wait to see it. I really do feel good about this settling move. I think that Guam and Siros [U.S. territories located in the western Pacific] might be good for a long vacation or a short-term interruption of your work, but I think they are mainly temptations to satisfy a deep need in a faraway place. I very much like to support your commitment to put down roots in New Haven. I think the stronger and deeper those roots will be, the more chance there will be to build community there. I think you have a real gift for building community and to bring people together in a real healing and helping way. I do not think you need to live together to do so, but that it might quite well be possible to form a community of people in New Haven who not only support each other but also realize together a new way of living in an old world.

I was fascinated by the contrast in your letter between your response to *Clowning in Rome* [Henri's book, published in 1979, about solitude, celibacy, contemplation and prayer] and your most urgent needs. I seriously believe that some of the places about which I talk in the book are places which can help you to be rooted without being "settled with title, salary and prestige." The solution—I think—is not in moving to another outer place but to another inner place. The great challenge remains to find the eternal in the midst of the temporary, to touch what remains in what passes and to love the ever living God in the love of the quickly passing family of people.

What I most desire for you is that you will soon become a father. Vincent van Gogh wrote to his brother Theo that art is the essence of life and that giving birth to a child is the highest form of art. I have a sense that there are levels of human experience we will only come in touch with when we become father or mother. Maybe it is in the child that we come closest to the Eternal in life and get a glimpse of the moment in which the deepest rootedness and the greatest detachment touch each other. There we are most human and closest to God.

Meanwhile I am giving a series of talks to the monks on Vincent van Gogh. His letters to Theo are an incredible source of spiritual insights for me, and his paintings and drawings are the form of art that most directly speaks to me. I took all my van Gogh books and van Gogh slides with me to the monastery, and the regular life allows me to read of it while I am here.

Van Gogh also helps me think about new ways of communicating. I have a sense that this material is better for a play than for an article or book. I wonder if it ever would be possible for me to write a short van Gogh play.* It is not a new idea since there are

---

* Henri did draft a script for a one-man play (fragments of which are in the Nouwen archives), and some of his talks on van Gogh for the monks of the Genesee and

a few around already, but my particular spiritual interest in van Gogh might allow me to do something that has not been done yet. While I am thinking about this I am involved in the making of a short van Gogh film with Gene Searchinger. He is an excellent film maker from New York. The Lilly Endowment gave a grant to the Yale Media design studio to make some films with professors, and they asked me to do a film with them on van Gogh. Well, it looks as if this thing will be done before Christmas and I wonder what it is going to look like.* Gene wrote me that he had done some very good filming of the *Night Café* in the Yale [University] Art Gallery and was now ready to do some filming of the *Starry Night* in the Museum of Modern Art in New York. I am supposed to write the "script" and provide the texts. But I start realizing more and more that you cannot simply write a text and then make a film with it. The pieces of film lead as much to the text as the text to the filming.

The life here is very good for me. The monks are very prayerful and very kind. The atmosphere is that of brotherhood and prayer, and it creates slowly some space in me to look through all my compulsions and needs and to catch some real glimpses of the living God. I see more and more how blind and deaf I can become for the Reality which is right in front of me and can lift me out of my prison. If I just let it happen. Indeed, love is stronger than death. That is what God keeps telling me. But I keep finding in myself the morbid tendency to contradict this and live as if death deserves more attention than love. The whole central idea of meditation is simply to pay attention to God and find your real self in

other settings had elements of theater, including Henri entering into the character of Theo van Gogh.

* This film ceased production after the death of Howard Weaver of Yale Media Design in April 1982. A film was eventually released by Searchinger in 1984 for the Metropolitan Museum of Art, the Rijksmuseum Vincent van Gogh and the Fondation Vincent van Gogh Arles, called *In a Brilliant Light: Van Gogh in Arles*, but it did not include footage of Henri. Draft scripts and other notes for the aborted film are housed in the Nouwen archives.

Him. If I keep paying attention to myself and my little world, I get more and more entangled in the old self, which really amounts to a death trip. I start really to see what Paul experienced on the road to Damascus and what happened to him afterwards. The lives of the saints keep telling me the same story. (I think I am going to buy myself Butler's four volumes of the *Lives of the Saints*;* the best way for me to get over my endless distractions is to look at God through the mirror of his saints. Maybe later I will receive the grace to speak to Him and be with Him more directly.)

Thanks for the clipping of the *Elephant Man*. I very much hope to see the play. My father is coming on the first of September to stay with me for a month, and I hope to see the play with him. I hope that you and Jet will also meet him soon.

I hope the new house and the new neighborhood is good for both of you.

Well, I better stop. Soon another bell will ring for Vespers.

Yours,
Peace,
Henri

P.S. Dear Jet,

This letter is as much for you as for Walt. But since it was so much a Walt-letter I wrote more on his wavelength than maybe on yours. But I hope you consider yourself part of the conversation. I very much look forward to seeing you on Orange Street. I wonder how close we are to each other.

---

* Alban Butler, *Butler's Lives of the Saints,* ed. Herbert J. Thurston and Donald Attwater (Notre Dame, IN: Christian Classics, 1956).

Henri's friend Jim Forest had moved to Alkmaar in the Netherlands to work with the International Fellowship of Reconciliation. Henri wrote to console him over the breakdown of his marriage.

FEBRUARY 28, 1980

Dear Jim,

Many thanks for your very kind letter. You have been very much in my prayers and thoughts. I made the mistake of planning a long letter to you and L. and this great plan never materialized since I kept waiting for that long free afternoon in which I could fully concentrate on writing you both. So big plans are like no plans and therefore I am just sitting here writing you, as I should have done long before, and not worrying too much about any great ideas or suggestions I might have.

I just have a great need to tell you about my friendship for you and my great desire to deepen that friendship in this so hard time for you. I deeply admire your spiritual strength and your ability to hold on to your Lord in the midst of the storms.

There is something incomprehensible about your pain. I am deeply convinced that you and L. had a beautiful marriage, that both of you were very happy with each other, that your life was full of joy and love. In no way do I even think that there was something wrong or lacking from the beginning. This makes it all the more incomprehensible, the more unreasonable. There are few explanations that help you. I keep having the deep sense that you are being tested very deeply. You are asked to cling to your Lord no matter what. You are asked to keep praying even when it might seem absurd. You are asked to enter the darkness of not understanding with an ever growing surrender.

In many ways you are only in the beginning of your life. I do not know what the Lord will ask of you. But I am deeply convinced he loves you with a very deep and special love, with a call that is quite radical. I also hope and pray that L. and you will be able to find each other again and recommit yourself to each other, but this might not be God's will for you. This is very much a desert time for you, a time of being lost, of having little to hold on to, a time full of temptations to give up, to become bitter and resentful. Your heart is very deep and wide, and it cannot be just yours.

I will soon give you a call. I am also planning to write L. and both of you, but I just need a little more space for that. But it certainly will come.

I am going to Rochester for a one-day retreat, and then I am going back to the Abbey for a few days. I look forward to that time. I also want to know if I might be able to help you in case you feel a need to get out of Alkmaar for a while and spend some time with friends or alone. I will be in touch with you about that.

Many good wishes. Many prayers and much peace and love.

Yours,
Henri

In the fall of 1980, Henri taught a seminar course on "Desert Spirituality and Contemporary Ministry." In response to a student who submitted a paper entitled "An Inconvenient Love: Coming to Humanity," Henri wrote a long, positive and challenging evaluation.

Dear Timothy,
Re.: An Inconvenient Love: Coming to Humanity

Your paper has touched me deeply. I am sorry it took me so long to respond to it, but I hope that my response still means something to you. I read every word you wrote and I felt a real closeness to what you wrote even when it remains hard for me to explain that feeling clearly. I could sense your struggle, your journey and your questions in my own soul without being able to always give words to them.

What struck me most deeply was your experience that being human was your weakness as well as your hope. I think that you touched here the center of the spiritual experience. "I was simply human. This was given to me, however, only after I could appreciate it, and, in a sense, ask for it—after three days of emptiness and tears." When I read this, I thought of a similar experience by Thomas Merton. After many years in the monastery he came to town and suddenly realized the joy of being human, the joy of being part of the human race, the beauty of being a weak, vulnerable human being like all other human beings. This deep sense of solidarity came to him as a true revelation and it filled him with joy. "I am simply human" was not a depressing experience for him but an experience that led him to true gratitude. (The most religious emotion!). And in that experience he was able to see his fellow human beings as people full of light and radiance.*

Your next step also deeply moved me, since I could so well identify with it. "I had to learn my humanity. I had to be shown my weakness in order to discover my freedom." Forgiveness became the way for you. How true that is. For me, forgiveness has been the

---

* Henri is referring to Merton's epiphany of 1958, recorded in his book *Conjectures of a Guilty Bystander* (Garden City, NY: Doubleday & Co., 1966): 140–141. "In Louisville, at the corner of Fourth and Walnut, in the center of the shopping district, I was suddenly overwhelmed with the realization that I loved all those people, that they were mine and I theirs, that we could not be alien to one another even though we were total strangers. It was like waking from a dream of separateness, of spurious self-isolation in a special world, the world of renunciation and supposed holiness. The whole illusion of a separate holy existence is a dream . . . There is no way of telling people that they are all walking around shining like the sun. . . . I suddenly saw the secret beauty of their hearts, the depths of their hearts where neither sin nor desire nor self-knowledge can reach, the core of their reality, the person that each one is in God's eyes. If only they could all see themselves as they really are. If only we could see each other that way all of the time."

most life-giving experience of my life. When I discovered not only that my weakness was my humanity but also that my humanity was a forgiven humanity, I truly found my freedom. "God helped me forgive myself in divine forgiveness and love. Assured that I am forgiven in a depth I do not know, I forgave myself and I forgave all the 'thems' of the past . . . and began to feel the freedom of God." Here you speak really to my heart. I am very grateful to you for articulating what is so hard to express. But I know from experience what you are speaking about, and I think that you have touched the center of the spiritual life.

One question I have to raise. Would it be possible to be more Christ-centered in your thinking? I have a sense that your experience and understanding form a very strong basis to know more fully and deeply the mystery of the Incarnation. By becoming one with us, God revealed himself as God to us. Thus the experience of our humanity as a forgiven weakness leads us to the heart of God's love for us and to the center of His forgiving presence in our life. Therefore I think that your story is the story with which you can come to know God's story better, and it is His story that makes our story worth living.

Thanks again for this very hope-giving and healing story.

Grade: Honors
Peace and love,
Henri J. M. Nouwen

P.S. It was good to know you during my last year at Yale. I pray that the Lord will continue to guide you and give you much hope, courage and confidence. Please do not forget me in your prayers.

❧

In 1980, after ten very good years as a professor at Yale, Henri had a deep conviction that his time there was coming to a close, and he was actively looking for and listening to where God was calling him next. One place he considered was Madonna House, a Catholic community of laypeople and priests founded by Catherine de Hueck Doherty based in Combermere, Ontario, Canada. The letter below to Doherty gives us a glimpse of his discernment process and the inner stirrings that were leading him away from teaching and into active ministry in Latin America.

Henri would resign from Yale after the spring semester of 1981.

DECEMBER 20, 1980

Dear Catherine,[*]

It has been a while since I wrote you. Many things have happened, and I like to keep you informed. At this time I am in Holland with my father to spend the Christmas vacation. I had a very busy but also satisfying semester at Yale Divinity School, and more than ever did I enjoy the kindness of the students and their sincere search for God in their lives. It was a real grace for me that I could speak with so many good people, and I have a sense that I have learned as much as I have taught.

Meanwhile, I have been thinking more about my future. It is clear to me that it is time to leave Yale after ten years there. I have a deep conviction that God wants me to move on, even when it is not clear yet what the direction is. Since my visit to Madonna House in August I have seriously wondered if Madonna House might be the place to start. Your prayers and your encouragement meant very much to me, and for a long time I thought that Madonna

---

[*] Letter to Catherine Dueck Doherty printed by kind courtesy of Madonna House Archives.

House was indeed the direction to go. The fact that you invited me to come to Madonna House and to stay there for a few months and the fact that the people at Madonna House showed me such kindness and hospitality seemed for a long time a part of a call to come to Canada.

But the more I thought about it and the more I talked with others and prayed about it, the more I started to question if I was doing the right thing. It is very hard for me to explain precisely what made me doubt, but by now I have come to the strong sense that Madonna House is not the place for me at this time of my life. This sense was very slow in coming. That is the reason that it took me so long to write you.

One of the main reasons for the decision not to come to Madonna House this summer is the growing sense that I have to continue with my studies in Spanish and in the Latin American Church. In 1971 I spent a summer in Bolivia to study Spanish, and since then I have made several trips to Latin America. But these trips always were very short and I never mastered the language enough to make me feel at home in a Spanish-speaking world. Now I feel that I have the time and opportunity to give all my energy to the study of Spanish and to the study of the Latin American situation. The Maryknoll Fathers have shown me a great willingness to help me and have suggested to me that I stay with them in Lima, Peru, to immerse myself as fully as possible in the Peruvian culture. They have offered the possibility to live in a parish and to be part of a group of priests who work with the poor. The more I think about this, the more I realize that this is not just a hobby but the continuation of a long interest and concern. At this moment I am considering going to Peru for at least one year and then slowly discern in which direction the Lord calls me.

Meanwhile, I am planning to stay in close touch with Father John Eudes Bamburger [the abbot of the Abbey of the Genesee] and his community. My relationship with the Genesee Abbey remains one of the most fruitful relationships of my life, and I hope to continue to spend time there to deepen my vocation and to ask advice. I hope to visit Father John Eudes in the coming months to discuss with him my plans. I also will visit my Bishop Cardinal [Johannes] Willebrands in the coming weeks to ask for his blessing and support.*

Well, this is what I have come to after much thinking and reflecting. I regret that I will not be able to spend more time at Combermere, but I hope and pray that you will continue to support me with your prayers.

The situation in our world is frightening, and many people experience deep anxieties. More than ever we will be tested in our faith. I hope and pray that the Lord will deepen our faith during these weeks of Advent and will fill us with a peace and joy which belong to his kingdom. Hope is not optimism and I pray that we all will be able to live hopefully in the midst of our apocalyptic time. We have a promise and God is faithful to His promise even when we are doubtful and fearful. As Paul says: "Our hope is not deceptive because the Holy Spirit has already been poured into us." I wish you and all the people at Madonna House a very blessed Christmas. Keep me in your prayers. I pray for you.

Henri

---

* As a diocesan priest of Utrecht, Henri required the permission of his bishop when he made changes to his ministry and life. Willebrands was Henri's bishop from 1975 to 1983.

In 1981, as he was preparing to leave Yale for the barrios of Peru, Henri received a letter from a man who wanted to know if humanity would survive the century.

AUGUST 11, 1981

Dear George,

I really don't know if our civilization will survive the century. Considering the growing threat of a nuclear holocaust, there certainly is a reason to wonder. But important for me is not if our civilization will survive or not but if we can continue to live with hope, and I really think we can because our Lord has given us His promise that He will stay with us at all times. He is the God of the living, He has overcome evil and death and His love is stronger than any form of death and destruction. That is why I feel that we should continually avoid the temptation of despair and deepen our awareness that God is present in the midst of all the chaos that surrounds us and that that presence allows us to live joyfully and peacefully in a world so filled with sorrow and conflict.

Please be sure of my prayers for you in these tempting times.

Peace,
Henri Nouwen

A scholar studying pastoral care had written for Henri's insights about handling pain in the terminally ill.

Dear Richard,

Thanks for your very challenging letter of July 15. It's not easy for me to respond satisfactorily to your letter since you raise so many important and sensitive issues, but let me just share with you some reflections. Over the last few years I have been increasingly aware that true healing mostly takes place through the sharing of weakness. Mostly we are so afraid of our weaknesses that we hide them at all cost and thus make them unavailable to others but also often to ourselves. And, in this way, we end up living double lives even against our own desires: one life in which we present ourselves to the world, to ourselves and to God as a person who is in control and another life in which we feel insecure, doubtful, confused and anxious and totally out of control. The split between these two lives causes us a lot of suffering. I have become growingly aware of the importance to overcome the great chasm between these two lives and to become more and more aware that facing, with others, the reality of our existence can be the beginning of a truly free life.

It is amazing in my own life that true friendship and community became possible to the degree that I was able to share my weaknesses with others. Often I became aware of the fact that in the sharing of my weaknesses with others, the real depths of my human brokenness and weakness and sinfulness started to reveal itself to me, not as a source of despair but as a source of hope. As long as I try to convince myself or others of my independence a lot of my energy is invested building up my own false self. But once I am able to truly confess my most profound dependence on others and on God, I can come in touch with my true self and a real community can develop.

All of this I am saying to restate my conviction that often deepening the pain is the way to healing because deepening the pain means to go to that place in me where I am really broken, sinful, dependent and where I'm no longer trying to stay in control but where I can reach out to God and to my fellow human beings without fear.

I agree with you that all of this has a lot of implications for care of terminal patients, and much more needs to be said in order to make these implications clear. I also agree that often much care is primarily concerned with reduction of pain and therefore often avoids the more basic core that often many people look for. However, I might not be as inclined as you are to make the sharp distinction between secular care and pastoral care. Many good psychotherapists, social workers and psychologists who are not thinking primarily in pastoral terms still will do a lot more than just pain reduction and often are able to lead people into a full recognition of their human situation, a recognition which has many qualities similar to the kind of confusion that I just spoke about in pastoral terms. So I tend to be a little more distant than you in making the distinction between secular and pastoral.

On the other hand, I very much agree with your suggestion that much pastoral care over the last decades has been so deeply affected by contemporary psychological ideas that often the true spiritual dimension of pastoral care has been lost. And I strongly sympathize with your feeling that much work needs to be done to develop a true spiritual-pastoral care for terminally ill people.

Finally, I have to say that I am not familiar with any writings that will help you to develop the idea of deepening and sharing pain. In this respect you are pretty much left to your own thinking. I also read Karl Rahner's death theology and didn't find it very helpful for my own thinking although I deeply appreciate much of his work.

These are just some thoughts that came to my mind after I read your letter, and I don't really know if they can be of any help to you. I really don't know how to test whether theoretical theology does call for application of "deepening the pain" to terminal care and caring for the bereaved within the main confessions of con-temporary Christianity. But I think that if you read more strictly spiritual literature, you might find much support for the general direction of your thinking. I, myself, have found that much of present pastoral care writing has lost contact with the main sources of Christian spirituality and, therefore, has become overly dependent on contemporary behavioral sciences. I really think that you are embarking on a very important project. But I also believe that you are very much in unexplored territory.

I wish you much courage and confidence in this project.

With many kind wishes,
Henri J. M. Nouwen

Henri loved clowns. He often used clowns as a way to describe being a minister. In this letter to a young couple working at a food program, Henri addresses their concern that they are being exploited by some patrons of the program.

AUGUST 31, 1981

Dear Judd and Evy,

Many thanks for your very kind letter. I really appreciate your taking the time to write me. I very much enjoyed our conversation and I only wish we could have had more time. I appreciated very much what you write about your frustration about the food program. I understand very well the questions you raise.

There is just one little observation I would like to make. Sometimes we have to dare to be fools for Christ. That means that sometimes we have to be willing to give food to people who don't really need or deserve it. And sometimes we have to be willing to work with some people who might even exploit us. Maybe that is as close as we can come to an experience of self-emptying. It is the experience of being useless in the presence of the Lord.

Understand me well, I am not trying to praise impracticality, nor am I trying to suggest that you should not stop doing the things you are doing when they prove to be counter-productive, but I am saying if you come in touch with the experience of being used or the experience of being useless, you might in fact be close to a true Christian experience, or closer than you sought.

Meanwhile, I keep you in my prayers and hope that your parish experience will be really filled with joy and peace.

I am enjoying my stay at the Abbey very much. I am praying with the monks and working with them in the bakery. Meanwhile I am still relaxing from the 10 exhausting years at Yale. If you ever want a few days of retreat, this might be the place for you.

Yours in friendship,
Henri Nouwen

Henri responds to a man who wants to know how he can experience God's love if he has never known human acceptance.

SEPTEMBER 3, 1981

Dear James,

Many thanks for your very kind and moving letter. I really did appreciate it that you took the time to write me and to share with me some of your deepest feelings.

What you wrote deeply touches me and I think that you are bringing me in touch with a reality which I truly can recognize in myself, even though I might not have written clearly about it. Your sentence "How does one give up the illusion and the longing for what one has never had?" really speaks to me.

We indeed need to experience God's love in true and real human relationships, and although hunger for human acceptance is like a bottomless barrel, I agree with you that without the experience of human acceptance, the experience of God's love and acceptance become extremely difficult.

During the last few months, I myself have experienced some real affectionate, caring acceptance from my friends during a difficult time in my own life. It was this human acceptance that helped me see God in a new way and allowed me to have a better experiential knowledge of what it means that God's love is deeper and stronger than any love that humans can give to one another; but without the experience of human love, the experience of God's love is very hard to come by.

All of this is simply to affirm what you write. I see in your letter, also, a true crying out for more human acceptance in your own life. I have a sense that the greatest mistake you can make is to make age a real factor. I have found that becoming older in no way means that I am less able or worthy to receive love and affection. I, therefore, hope that you will not deal with your feelings of adulation as an unchangeable and fatal event. In fact, many of your experiences in your life might enable you to more fully understand the true meaning of giving and receiving human and Divine love.

God's ways are remarkable and He can truly break through all human limitations and restrictions; so be hopeful and expectant and pray fervently that the Lord will give you what you most deeply crave. You really deserve it and the Lord will not let your prayer go unanswered.

I hope and pray that one day we will meet again and have an opportunity to share our ideas and experiences with one another.

By separate mail, I am sending you a book with prayers which I recently published and I hope that this might be of some meaning to you.*

Sincerely yours,
Henri

"Protestants have chewed on the Gospels without being fed" is a sentence from a letter from Henri's Quaker friend Mike Sibley. Sibley writes to Henri after attending a Catholic Mass at the Abbey of the Genesee and expresses his "muddled" response to the experience, which has stirred a spiritual hunger he can't quite name.

As he writes to Mike and his wife, Pat, Henri is about to leave for Bolivia, where he will join the Maryknoll Fathers for orientation and language study before beginning parish ministry in Peru.

OCTOBER 6, 1981

Dear Mike and Pat,

Thanks so much for your very kind, open and challenging letter which you wrote me on September 21.

Regretfully, it took me a while to respond. This was not only a lack of time, but also because of my need to think a little more about your letter. There are many things I would like to write to you in response, but I think I will just mention a few.

Knowing you both has been a real gift to me. I have always felt a deep, human affection in both of you, and the more I come to know you, the more I have been grateful for this friendship.

At the same time, I have also become aware of a spiritual hunger in you which was not being satisfied. It always seemed to me

---

* Henri is referring to his book *A Cry for Mercy: Prayers from the Genesee* (Garden City, NY: Doubleday, 1981).

that in some way or another, you had not been fully introduced into the great mysteries of the spiritual life. I strongly feel that you know a lot about it and, in many ways, more than I do. But, at the same time, I realize that the experience of God as I have been privileged to enjoy it within the Catholic community has never really been fully part of your life.

Your letter, as well as your remarks that you had both experienced a certain desire to be more intimately connected with the Catholic Church, has made me think a lot. I, indeed, feel that it would be extremely important for you to explore this deep hunger which exists in both of you. I see this hunger as a desire for a more full and intimate communion with the Lord Himself and for a deep understanding of a radical transformation which becomes possible in and through Christ.

I have a deep and growing admiration for the Quaker tradition. My increasing contact with Pendle Hill* has deepened my sympathy for the Quaker way of life, but what I miss there very much is the sacramental presence of the Lord. In my own life, the Eucharist is the center. There the Lord comes to us as food and drink and transforms us into true new beings. The Eucharist, and indirectly all other sacraments, makes the Christ life something radically different from a life inspired by the ideas and the stories about Jesus. The sacramental life is a life by which we become living Christ, in which we truly die from the old man and woman in us, and in which Christ becomes the center of our identity. This is the mystical life. Mystical life is the real life. It is the life of the spirit of Christ within us. It is the life which makes it possible for us to say, "Not I live but Christ lives in me." I have a sense that you both are very open for this, and in fact, know more about it than most people (even most Catholics!).

One thing I would like to say to you is, do not stop searching in

* See letter to Mary Ellen Neill, June 3, 1979, for more information on Pendle Hill.

this direction, and do not let the fear of losing a supportive social milieu become the dominant factor in your decisions.

I am, obviously, not sure if you should become a Catholic, and you know me well enough to realize that that is not something I try to "accomplish." But I sincerely feel that you should follow the movements of the spirit which might lead you in the direction of the Catholic Church, and I frankly feel that this movement will not lessen, but in a mysterious way will strengthen your ties with your Quaker friends.

Just last week when I was in Pendle Hill, I heard about a course on the seven sacraments which is offered in Philadelphia by a Quaker, a former professor from Earlham College [a liberal arts college in Richmond, Indiana, founded by Quakers].

All this is just some quick responses to your letter, and I hope that we are on the same wave length.

I certainly want to say that I want to be of help to you in your search, and do not hesitate to write and ask for books, literature or tapes on the subject. I would love to help you as much as I can.

Thanks so much for your very beautiful letter.

Best wishes,
Yours,
with affection and love,
Henri

In the new year of 1982, Henri's friends Jim Antal and Cindy Shannon announced their engagement. They asked Henri to be the officiant at their wedding. In the following letters, Henri helps the couple prepare for their marriage.

Henri is writing from Lima, Peru, where he is a parish minister for a poor barrio outside the city. He will stay in Peru until March 1982.

JANUARY 6, 1982

Dear Jim and Cindy,

Many thanks for your phone call and the kind letters I received when I came to Peru. I send you both my warm wishes and many congratulations. I very much hope and pray that the months to come will be months of quiet preparation and a true time of engagement. It is so important to prepare yourself spiritually for marriage. Please don't get entangled in problems around dress, cakes, rituals, receptions, folders, programs, gifts, etc. They all belong to the devil's trappings. Let your families worry about that. Spend a lot of time together, in Spenser, at the Genesee or any place that belongs to God.

Try to learn to pray together. The liturgy of the hours may give you a way. Try to be very ascetical about "issues." Nuclear war, hunger, ecology, sports and even photography might become distractions in a time that should be first and foremost for both of you. Be sure to buy a lot of flowers! They are beautiful but they also die soon. Just as you both!

I look forward to being with you.

I am enjoying Lima very much. A city full of history and real life. Within a week or two I am moving to a poor barrio to work and live there. I am looking forward to that.

May the Lord bless both of you in the months to come.

Love,
Henri

P.S. Many thanks for your comments on my diary.* They were helpful and encouraging.

---

* Henri kept a diary of his experiences as a missionary. It was published as *¡Gracias!: A Latin American Journal* (San Francisco: Harper and Row, 1983). He gave Jim and Cindy a copy of an early draft manuscript for review and comments.

Henri continues to prepare Jim and Cindy for their marriage. Here he focuses on the wedding.

JANUARY 29, 1982

Dear Jim and Cindy,

Many thanks for your card and letters. It was really good to hear from you both, and I have already entered with you into the time (kairos!) of preparation. I pray for you during the Eucharist and during the liturgy of the hours, I think of you often and I am with you in this "advent" period of your life. God loves you both deeply, unconditionally and most generously. Be sure to celebrate that love with which he embraces both of you, in prayer, in Eucharist, in meals and in good visits to friends. If you have time, read a good book on marriage. I think that the German theologian Kasper wrote a good one.*

Thinking about the wedding, I can only say one thing. The wedding belongs to Cindy's parents! This might sound strange, untrue and not very modern, but without realizing this you will have only problems! My own parents, when they married, had many ideas about when, the how, and the where, of their wedding, but it happened as my grandmother wanted it. And all the weddings I have been part of, including John [Mogabgab] and Marjorie [Thompson], were clearly orchestrated by the parents of the bride. (By the way: this was also true for the way my ordination to the priesthood was celebrated!)

You have to be aware of the symbolic meaning of this. It is the last time that parents can say: "She is our daughter, and we will make that clear to you, who want her as your wife." Personally I

---

* This might be Walter Kasper's *Theology of Christian Marriage* (New York: Crossroad, 1981).

feel that it is important for the son-in-law to give his mother and father-in-law all the honor they deserve. It really is their day, their feast, their chance and their way to hide the painful truth that they are losing their child. I am not saying that you should not make your desires clear and express them with conviction. Cindy's parents deserve to know your ideas about it all, but then . . . they have to be given the freedom to set the tone themselves. You will be able to do it your way after July 10th, not before!

This can also set you free to do other things together that really counts. Days to Spencer or Weston [Priory], or days on the beach or days reading poetry, or days of joyful silence. I will send you both a little gift to help you both to prepare yourselves. (Might take a month to get to you!).*

I am very glad to be part of your life together.

Love,
Henri

Henri took friendship very seriously. In one case, at least, he made a formal request of friendship, and the other person took five years to say yes. It was not because he didn't want to be friends with Henri; he simply knew that friendship would mean being available at any time, being completely open with his inner life and giving and receiving love, support, encouragement without limits. This style of friendship was not for everyone, and there are many people for whom it was simply not sustainable. Henri often referred to his friendships as "gifts from God" and endeavored to live his relationships with the same kind of attentiveness and discipline with which he approached his priesthood. In a journal entry from his last year he wrote:

---

* Henri sent the couple a psalter (a volume containing the Book of Psalms).

*"Friendship requires trust, patience, attentiveness, courage, repentance, forgiveness, celebration and most of all faithfulness."**

As we read through the letters in this volume, we can notice a progression in how Henri defines and lives his friendships. In this letter to Jim Forest, we see him grappling with the questions of how much of his struggles to confide and what the boundaries of friendship for priests are. In the same way that he viewed marriage as a ministry, he saw the spiritual dimension of friendship and endeavored to live his relationships in a way that acknowledged the presence of God in their intimacy.

Henri writes from Lima, Peru.

FEBRUARY 3, 1982

Dear Jim,

Your very good letter from Holland written on Dec. 23, '81, came to me on Feb. 3, '82! It was really good to hear from you. I very often thought of you especially during the Christmas days, and I wondered how you were doing. I am really grateful for your very warm and intimate letter. It is truly a letter of a good friend, and while reading it I experienced the power of your love, your kindness and real friendship. I have missed hearing from you and it was great to hear from you, not just about the many things you are doing but more so about the inner side of things.

You are touching an extremely important area that has kept me very much pre-occupied the last year. It is indeed the question of mutuality in friendship and true confession. I am exploring the deeper levels of friendship, of risk-taking, of forming a community of confessing Christians. I am becoming aware of the power of confession and forgiveness through deep mutual friendship. Somehow I start feeling that there also is hidden the deepest meaning of the sacrament of reconciliation.

---

* *Sabbatical Journey: The Diary of His Final Year* (New York: Crossroad, 1998), 7.

You have confessed much to me. I have confessed little to you. As long as this is true, we cannot love each other in the deepest way that our faith in Jesus allows us. I have struggled with this a great lot over the past months, and I have taken a few great leaps of faith with some very dear friends and this has brought me closer to them and to God and has slowly revealed to me the deep meaning of confession, repentance and forgiveness.

But there is a right time for this too. I love you very much. I am grateful to God for your entering in my life. Your openness, your vulnerability, your pains and agonies have all made me love you more and made you a more vital part of my prayer. But I have not given you the chance to love in that same way. I have remained a priest-friend in the way that my priesthood became a way to prevent you from being a truly deep and intimate friend. I see this now more clearly and feel excited about the new possibilities in our relationship that are opening up.

When you visited me in the Genesee, I was very grateful that you came. It was a true gift for me. But somehow it was not the time for confession for both of us. There wasn't much time, and we could hardly come to that moment of mutual silence and solitude in which a fellowship of the weak can exist.

I just want you to know that I feel very close to you and know that someday the Lord will lead us to a new place where we can be together in a new way and experience together the freedom His love gives. I do not know when that will be, but I trust that we both will know when the time has come. In a deep way I know that my struggle with God, with prayer, with loneliness, with sexuality, with intimacy, with understanding, with ministry should become part of your struggle. I know that my love for you makes me desire that I can let you touch my wounds and my most interior places. I know that maybe I can heal you better with my weaknesses than with my strength. But it asks a great faith, a great hope and a great love, and at times I feel so terribly small and fearful. But we can support each other in our desire to live bravely, fully trusting that

God's grace is immense and wants to set us really free. Dear friend, we have just begun!

Meanwhile, I am living in Lima with the Maryknoll priests in a parish of 120,000 people. I wrote a long diary which you are welcome to read.

I will stay here until April 1, then return to the U.S. In August or September I will come to Holland and stay there for a while. Meanwhile I will decide if and how I will work in Peru in the coming years.

I hope that the Lord will soon bring us together and reveal His abundant love to both of us.

I pray for you and trust in your prayer for me. Thanks so much for your pictures of your little ones. Enclosed is a picture of one of my many new friends in Lima.

Peace and love,
Henri

A third letter to Jim and Cindy about the covenant of marriage.

FEBRUARY 26, 1982

Dear Jim and Cindy,

Thousand thanks for your Spirit-filled letters. Your letters really radiate freedom and love. I can sense your joy, your energy, your inner peace and your deepening love for each other. Love casts out fear, and how powerful are we when we are free from fear! I can feel the growing freedom from fears in both of you and know that you are coming close to that love that can move mountains!

I hope June Hagan, my secretary at the Abbey, sent you the Psalter. It is a good book to read together. When two people who love each other focus on the same word of God, there is a triangle that no human being can break.

I pray for you as you both prepare yourself for the great covenant of love. Keep in mind that your love for each other is to become a living sign of God's real presence in this world. Marriage therefore is a sacrament. It makes visible and realizes the presence of the Lord in the midst of this war-ridden, anxious, chaotic world. It speaks of life where there is death and of hope where there is despair.

I am so glad with your growing "defenselessness." There it is that God pours out His creative love, and there it is too that you can become lovers who can embrace with that divine love all the suffering people of the world.

I keep you both in my prayers every day.

Love, Peace, and Joy,
With an embrace from
Henri

This is a letter to a priest about the place of love in the classroom. Henri taught a course on "Compassion" at the Pontifical Gregorian University in Rome in the spring semester of 1982. His book Clowning in Rome: Reflections on Solitude, Celibacy, Prayer, and Contemplation *(Garden City, NY: Image Books, 1979) was based on his lectures there.*

Henri is back from Peru and spending four months at the Abbey of the Genesee.

APRIL 2, 1982

Dear David,

Thanks so much for your beautiful letter. It was so good to hear from you again. Very often I have thought of you and our good time in Rome, and it feels very good to be in touch with you again.

What you write about your relationship with your students really speaks to me very directly. If there is anything that I have learned from teaching, it is that loving your students is the basis for a real learning process from both sides and that indeed this love has to be expressed concretely and directly. I am so glad that you were able to discover this and act on this insight.

The mystery of it all is that as you start loving your students, often you start experiencing their pains more deeply yourself. But, as you well know, in this life love and pain are never separated, and I guess that it is the place where suffering and love both meet that God is most present.

I just returned from Peru, where I had a most blessed time. I spent three months there—two months working in a parish and one month visiting different people and places. I am now sorting out many impressions, and I am trying to discern if God calls me to work there for a much longer period of time. Please keep me in your prayers in this time of decision-making.

If you are ever interested in making a short retreat, the Abbey might be the ideal place for you. I very much hope to stay in touch with you.

Best wishes and with many kind greetings.

Yours,
Henri Nouwen

Henri writes to a reader of his book Genesee Diary.

MAY 13, 1982

Dear Dr. Holmes,

Many thanks for your most kind letter. I really did appreciate your warm response to *Genesee Diary*. That really means a lot to me. I was especially grateful for your realization of solidarity with other people on the path. Yes, you are not alone in your struggles. At the same time it remains true that your journey is a unique journey and that the Lord loves you in a very unique and special way. I think that it is precisely in this tension between solidarity and uniqueness that our spiritual growth takes place.

    I'm certainly not surprised that my book did not change your life. Writing it did not even change mine! But the true task of life might be the task to live our life faithfully in communion with the Lord than to change it. Be sure of my prayers for your vocation and your journey through life.

Sincerely yours,
Henri Nouwen

This is a letter to a young man working in a primate research center in Puerto Rico who wrote with questions about how to respond to the injustice he sees in the world.

Dear Paul,

Many thanks for the wonderful letter which you wrote me. I really
do appreciate you telling me about your life, your interests, your
concerns and your frustrations. Your letter really makes me feel
close to you, and I'm very grateful that you took the time and energy to contact me in such a personal and real way. I obviously
have heard at different times about you from your mother, and
from what she told me about you I had become very aware that we
are totally kindred spirits.* As you probably know, I just returned
from Peru, where I lived for three months in a quite poor area of
town. In many ways I experienced there the same things about
which you write to your friends—a lot of noise, a lot of movement,
a lot of dogs, a lot of TV confusion, lack of water, lack of space,
lack of energy, much drunkenness and many frustrations.

I lived with a very poor family for a month and thus was really
able to become part of this way of living. Although I experienced
very much the oppression and exploitation about which you write,
I also discovered many truly human treasures which we, in our
First World affluence, have lost touch with. I saw a lot of beautiful
family relationships. I saw a lot of real joy, gratitude, spontaneity, ability to celebrate and an immense amount of true human
affection. Especially the children taught me a lot. The openness
and playfulness really brought me closer in touch with the living
Spirit of God than many theology books will ever be able to do.
I hope that you too will be able to taste some of the Spirit of the
people because I am deeply convinced that we only can work for
the liberation of the people if we love them deeply. And we can
only love them deeply when we recognize their gifts to us. I am
deeply convinced of the importance of social change and of the

---

* Henri is referring to Mabel Treadwell, one of his administrative assistants in
1982.

necessity to work hard to bring about a just and peaceful society. But I also feel that this task can only be done in a spirit of gratitude and joy. That is why I am more and more convinced of the importance to live in the Spirit of the Risen Christ. Christ is the God who entered into solidarity with our struggles and became truly God with us. It was this solidarity that led Him to the cross by which He overcame death and evil. Believing in the Risen Lord means believing that in and through Christ the evil one has been overcome and that death no longer is the final word. Working for social change, to me, means to make visible in time and place that which has already been accomplished in principle by God Himself. This makes it possible to struggle for a better world not out of frustration, resentment, anger or self-righteousness but out of care, love, forgiveness and gratitude.

One of the persons who best understood this was Dorothy Day. She was a true Christian anarchist. She deeply believed that we are responsible for ourselves and our actions and that our lives should be built on deep respect and love for our brothers and sisters. I hope you will have the time to read her beautiful autobiography, *A Long Loneliness.* I'm sure you will recognize there many of your own struggles and concerns and find also new perspectives for them.

I'm very glad to hear that you would like to be a researcher. That will give you a solid ground while allowing you also at the same time to keep your eyes open for the struggles and pain of the people. One day I hope you will write me a little more about your work with the primates.

Meanwhile, I'm spending two very quiet months in New Haven. I have acquired so many new impressions during this year that I needed some time alone for prayer, meditation and quiet writing. Two close friends are supporting me in this retreat. We come together every night for two hours to pray and celebrate the Eucharist. The rest of the day I'm spending in reading scripture and sorting out the many feelings, emotions and ideas that crowd my heart and mind. It is really a time of discernment, and I hope I will come out of it with a much better idea about my vocation.*

Thanks so much again for your wonderful letter. I'm glad to be in touch with you. Be sure of my prayers for you and my sincere hope that the Lord will fill your heart with a deep joy and peace.

Yours,
Henri

In this letter to Father Peter Byrne, the then–regional superior of the Maryknoll Fathers, Henri describes his inner state of uncertainty in regard to his future in the light of his recent stay in Peru. He recognizes that what he most needs is a retreat for quiet reflection on his next moves. An invitation to Harvard University is mentioned, which sheds light on the number of people and places that were calling for his attention at this time.

He writes that he is editing his diary notes so they can be read by friends. Each of his books went through the same process—first they were typed from handwritten drafts and comb-bound for comments by friends, and then later, with their encouragement, the typescript would be prepared for publication.

MAY 20, 1982

Dear Pete,†

Many thanks for your good letter. It was really nice to hear from you. It was especially nice to hear about the way you celebrated

---

* This kind of structured retreat with friends was a regular practice for Henri. In this case, the retreat was as much about his struggle for friendship and intimacy as it was for discernment.

† Letters to Father Peter Byrne printed by kind courtesy of the Maryknoll Mission Archives.

Holy Week in the Altiplano. I'm still having very beautiful and rich memories of my time in Peru. Your generous hospitality and personal kindness to me have really made that a special time for me. I'm now looking back over my diary notes, and I'm editing them so that they can be made into a readable manuscript which I can present to some friends. I hope to have this work done within a month or two, and I plan to send you a copy to ask for your own impressions and response.

Currently I've come to a place where it seems important for me to sort out my many feelings, ideas and impressions and to really discern God's will for my future. I've decided to cancel all further appointments and to make a two months retreat with friends at Yale. I'm now living in a very quiet place in New Haven, spending most of my time with prayer, scripture reading and meditation. I feel it's very important that whatever I will decide for my future is a real response to the Lord's call and not just another exciting thing that I want to do.

A few weeks ago I visited George Rupp, the dean of Harvard Divinity School, who expressed a very strong interest in having me relate in some way or another to Harvard's program in Theological Education. He and I have been wondering if my eventual work in Peru could in some way be integrated into the educational work of Harvard Divinity School. I myself am still very confused about all of this, and I strongly feel that this is not yet a time for decision making. Somehow it seems that my priority right now should be to deepen and strengthen my spiritual life and to listen very carefully to God's voice. This is certainly not easy for me since I'm such a restless and noisy person. But I think that I am at least giving it a good try.

So this gives you a better idea of where I am. I very much hope that you can stay in touch.

With best wishes in friendship,
Henri

🎔

As promised in his letter of May 20, 1982, Henri is writing to Father Peter Byrne again to send him a copy of his diary. He has secured a book deal with a working title: Latin American Diary. Henri is concerned to get Peter's blessing on what he has written, especially parts that might be construed as a negative portrayal of the Maryknoll community. He recognizes the danger of publishing such a personal book but is committed to telling the whole story, including his struggles with depression and frustration, because they are "a true part of my total journey."

He writes from Pendle Hill, where he is giving a five-week retreat.

Dear Pete,

Within a few weeks I hope to send to you the edited copy of my Latin American Diary. Harper and Row is very eager to publish it, and many of my friends who have read it encourage me strongly to do so. But I do not want to consider publication without you and [Maryknoll Father] Gerry McCrane having been able to see and criticize it.

I very much would appreciate if you could take the time to read this critically and to let me know if there is anything that would better remain unpublished. I do not want to harm, hurt, offend or embarrass anyone, any family or any institution with this writing. If the publication of this diary would not be a contribution to Maryknoll's mission, I prefer it to remain unpublished. The many people who have read this manuscript have found it very helpful and stimulating, but I want to be sure that the diary is real positive fruit of my six-month journey to Latin America.

As you will see, there are parts in this diary that express my own inner struggle with depression and similar feelings. In the context of these experiences, sometimes negative feelings are expressed. Since these experiences are a true part of my total journey, I prefer to leave them in. But if you feel that this would be unwise for some reason or another, please let me know. I also would appreciate, if you would be willing, letting me know where I might be wrongly informed. I need to make changes in this respect.

I realize that I am imposing this whole thing on you, but I took the freedom to do so since I know how you are interested in my reflections on these six months and I very much value your judgments and criticisms.

Meanwhile, I am giving a five-week retreat at Pendle Hill, a Quaker Study Center near Philadelphia, and I am enjoying it very much.

I am still considering very seriously returning to Lima in 1983 but probably will take a few more months to make a final decision on this.

I hope you and all the friends in Lima are doing well and that the Lord continues to fill you with joy and peace.

Yours in friendship,
Henri

Henri writes to a monk he befriended at the Abbey of the Genesee who had written with concerns about inclusive language.

JULY 20, 1982

Dear Brother Alexis,

Many thanks for your kind letter and reflection. I appreciate hearing from you even though at times I have quite a struggle to decipher your handwriting. But I guess you like to test my patience a little bit!

Though I understand your uneasiness with women who cannot use the word "Father" for "God," I still feel that it is important that we listen carefully to the problems that many thousands of women raise concerning inclusive language.

The fact is that many women have left the church or are growingly uncomfortable with the liturgy because of its exclusively male language. For us men this sometimes is hard to fully understand. I feel that we are called to listen carefully to the voice of the women since they want to bring us in touch with the quality of God that we may have overlooked unconsciously and unwillingly. Meanwhile, I am enjoying the conference very much. We are now in our fourth week and are reflecting on "The Passion and Resurrection of Our Lord."* It is a very blessed time.

I am looking forward to being with you again at the Abbey and especially to celebrating the twenty-fifth anniversary of my ordination.

Many thanks for your letter. Please keep me in your prayers.

Yours in friendship,
Henri

Henri is writing to his friends Albert and Dee, whom he married in 1971. The two have moved away from formal religion, and Henri is honest in his feelings of pain that they are no longer "nurtured by the Body and Blood of Christ in the Eucharist." He comments on communism, capitalism and Christianity as well as his unconditional love for his friends no matter what their views may be.

---

* Henri is referring to a five-week retreat he taught at the Pendle Hill Summer Institute, as mentioned in the previous letter.

Dear Albert and Dee,

Many thanks for your wonderful letter. I really was very grateful to hear from you. During the time of the celebration of the twenty-fifth anniversary of my ordination, my thoughts often went to both of you. In many ways I found myself missing your presence here.*

Your friendship means very much to me, and I cannot really think about my life and the many joys and pains without seeing you as part of the picture. I love you both very much and feel that your being there and my being here is not without many bridges and connections that run very deep.

Thank you for your remarks on our spiritual journeys. I really do not have any problems with your being a dedicated Communist, but it does cause me often much pain that you no longer are nurtured by the Body and Blood of Christ in the Eucharist. I still have a very vivid memory of your wedding and the bread we shared then. I always had hoped that that spiritual event would become a mark for your life together as a family.

Personally, I feel that Communism and Christianity are a lot closer than Capitalism and Christianity and my recent six-month trip to Latin America has referred me very much to that way of thinking. But I also feel very strongly that the death and resurrection of Christ is the greatest event of history and that our ultimate connectiveness [sic] with that event has the potential to make us into people who truly participate in the divine mystery of creation and redemption. I also want you to very much know that my friendship with you is unconditional and based on a deep

---

* Henri celebrated the twenty-fifth anniversary of his ordination at the Genesee Abbey on August 6, 1982. More than a hundred of his family and friends gathered in honor of the occasion, celebrating Mass, sharing a meal and sharing anecdotes about Henri. A large tent was set up outdoors, equipped with a podium for speeches and dining tables from which guests were able to watch the speakers and converse.

affection that I felt from the very moment we met, and I trust that this affection is speaking a language that transcends whatever difference we might have when it comes to expressing ourselves in ideas and words.

I hope the move to your new home will give you much joy and peace. I hope and pray that one day soon I can see you in your new place.

Thanks again for your wonderful friendship.

Peace and love,
Henri Nouwen

This is a letter to a PhD candidate who had written with questions about Henri's approach to pastoral theology.

SEPTEMBER 4, 1982

Dear Mark,

Many thanks for your kind letter. You really want to put me to work!

The many questions you raise are very hard to answer for me, since I am not such a well-organized person as your inquiry suggests.

Instead of answering your questions I simply prefer to tell you that I consider myself primarily a priest who wants to minister as concretely and directly as possible to the people with and for whom I live.

I have never been very concerned about any particular themes, method or approach. Nor have I tried to make any particular contribution to pastoral theology. I also do not think that I know what the greatest concerns and the biggest needs of contemporary pastoral theology are.

When I think about my life and my work, I think about it more as a way of being present to people with all I have. I have always tried to respond as honestly as I possibly could to the needs and concerns of the people who became part of my life, and I have tried to respond with whatever my own life has taught me.

Jesus' invitation to "lay down my life for others" has always meant more to me than any physical martyrdom. I have always heard these words as an invitation to make my own life struggles, my doubts, my hopes, my fears and my joys, my pains, and my moments of ecstasy available to others as a source of consolation and healing. To witness for Christ means to me to witness for Him with what I have seen with my own eyes, heard with my own ears and touched with my own hands.

I do not remember ever having to sit down "to write a book." The publications that you know are more a result of speaking with people, sharing my own life with them and trying to give words to what often remains hidden under the threshold of our consciousness.

I have always felt that the center of our faith is not that God came to take our pains away, but that He came to share them and I have always tried to manifest this divine solidarity by trying to be as present to people in their struggle as possible. It is most important to be with people where joy and pain are experienced and to have them become aware of God's unlimited love in the midst of our limited abilities to help each other.

I don't have a real answer as to who has influenced me the most. If I am honest about it, I think that I am most profoundly influenced by the people I try to minister to. Books, as a whole, have had very little lasting influence on me; often it is people who do not write books that have a greater impact.

Besides the people that you mention that have played some significant role in my education, two others could be mentioned— John Henry Newman and Vincent van Gogh. Although these two are very different people, they both showed me a very great sensitivity for the sacramental quality of existence.

Well, I hope this will not disappoint you too much! Be sure not to treat me as a systematic theologian. I am primarily a person who wants to witness to the real presence of God in our lives.

May the Lord give you much hope, courage and consolation,

With prayers,
Henri Nouwen

This letter is to a good friend who has lost his partner to heart disease. It was originally written in Dutch and is signed, "Harrie," which is how Henri was known to his Dutch family and friends.

Henri mentions his decision to accept Harvard's offer to teach in its Divinity School faculty. He also intends to keep doing pastoral work in Lima, Peru.

Henri writes from his family's vacation home in Losone, Switzerland.

OCTOBER 5, 1982

Beloved Piet,

The world is so vast and so threatening. Love is so tender and delicate and creative. I think about you every day, I pray for you every day and I realize how much you mean to me. The death of Frederik has touched me so deeply and moved me so deeply that for days I could only think about you, your love, your pain, your worries, your faithfulness and now about the sorrow and strange joy that embraces you. I remember as though it was only yesterday the day you first told me about Frederik and the day I first visited you on your houseboat. I can still feel the feelings I experienced on your part and the security which surrounded me when I spoke with you about my own pain and loneliness. Of the many people I met at the Transitorium [one of the main campus buildings at the Utrecht University], you are the only one I have continued to see as a friend and who made me feel that I was understood in a new way. You once brought me flowers to my room in Utrecht, and Frederik once said: "We are really proud of you." This was an experience that opened up something in me that always had remained closed until I met the two of you. A new space, a new sound, a new connectedness.

Thanks to you I got to know Frederik. Despite the fact that we saw each other so seldom and despite the fact we seldom corresponded with each other in recent years, I can no longer imagine my life without having to think about you and Frederik. When I think about Frederik, feelings are emerging in me that I have received from him, feelings of understanding, patience, generosity, tenderness, interest and real love. I have often hoped that you would come to visit me in New Haven, and I have often longed to involve you more deeply into my life. Even in a foreign land, you, together with Maria and Louis ter Steeg, remained the nearby and familiar faces that caused me to long to return to my friends.

I write all this to you because it is true, although I would not have been able to express it until I heard about Frederik's death. I realize now how deeply I love you and him and how deeply grateful I am that it is through you that I got to know him. The "small" words and gestures I received from Frederik are carved into my heart as one of the many signs that God is indeed love, a sign that has indeed been life-giving for me.

Love is stronger than death. You know it and I know it. But I pray for you that this knowledge will descend deeper and deeper into your heart and bear fruit there. I feel your sorrow, your moments of deep loneliness. I feel them because I have always felt them. That's why I experience you now as being so close by. I also feel that strange love of God that envelops you, a joy that is hidden in sorrow. Jesus spoke those mysterious words: "It is best for you that I leave you now . . . so that my Spirit, the consoler, can come." I will continue to pray for you that Frederik's life, but also his death, might bring you closer to God, the consoler.

Beloved Piet, I would love to talk with you about Frederik and about myself. But especially about the Lord who has brought us together in his love. I hope this will be possible soon.

As for myself, I have been in South America for six months, and I am deliberating as to whether I should go back for a longer period of time. It looks like I will be associated with Harvard shortly in such a way that I will be able to combine pastoral work in Lima, Peru, with teaching regularly at Harvard. Details still need to be worked out, but the direction is clear.

I strongly hope that Matthew [Piet and Frederik's foster son] is doing well, send him my sincerest wishes. I hope that you will be a genuine consolation to each other during this time.

Would you ever have the time or peace, please write or phone me. That would mean much to me. I am at the moment (until November 10) in Switzerland.

Many affectionate greetings,
Harrie
[Translation from Dutch by Peter Naus]

A letter to his friend Jim Antal about how to respond to the demands of parishioners.

Henri mentions his most recent book project, Peacework, *about the spirituality of peacemaking. This theme would preoccupy him for several years, but the book would not be published in his lifetime.**

Henri writes from Switzerland.

---

* In 2005, it was published as *Peacework: Prayer, Resistance, Community* (Maryknoll, NY: Orbis).

Dear Jim,

Thanks so much for your good letter. It is a true grace to hear from you and very concretely experience your deep love and friendship. It is a truly life giving gift.

I have been thinking about your struggle with the parish. I feel more and more that what you are experiencing is the true pain of the man of God. You have created a hunger that you cannot still and a thirst you cannot quench. You created your own problem, and that was your task. But it may be that the response is not only gratitude but also ardent desire, impatience, irritation with your limitations and even criticism. Be sure to take all of this into your prayer and let Our Lord purify you. This is the true cross, the suffering, that leads to glory. Try to be very gentle, very open and very forgiving. Let Cindy and your best friends be part of your struggle, but do not let your parishioners become the subject of your inner struggle.

You are tasting something of the mystery of God's majesty. Those who want more and more and more are truly searching, even when they may hurt you in the process. Be sure to teach all your people to pray. Speak to them about prayer. Show them how to pray (including how to sit, where to sit or stand or kneel, etc., when to do it, etc.) and do it with them, young and old. Never go to a meeting, small or large, without inviting people to pray. The Lord will respond and also give you added strength.

Here all is well. I live as a hermit and try to struggle hard with my Lord! I try to be faith-full and stick to it even though at times I am tempted to run off into the Alps, into town, into the lake, into self-complaint, morbid feelings of loneliness or illusion of misunderstood visions! I am especially trying to deal with the intimate connections between my inner pains of sinfulness, shame, guilt, depression and self-rejection and my faithlessness in regard to the Church (relationships with Word, Sacrament and Authority). It is an agonizing struggle but worth it since I am only fifty and can still start a new life!

I read and write about peace and peacemaking. Chaim Potok's book *The Book of Lights* speaks deeply to me. I also read *Waging Peace*, edited by Jim Wallis. Very helpful. Meanwhile, I read Old and New Testament with the peace question in mind. A lot about "the Great Day of God's Anger" (Rev. 6, 17; Joel 2:11; Rom. 1, 2; 1 Col. 8 [?]; Lamentations 1.12; Isaiah 13:9–10; Amos 2.9; Zechariah 12.9–12; Daniel 7, 13–14; 9.27; 11, 31; 12.1; Rev. 1.7) ! Very shocking but also liberating. I have not dared yet to write about it. It feels like touching the Sun!

Love,
Henri

This is another letter to Jim Antal assuring him of his friendship and love. Henri is candid about his struggle with loneliness and his emerging insight that this is linked to what he calls "unfaithfulness to the Church." Henri mentions his hope of joining Jim in a run along the Charles River. This is a reflection of Jim's and other friends' persistent attempts to encourage Henri to pay more attention to his physical health.

OCTOBER 30, 1982

Dear Jim,

Your letter is a real oasis in my desert. I can't tell you how healing and consoling your gentle and loving words are for me. Your affection, your tears, your care and real friendship are a true gift of God for me. More than ever I am aware of the power of the word. Your words are words with new life, and they truly give life. I am so thankful for your courage to express yourself so directly, openly and [with] vulnerability, and thus to become a real source of grace. If you ever have any doubts about your vocation to the ministry, let me take that away simply by saying that your ministry of friendship and love to me is enough to be able to dissolve any possible doubt.

Let me try to tell you what is happening to me. I am starting to realize that my deep experiences of loneliness are connected with my unfaithfulness to the Church. I suddenly realize why the Church is called the "bride" of Christ. My relationship with the Church is a marriage relationship, and my "liberal" past has been a form of unfaithfulness. Sure, the Church is not without its many weaknesses, but you don't love your bride because she has no weaknesses. A celibate is not a bachelor. It is a person with a unique connection with the Church and therefore with a special call to faithfulness, obedience and love. Here I am rediscovering this, and it means a true experience of repentance and a true desire to love in a converted way.

I also discover that only as a deep faithful lover of the Church I can take risks on the level of peacemaking. You can only risk your life when you are in love. My lack of courage and outspokenness in many crucial issues of our time is clearly connected with my spiritual homelessness.

It means a lot to me that you are willing to support me in this struggle. Your love and friendship as well as Cindy's make this possible.

I look forward to seeing you soon. On Nov. 10 I will be back in Boston. I very much want to share with you my writing on peacemaking. I finished $2/3$ of the text. I hope to have a first draft when I return. And indeed, how good will it be when we can run along the Charles River together!

Thanks for writing about your struggles at the School.* No, the solution is not a social solution. Religion is not spending social time together. Ministry is to point again and again to the Lord. He

---

* Jim was a high school chaplain.

alone can bring us what we need. It is so important to discern constantly if our words and actions bring others closer to God or not. It
is a very important criterion on our work. In fact the only criterion
that works! Once you live and work with that criterion you will be
at peace even when people criticize you or show anger or hostility.
The word of God is a sword that often divides people. But without
that word the world cannot find peace. Be strong and have courage.

See you soon.
Love,
Henri

*Henri used letters to build friendships and networks. He would almost
always write letters to couples, including the spouse in his words and men-
tioning children or common friends if they have them [these have been
edited out of most letters published here]. In the case of Jim Antal and
Cindy Shannon, however, he often wrote to them separately, signaling a
close friendship with each of them.*

*In this letter to Cindy he responds to struggles she shared with him
about her changing relationship with her family as she gets older. He also
addresses the importance of stories when teaching children.*

*Henri had just moved to Boston in preparation for his teaching responsi-
bilities at Harvard Divinity School. He would begin as a lecturer giving public lectures and retreats about the Christian spiritual life and by fall 1983
accept a professorship of divinity. The plan was to teach one semester per
year in 1984 and 1985 and work in Latin America the rest of the time. He
lived in a university-operated apartment on Ware Street, before moving into
the Carriage House, a part of the Center for the Study of World Religions.*

OCTOBER 30, 1982

Dear Cindy,

Thanks so much for your good letter and very caring words. I have thought that you are struggling with the integration of two calls: "Love your father and mother" and "Leave your father and mother." Both are divine "commands," and the struggle is to make them both true. Somehow loving asks for leaving, precisely since love is not simply emotional and filial attachment, but spiritual love that leads your parents and sisters closer to God, the source of all love. I think the struggle to make this true is a life-long struggle, often with feelings of shame, guilt and even anger. But we have to live through it all. It is God's way to purify us and to make us re-claim God as our Father, Mother, Brother and Sister.

Keep telling stories. The stories themselves will teach the children, now and later. All that counts is knowing and living the story. Don't explain, apply, exegete, analyze or comment too much. Let the children act out the story and they will know what it means for them individually. The story is the place where we can feel at home.

I enclose two very beautiful cards for your prayer books. Look at the space between the fingers. That space makes all the difference. Created in love and created free—.

Love,
Henri

Henri received letters for all kinds of reasons, and in this case it was to answer a questionnaire about paranormal experiences.

DECEMBER 9, 1982

Dear Bruce,

Many thanks for your very wonderful letter and for your questionnaire. I really do not know how to answer your questions, but I thought I would write you a short note.

I don't have any memory of the experience of being removed from my normal mental state of mind during a sermon. As a whole I cannot witness to any kind of experiences of the nature to which you refer.

The only thing I could mention would be the experience that quite often people to whom I have spoken hear more than I myself planned to say or intended to express. At different times I have come to realize that God spoke through me although I expressed myself in a very limited and broken way. Often I have been deeply moved by the awareness that people really heard God speaking to them, even though I was far from a perfect instrument. In that sense I have had a real experience of what it means to speak in the name of the Lord. I do not really think that the terms such as "experience of profession" can be applied to my experiences, but I must say that preaching is one of the most profound and meaningful tasks of my life. Often I felt that God really revealed Himself to me in new ways through this ministry.

Thanks again for your kind letter.

I hope this will help you a little bit.

Yours,
Henri Nouwen

This is a letter to a grieving widow.

Dear Mrs. Walsh,

Many thanks for your very kind note. I was really glad to hear from you.

I want you to know that I keep you very close in my thoughts and prayers. I know and understand how very hard these days must be for you. Your husband was such a wonderful man and has given you so much, and after 54 years of marriage, it is very hard to be alone. It certainly will take quite a while to let him go, because even though he has died, in many ways the reality of his death can only slowly be accepted. I am very grateful and glad that you had such a wonderful life with him because that will make it possible for you to live on in gratefulness and peace.

You still have an important task in life—a task of prayer and a task of service and a task of simply saying "Thank You" for all the good things the Lord has given you. I am sure your husband will continue to help you in the fulfillment of this task because, as you know, his absence also means a new way of becoming present. He is becoming present to you now as a spiritual support in your life as a Christian, and his memory will be a real strength to you in the years to come.

I still experience my mother's guidance in my life even though she died four years ago. She continues to be a source of hope and courage to me. Although I miss her very much, I also know that it was good for her to go so that she could be with us in a new way. I am sure this will be true for you and your husband. Just as Jesus' leaving was good for his disciples, so the leaving of those who are close to us can also be good for us. This might be very hard for us to accept and understand, but it is a truth that can give us a lot of consolation and comfort.

I am glad that you liked the flowers.

With many kind wishes,
Yours,
Henri Nouwen

Not every letter Henri received was from a soul in trouble! Here he writes to a woman whose problem is that she has a wonderful life but is longing for a more personal, intimate and direct relationship with God.

FEBRUARY 3, 1983

Dear Ruth,

Many thanks for your very lovely letter. I am grateful to you for writing me about yourself and your family, especially about your desire to grow closer to the Lord.

You have, indeed, lived a very rich and beautiful life, and God has blessed you in many ways. I guess in our culture there are few people who could say the things you can say and tell the stories you can tell.

In some way I feel that God has been very active in your life and has been very generous to you and your family. What you seem to ask for is for more intimate, direct, personal contact with Him, a way of experiencing Him more directly. It is a beautiful desire to have, and the desire itself shows God's special love for you.

I, obviously, do not have a simple answer to your question, but two things come to mind. First of all is gratitude. Maybe you could try to develop a prayer of gratitude. Many people find it hard to be grateful. Many people feel that they need more than they have and are often angry that they do not receive what they want. You have the experience of being given many good things, and, therefore, it will be easier for you to live a life of gratefulness. Gratitude is one of the greatest Christian virtues. "Eucharist" means saying thanks, and if you could say thanks, not just for what you have received, but also for all the gifts God gives to his people, your life would become more and more a Eucharistic life, a life in which you say thanks to the giver of life.

Secondly, I think that your life can be more and more a life of intercession. Jesus' suffering is for all people. He came to bring all people closer to His Father. One of the greatest vocations we as Christians have is to pray for others. To pray for the many people who we know as well as for the many we don't know but of whose suffering we are aware. My sense is that you will come closer to the Lord Jesus the more you pray for others, because Jesus came for others and praying for others is entering more deeply into the mystery of His divine intercession. There are so many people who need our prayers, and to take the time to lift them up to the Lord is one of the greatest services we can perform.

Maybe you can buy a notebook in which you can write down all the people for whom you want to pray. I am sure that book will fill up very soon, and you can take that book with you in your prayer and ask the Lord to touch all the people whose names you have brought together. Doing so, you certainly will experience more fully the love of Jesus.

I think that a life of grateful prayer and a life of intercession for others will bring you the goal you seek.

There is much more to say about this, and I am quite willing to write you again when you desire that. I just hope that these few thoughts at least will point in a direction that might be helpful to you. If not, please let me know and we will try other ways.

Be sure of my fervent prayer for you. My conviction is that those who desire to come closer to the Lord will be richly rewarded. Be sure to ask the Lord to give you the gift of prayers. It is the greatest gift He wants to give.

Sincerely yours,
Henri Nouwen

Henri's diary about his seven-month stay at the Abbey of the Genesee elicited a strong response from many people. Earlier, in the letter from May 13, 1982, we read how Henri responded to a reader who was disappointed that he had not been able to change as a result of his contemplative sojourn. In this letter, written nearly a year later, the issue has come up again, and this time Henri has a slightly different response.

APRIL 26, 1983

Dear Tom,

Many thanks for your very kind letter. I really appreciated deeply your honest response to *The Genesee Diary*.

I can very well understand that you felt disappointed with the conclusion and often I wished I could have written something else, but I felt I had to be honest and tell the whole truth. Now when I look back at those times, I think that many changes have taken place but maybe not the changes that I had hoped for.

The mystery of God's Grace is that He often changes us in ways that we were not planning on and that sometimes we do not have eyes to see or ears to hear these changes in ourselves. I deeply believe that God is always active in us and always molding us into new people.

During the last few years I have been able to make some very important decisions. The most important decision is to dedicate a large portion of my time to working in Latin America, and this

decision is not independent from my time at the Abbey. I am realizing that my desire to work with the poor is intimately connected
with my life and time at the Abbey. The contemplative life and the
life with the poor seem very intimately connected. So maybe there
is less reason to be disappointed than seemed to be.

Thanks so much for writing.

Sincerely yours,
Henri Nouwen

*In the previous letter, we read that Henri has made a decision to spend
more time working in Latin America. By December, when he writes this
next letter, we see that his plans have changed dramatically. Instead of
working in Latin America, he went on a ten-week, United States–wide
tour to speak about it. It was a reverse mission taken up after accepting
that his strength was not in daily missionary life but in galvanizing awareness about US involvement in Central America and articulating the gospel
message of how to respond to injustice, corruption and violence as a Christian.*

*This letter also mentions L'Arche for the first time. L'Arche Interna-
tional is an organization founded by Jean Vanier in France in 1964 for
people with mental and physical handicaps. Vanier had reached out to
Henri in the late 1970s (he wanted to use a quote from one of Henri's
books), and the two men had corresponded thereafter. Vanier would be a
guest lecturer in Henri's classes at Harvard. In 1983, Vanier invited Henri
to visit L'Arche. This visit would prove to be an important one for Henri,
as we'll see.*

DECEMBER 9, 1983

Dear Cindy and Jim,

Many thanks for your wonderful letter. It always is a gift to hear from you.

While I was traveling through the U.S. and lecturing about Central America, I became aware that while I was exhausting myself to prevent war, the chances of war were increasing. This has helped me to realize that sometimes the power of evil seduces us to work for peace in such a way that we come close to losing our soul. Peace Pilgrim helped me see how important inner peace is.* It is that sense of God's presence in our life that allows us to trust in the power of God's peace even when we do little. Living in L'Arche with the handicapped also opened my eyes to that peace that does not belong to this world but can be found here already.

Be sure to make this inner peace your utmost priority. I say this to myself as much as to you. When we radiate the peace of Christ we are peacemakers, and then our peace activism can witness to this inner peace. But without that inner peace our actions easily become instruments of the powers of war and destruction.

Jesus' words "Pray unceasingly for the strength to survive all that is going to happen and to stand with confidence" are of crucial importance for us in these days. Prayer should be our first concern. Without prayer even our "good busyness" will lead to our destruction. If there is anything that I learned from my lecture-preaching tour, it is this newfound insight that I want to share with you.

Maybe you should make a prayer room in your house or at

---

* Peace Pilgrim was the chosen name of Mildred Norman Ryder (1908–1981), an American, nondenominational pacifist and peace activist known especially for walking more than 25,000 miles over twenty-eight years across the United States for peace. Henri used her writings in his 1984 "Introduction to the Spiritual Life" course at Harvard and kept a resource file with newsletters from the organization that formed after her death in 1981.

STOP,* a place to where you can go and often return and let God speak to you. I more and more think of myself as the lost sheep entangled in the bushes. I need to be found by Christ and set free from my many meetings, discussions, planning sessions, strategies, etc. I need to become very poor and very simple so that I can be picked up by the Lord and led back to His home.

Never forget the words: "In the world you will have trouble but be brave, I have overcome the world." Every time you spend silent time in your prayer room, you celebrate Christ's victory over the world (over death, over the evil one) and allow yourself to taste already now the peace that comes from this victory—

It is so important for the people around you to see that peace of Christ reflected in your eyes, your hands and your words. There is more power in that than in all your teaching and organizing. That is the truth we need to keep telling each other.

I love you very much and pray for and with you every day. I also know that 1984 is going to be a very liberating year for both of you and for me. Our friendship makes me so sure of that.

Peace and Love,
Henri

Letters to Henri were often from people in crisis. In this case, he is writing to a friend whose husband is struggling with brain damage after a stroke and whose youngest son is in trouble with drugs. She is losing her ability to cope.

Henri writes from L'Arche in Trosly-Breuil, France, where, back for the second time, he is undertaking a four-month stay. He is unclear about

---

* Student/Teacher Organization to Prevent Nuclear War, a national organization Antal founded while a high school chaplain.

staying at Harvard Divinity School and at Vanier's invitation is exploring a potential call to L'Arche.

SEPTEMBER 11, 1984

Dear Barb,

After reading your very pain-filled but also very grace-filled letter I had only one desire: to come and visit you. More than anything I wanted to spend some time with you to offer you my love and friendship and to learn from you who has been tempted so much.

I cannot come to you now, since I am in France with Jean Vanier and his community for the handicapped. I so much wish you could also be here, since this is such a place of consolation and comfort.

I realize that I cannot come to you and you cannot come to me. But there is a special solution. My closest friend John Mogabgab, who worked with me for five years in Yale, and his wife, Marjorie Thompson, who is a minister at the Presbyterian Church in Stanford, live close to you, and I have written them to ask them to visit you. This would be a real good thing because we all belong to the same suffering body of Christ and we can comfort each other as members of that body. Please receive John and Marjorie with love, and you will receive me. Later I hope to visit you myself.

Meanwhile, I simply want to ask you to trust that the Lord will continue to give you the strength to live through your pain with your husband and your son. Your letter shows that you have a great faith, courage and confidence even though you yourself do not feel it as much. But God has not left you alone. I am sure that He will give you all the strength you need to be faithful in the midst of your agony.

Be sure not to lose your life in the lives of your husband and son Robert. Their lives are best served when you can claim your own life as unique and different from theirs. I know this is easy to write, but I write it to encourage you to take some time for yourself, to read, to pray, to go out with friends, to enjoy nature, to listen to music, to breathe your own breath! Your life is unique in God's eyes, just as Robert and your husband's life.

I very much hope to be of any help to you that is possible. I am confident that the Lord will show us how we can best be for each other. Somehow I feel that your suffering will bear many fruits even though they are not visible yet.

Be sure of my fervent prayers for you and your husband and son Robert.

Peace and love,
Henri

Over the years, Henri found numerous places to write. One of these was St. Bede, a Benedictine monastery in Eau Claire, Wisconsin. His host was Sister Connie Ostrander, OSB, the prioress of the community, whom he met in 1983 while keynote speaker for a National Catholic Education Association (NCEA) conference. Ostrander and Henri shared a religious vocation, and many of the letters they exchanged over the years are words of encouragement and witness.

Even as his own vocational path remains unclear, he writes with certainty to his friend Connie that St. Bede must provide a refuge of prayer and contemplation for people who are "so hungry for God."

SEPTEMBER 16, 1984

Dear Connie,

Thanks for your good words and the lovely photographs of Tessie.*
I send her many kisses from France. Tell her that "Uncle" Henri loves her and waves to her from the other side of the ocean.

I start my thirty day retreat at the end of the month. Keep me

---

* Tessie (Tess) is Sister Connie's niece.

in your prayers. I need many conversions to be able to be what I am called to be.

I often think of you and the community. I so much hope that St. Bede will be a real place of prayer and contemplation. It needs to be that to be a leaven in our world. I so much hope that many will spend long hours in the presence of the blessed Sacrament. It is the place from where true healing and new life comes forth. It also is the place where we come to know our true call.

Reform and renewal always means a return to contemplative prayer. Many, many will come to St. Bede when they realize that it is the place of unceasing prayer. People are so hungry for God. They look for people who can let them drink from the well of eternal life. Make your home into such a well, and you will be rewarded with true peace, true joy and a very fruitful ministry—

Thanks again for all your friendship and support. Greetings to all.

Love,
Henri

Henri writes to his friends Baldwin and Roni on the occasion of the birth of their second child. Although his friends have moved away from religion, he encourages them to "seriously consider" the spiritual life of their child. Henri writes to his friends while on a thirty-day retreat at L'Arche.

SEPTEMBER 20, 1984

Dear Baldwin and Roni,

Many joys with Nora. While I am in France, my assistant told me about your new Baby. You both and Lee must be very glad and I am glad with and for you.

It was great to hear from you again when I was in LA.* I tried to reach you but did not succeed. I also didn't have your right address anymore, so couldn't write.

I often think of you and pray for you. I regret the minimal contact, but I trust that our lives will grow closer again as we move into the future. I am for four months with Jean Vanier and his community of handicapped people in France.

I am making a thirty-day retreat with a Belgian Jesuit and struggle hard to deepen my relationship with Jesus. I am more and more convinced that only with a deep and lasting connectedness with God will I be able to fight the many demons that surround me. I just returned from Guatemala and saw, as never before, how the forces of light and the forces of darkness are in battle. Both great Saintliness and great Evil are manifest.†

In the Spring semester I will be at Harvard to teach. For the next five years I probably will be half time at Harvard and the rest of the year trying to travel, write, give retreats, etc.

I hope and pray that you will consider seriously Nora's spiritual life. Offer her the light of Christ and a journey supported by the grace of Baptism, Confirmation and the Eucharist. I guess that much of that has lost its meaning for you, but I hope and pray that you continue to think about introducing your children into the life of the Spirit. There is such a wealth of true life hidden in the Sacraments, and I feel, ever since my role in your wedding, that I have to keep calling you to that place of healing and grace.

Your picture in the ocean with Lee [their son] still hangs in my

---

* Henri may have been in Los Angeles to visit friends at the Los Angeles Catholic Worker.

† Henri traveled to Guatemala with Peter Weiskel, his friend and administrative assistant, to visit Father John Vesey, the priest who went to live in the village where Father Stanley Francis Rother was murdered by a rightist death squad of the Guatemalan military for being an outspoken advocate for the poor. Henri published a book about his experiences in Guatemala entitled *Love in a Fearful Land: A Guatemalan Story* (Notre Dame, IN: Ave Maria Press, 1985).

study and makes me think of you often. Maybe I should have a new one since it has been such a long time!

Let us stay in touch. Somehow we need each other. I am sure of that. I love you both very much. Be sure of that!

Love,
Henri

In 1984, two friends of Henri, a married couple, entered into a marital crisis.

In this first letter of many included in this volume, Henri writes to Cynthia. Her husband, Ronald, has started seeing another woman, and she is devastated. The original letter is seven pages and handwritten.

SEPTEMBER 24, 1984

Dear Cynthia,

Your letter is a real gift to me. I am very grateful to you for writing and telling me about the terrible pain you are experiencing. I didn't know if you wanted me to know about your struggles and therefore didn't know how to offer you my support and deep friendship. But now I feel that you have given me a new freedom to write you and express to you my feelings, thoughts and hopes.

Let me first say that I start a thirty-day retreat this coming Sunday. For a whole month I will be in silence and prayer together with five Jesuits (one from Colombia, one from Italy, one from Holland and two from Belgium). We will be directed in this desert experience by a Belgian Jesuit who also guided my day retreat last year. I tell you this because I want you to know that during this time you and Ronald will have a very special place in my heart and I will spend many hours praying for you, your life, your family and your future. I also wanted to write you this letter before the retreat so that you know how close I feel to you and how dear you are to me.

Your feelings of being lost, unloved and a failure, your anger and rage, your fears for your children and your future. . . . I know how much agony and pain they create. Being so alone, so rejected, so offended, so betrayed must really rip you apart and wound you deeply.

Ever since I have received your letter, I have wondered how I could best help you at this so critical moment of your life. Let me simply write you what came to my mind most strongly. Most of it came from my own experience, and I hope that you can receive it as words of someone who loves you very much.

It seems crucial to me that now, more than ever before, you realize deeply that your worth and value does not depend on any-one else. You have to claim your own inner truth. You are a per-son worth being loved and called to give love, not because anyone says so or act so [sic], but because you are created out of love and live in the embrace of a God who didn't hesitate to send His only son to die for us. The crisis you are living through now is one of the most difficult crises for anyone to have to live through, but it can become the most important moment to claim your own inner value as a person and a woman. Your being good and worthy of love does not depend on Ronald or any other human being. You have to keep saying to yourself: "I am being loved by an uncondi-tional, unlimited love, and that love allows me to be a free person, center of my own actions and decisions." The more you can come to realize this, the more you will be able to forgive Ronald and love him in his brokenness. Without a deep feeling of self-respect you cannot forgive and will always feel anger, resentment and revenge. The greatest human act is forgiveness: "Forgive us our sins, as we forgive those who have sinned against us." Forgiveness stands in the center of God's love for us and also in the center of our love for each other. For us people, loving one another means forgiving one another over and over again. The reason that forgiving is so very hard for us is that we do not really believe that we are deeply loved by a love that is faithful, because it is God's love.

I also want to respond to the idea that Ronald never really liked you or loved you deeply. This a real "trap." Every time someone says that retrospectively he or she didn't really love us, we have to think strong and realize that love among people is not first of all a feeling or an emotion or a sentiment but a decision of the will to be faithful to each other. You and Ronald love each other first of all because you both have willed to live together, care for each other, offer your children a safe home and grow always closer to each other. There really are no people whom we can love with unlimited feelings of love. We are all imperfect, broken, sinful people, but we are able to love one another because we are able to *will* to be faithful and constantly forgive each other's unfaithfulness. I have known you and Ronald well enough to say that you are both very talented people with great gifts of heart and mind, that your marriage vows were based on real affection, real mutuality and real sharing. Your will to love each other is based on a very beautiful foundation which, I think, is strong enough to survive the painful crisis you are going through. Cynthia, there is nothing wrong with you and your decision to be married is not ever based on the condition that there never should be anything wrong. It is based on the beautiful truth that God loves you and Ronald so much that he brought you together to be a sign of hope to each other, to your children and to your friends by a faithfulness that has been made possible because of God's love.

This all may sound a little distant considering the enormous concrete pain you are experiencing. But I still want to write this to you because in times of deep emotional pain it is so important to hold on to the truth we know even though we do not feel it. I am deeply convinced that new feelings of peace and joy will again be given to you when you hold on to what you know to be true in the midst of your darkness.

I also want you to know that I do love Ronald very much, now as much as before. He is a very important and very loving friend for me ever since I met him in Notre Dame. I want to be faithful to that friendship even though I suffer from what he is doing to you, to his children, to himself and also to me. This sin and his unfaithfulness is real and cannot be just talked about lightly. To the contrary, this time is a crucial time for him. He has to make a very important decision. He has to reaffirm his marriage vows, break all contacts with the person he has been seeing, ask forgiveness and start living a new, converted life. That is obviously not all that easy, but he has friends who want to support him and show him the way. I want to do whatever I can to help him in choosing that way and becoming the husband and father he promised to be. My love for him is very strong, and I hope to show him that.

Dear Cynthia, you and Ronald are very important friends. Your life and my life will never be lived in separateness. God has given us to each other, and we are meant to be signs of hope to each other, especially in moments like these. You do not only mean much to me but also to my family, and we all want to see your family to be strong and loving and full of joy and peace.

Please do not give up. Trust that new light will appear and that much will depend on your own choice not to give in to self-rejection but to trust that you have the strength to offer new life to Ronald, your children and your friends.

I pray for you with great conviction and hope. I love you dearly and hope that my love can be a real support for you in these dark days. Trust in God's love, but also in Ronald's ability to show you that love again. Your life is just beginning! I am praying that this painful period in your marriage will lead you and Ronald to an always deeper commitment to God and to each other.

Yours with love and prayer,
Henri

Henri did not choose sides or judge his friends. Just after writing to Cynthia, Henri writes to both his friends with words of encouragement.

SEPTEMBER 1984

Dear Cynthia and Ronald,

I pray for you as I prepare for a thirty-day retreat. I am very aware of your struggles. Please be faithful at all cost! The Lord has given you a great treasure: each other and the children. He wants to keep you together in his love. Do not forget to pray together even when it seems hard or close to impossible.

I very much want to stay in touch and know what is happening with you.

Stay in touch with the women of Madonna House. Their prayers are very healing and very strong. I know this from experience.

I will take you with me into my thirty-day desert experience. I offer it to the Lord for you both and trust that he will touch you deeply with his healing presence. Think of this time as a time of purification and renewal. Your life together has just begun. Give it a real chance to grow stronger and deeper. I love to support you in that with all my heart, love, strength and hope.

Love,
Henri

In late summer 1984, Mark O. Hatfield (1922–2011), a Republican senator from Oregon who had a reputation for independence and integrity,

came under suspicion in an ethics investigation.* Henri first met Hatfield
in regard to US foreign policy in South and Central America in the 1980s.
    Henri writes to Hatfield about how to handle the injustice and pain of
being unfairly accused.

SEPTEMBER 30, 1984

Dear Senator Hatfield,

Just during the last weeks, I have become more acutely aware of the
very difficult months which are behind you and the struggles you
are still facing. Jim Towey wrote me a wonderful letter in which he
shared some of the pain you have had to suffer and in which he
expressed in a most moving way the deep affection he has for you
and your family.†

    I am in France, living this past month with Jean Vanier and his
community of handicapped people. It is a very special grace for me
to live among people who suffer deep wounds but whose wounds
have become the places where God's compassionate love is becoming most visible. Living in a fellowship of the weak, I am learning
much about the mystery of God's presence among his people.

    Tonight I am starting a thirty-day retreat together with five Je-
suits who also came here. It will be a period of total silence with
no other task but prayer. A Belgian Jesuit will guide us in the Spiritual Exercises of Ignatian spirituality during these thirty days. I
am writing you this because I want you to know that you will have
a very special place in my heart during this month. I know it is
going to be a very intense, demanding and even trying month for
you, but I hope that the knowledge that you have a friend who lifts

---

* In January 1985, the Senate Ethics Committee dropped its inquiry and
recommended no action against Hatfield; http://www.nytimes.com/1985/01/16/us
/ethics-panel-finds-no-corruption-in-hatfield-dealings-with-gree.html.

† Jim Towey was senior adviser to Hatfield. He later served as director of the White
House Office of Faith-Based and Community Initiatives. Henri and Towey became
friends and corresponded regularly. Henri wrote this letter to Hatfield at the behest
of Towey.

you up daily to the Lord will be a source of consolation to you. The thirty-day retreat is like a desert experience in which one is invited to fight the demons and purify one's heart in order to be able to be a faithful servant of the Lord in this world. It is certainly not going to be an easy time for me since there are so many demons waiting to possess me, but like the Lord's own time in the desert it is a time to deepen and reaffirm one's choice for life and the Lord of life. You will be with me in this time, and I have a deep conviction that our lives are connected in such a way that the Lord will not touch me with his love without also letting that have its effect in your heart. So please trust our unity in this time during which you are very busy and during which I am very free.

I have been thinking a lot about the agony you must have been experiencing. What is more painful than seeing your own integrity being questioned by a press behaving like a "roaring lion looking for someone to devour" (1 Peter 5:8)? I can hardly think of a suffering harder to undergo. Our name and reputation as sincere, honorable, trustworthy people belong to the core of our being, and when we are being attacked right at that place we are most tempted to give the demon a foothold in our heart.

How to live in such a period of threat and temptation is the great spiritual question. I would like to write you a few reflections on this question even though I have no full answer. My own life is so broken and tainted with sin and ambiguities that I do not have the clarity of vision that is required. But I hope that you are willing to receive these reflections as coming from a friend who deeply respects you, sincerely loves you and eagerly wants to offer you support and friendship during these hard times.

As you know so well, the great temptation of every human being and—I dare to say—especially of a politician is to let his identity be determined by the people who surround him, support him, vote for him, etc. The truth is that we are not who people say we are—good or bad—but we are people infinitely loved by God even though we are sinners. To this truth you have to return over and again. In these months your greatest temptation is to be only concerned to prove to your "enemies" that they are wrong in what they say of you. The more you fight your enemies, the greater the danger is to get caught in their nets. I am still very grateful for your advice not to become "too political."* You warned me of all the manipulations and blackmail I would become subject to. You said, "Remain a man of the Spirit of God, and you will do more for politics than when you try to become too much part of the life of the politician." You were so helpful to me there. I knew you spoke from your heart. You knew that finally the only one we should cling to is our Lord himself. I urge you to cling to him in a very special way. Your true name is the name God has given to you, and no human being can take that name away from you. Nor you nor I can predict your political future. You might or might not be able to convince others of your integrity, and it might be that you will have to suffer a very painful alone-ness in which you have no other company than the Lord himself. Do not be afraid for that. Look at Him when He remains silent before Pilate. Look at Him too when he remains obedient to his Father in the knowledge that the Father will never leave him alone: "The time will come . . . when you will be scattered, each going his own way and leaving me alone. And yet I am not alone, because the Father is with me" (John 16:32).

I realize that this is one of the hardest periods of your life, since one tries to do harm to you in the center of your being. But it also is the true hour of faith and fidelity. It is a time of dying with Christ. It is dark and lonely, but when you know that your heart is united with the heart of Christ the powers of darkness will not destroy you. If within a few months you will be re-elected and all investigations will have restored your full honor, you can be very grateful but do not have to be exuberant saying: "I always told you

---

* Henri may be referring to his 1983 speaking tour, "An Interrupted Journey: Peacemaking in Nicaragua and Peru."

so." But if you will not be re-elected and not receive the satisfactory response you expect, you may feel sad but do not have to become depressed, resentful or bitter. In both situations you can become more compassionate, that is, a man who suffers with Christ and thus gains the life that even death cannot destroy.

There is a joy deeply hidden in the heart of the suffering Christ. It is a joy that is not alien to you. You have tasted it already. It is the joy of the children of God who know their weakness and broken-ness but who always continue to experience the abundance of his forgiving and recreating love.

I have wondered what would help you in your life of prayer dur-ing these days of struggle and temptation. I think that this is the time to learn the "prayer of the heart." I have asked Peter Weiskel, my assistant at Harvard, to send you the book *The Art of Prayer.** I consider it one of the best books on prayer. It is an anthology of writings of 19th-century Russian mystics. It is not a book to read but to meditate with. One or two sentences may be enough to nurture you for a long time. The introduction may be worth reading first, to give you some idea what is meant by the "prayer of the heart." It is the prayer that teaches you to live in the house of God already, now even though you are still surrounded by the dark powers of this world. I hope this book will give you much consolation and new strength.

Meanwhile, know that God holds you in His love and that I pray for you daily in the solitude of the retreat.

I am wishing you much hope, courage and confidence.

United in Our Lord,
Henri J. M. Nouwen

---

* *The Art of Prayer: An Orthodox Anthology*, compiled by Igumen Chariton of Valamo; trans. E. Kadloubovsky and E. M. Palmer; ed. with an introduction by Timothy Ware (London: Faber and Faber, 1966).

Letters are a good way to catch up and stay in touch. Here is a letter from Henri to his friends Cindy Shannon and Jim Antal reporting back about his experience while on retreat ("pure grace") as well as notice of his busy schedule of traveling and writing. He has three books on the go!

He comments on money, urging Jim to do what needs to be done for a new social justice initiative and to trust that the "money will come."

NOVEMBER 10, 1984

Dear Cindy and Jim,

Many thanks for your wonderful card and letter. The retreat was a tremendous experience.* Pure grace. A truly new encounter with Jesus and a rededication to a life of ministry with, in and for him. My depression and fatigue are completely gone. I have never felt so good in ten years! Thanks so much for your part in this. I hope we soon have a chance to talk about it all.

Do what needs to be done! Money will come. I am sure of that. The children of the light need to be at least as smart as the children of the darkness! A computer and good wiring of the house seem to be minimal requirements for getting the Good News around! (Mens sana in casa sana!†) I am sure you are diplomatic and tactful enough to let your staff take a few undiplomatic and untactful risks!‡ The Lord won't leave you bankrupt (ask Mother Teresa for advice on this!).

I am very excited about being in Europe again. I am learning much about French spirituality, French art, French cooking, French language and especially French Saints (Thérèse of Lisieux,

---

* Henri is referring to his Ignatian retreat, referenced in earlier letters.

† Latin phrase meaning: "A healthy mind in a healthy home."

‡ Jim had just become the new executive secretary of the Fellowship of Reconciliation, the oldest and largest interfaith pacifist organization in the United States.

Curé of Ars,* Margaret Mary Alacoque, Bernadette Soubirous, Vincent de Paul, Charles de Foucauld, etc., etc.). After Thanksgiving I will go back to France and visit Paris, Taizé and Ars.

Peter [Weiskel] and I have nearly finished a small book on John Vesey and his work in Guatemala.† Meanwhile I am still working on the peace book and on the book about "Intimacy, Fecundity and Ecstasy."‡

I hope and pray the baby "feels good." The months are moving along fine, and I hope to be close by when the time has come to fulfillment.

Be sure to keep some kind of inner and outer space for yourself. It is very important that you are not always overextended. In the U.S. it seems that every situation quickly becomes urgent or even emergent. But it might be a lack of faith after all. I realize this when I notice the French taking 12–2 pm to have a leisurely dinner every day! For them everything seems less urgent than a good meal!

Peace,
Henri

After careful discernment, Henri resigned from his position at Harvard Divinity School in July 1985. He is now living for a year in L'Arche in Trosly-Breuil, France. He is happy with his decision, writing "All is well here, very well indeed." Life has not slowed down, however, and he is as busy as ever with traveling, speaking and writing.

---

* Saint Jean-Baptiste Vianney.

† See letter to Baldwin and Roni, September 20, 1984.

‡ This was published as *Lifesigns: Intimacy, Fecundity, and Ecstasy in Christian Perspective* (Garden City, NY: Doubleday, 1986), the first of many books inspired by Jean Vanier and the handicapped people Henri met at L'Arche.

The move to L'Arche was primarily a personal one. Henri was exhausted and lonely, and he needed a home. Jean Vanier recognized this longing and invited him to Trosly-Breuil to live with him, his mother, Madame Pauline "Mammie" Vanier, and the community of handicapped people and their assistants at L'Arche.

Henri's writing followed this change of place and focus. It moves away from the political arena of justice work in Latin and Central America toward peace work in the inner landscape of people's hearts. His manuscript on peacemaking was set aside for a treatise on human intimacy (Lifesigns: Intimacy, Fecundity, and Ecstasy in Christian Perspective). *This book was written in direct response to Vanier's interest in human sexuality, which found expression in* Man and Woman He Made Them, *for which Henri wrote the foreword.*

Henri provides his friend Cindy Shannon with an update on his activities.

AUGUST 8, 1985

Dear Cindy,

Many thanks for your very kind letter with all the good news about you, Jim and Luke.

I look forward to receiving the pictures of Luke. Be sure to include pictures of Jim and yourself.

Thanks for your response to Jean's book.* I am very glad to know that you like it so much. I also feel that that book may be important to Jim when he reflects on a response to Richard Foster's article in *Sojourners*.† We talked about this article on the plane to San Francisco. Jean's vision on human sexuality might prove to be very important for future discussion. It might help us to

---

* *Man and Woman He Made Them* (Mahwah, NJ: Paulist Press, 1985). Henri wrote the foreword, calling it "A truly inspired book with profound insight into the mystery of human sexuality."

† Henri may be referring to Richard Foster, "God's Gift of Sexuality: Celebration and Warning in the Context of Faith" (*Sojourners*, July 1985). Foster is a Christian theologian and author in the Quaker tradition.

find the right tone of conversation while being very careful in dismissing age-old wisdom based on tradition, scripture and human experience. It is quite understandable that issues around human sexuality create more response than even the nuclear issue. They go to the core of our humanity. Therefore it is very important to be very thoughtful in our writing and talking about sexuality and not jump too fast on any bandwagon, whether church or fundamentalist, conservative or progressive. We need a real new way of thinking about this, and I think that Jean Vanier can help us much.

All is well here, very well indeed. I just revised (practically rewrote) *With Open Hands*.* I had never read it in English (I wrote it in Dutch) and was shocked to realize that less than a third of it made any sense to me. I wonder how and why it ever became popular. (Probably because of the pictures!).

Now I am re-working the *Sojourners* article.† Tomorrow I go to Ireland for a few days. I take a boat from Le Havre with an Irish group of handicapped people who return to Ireland after a month in Trosly. The boat takes 20 hours! I will stay with friends in Cork.

Love to Jim.

Peace,
Henri

---

* This is Henri's book about prayer published in 1971 as *Met Open Handen: Notities over het Gebed* with photographs by two Dutch friends, Ron P. van den Bosch and Theo Robert. The English translation was published as *With Open Hands* (Notre Dame, IN: Ave Maria Press, 1972).

† Henri may be referring to a three-part series of articles he published in *Sojourners* on the theme of intimacy that would be published as *Lifesigns: Intimacy, Fecundity, and Ecstasy in Christian Perspective* (Garden City, NY: Doubleday, 1986).

Anne Hommes and her husband, Reverend Tjaard Hommes, met Henri through Father Don McNeill. Reverend Hommes and Father McNeill started a Pastoral Theology program at Notre Dame University. Reverend Hommes was also Dutch and was in a similar academic discipline as Henri. The two quickly became friends.

In this letter, Henri is responding to questions from a young student of Anne's, I Putu, about his formation and influences.

SEPTEMBER 9, 1985

Dear Anne,

Your letter is quite a challenge. I do not have any "green upholstered door" experiences that could help I Putu. You can tell him that I was a very hard working, somewhat anxious, not too smart young man, who struggled hard to make it through gymnasium [European equivalent to U.S. preparatory high school], who decided to become a diocesan priest, partly because he didn't think he would ever want to study more than was necessary to become a priest.

Maybe my somewhat low intellectual self-esteem and my great need for friendship has made me more inclined to share my struggles and uncertainties with others than usually happens among scholars. For a period in my life I bragged on my weaknesses in the wrong way: I used them to avoid difficult positions and responsibility and to evoke some sympathy and even a smile. Later, when I had more self-confidence, I continued to speak about my inner struggles as a source of self-understanding but also as a way to deeper solidarity with others.

Now I am working with mentally handicapped people! Notre Dame Yale and Harvard now seem like a long complex route to reach the poor in spirit. I do not regret any part of it. God has been very very good to me.

Merton had some influence on me, but not too much. He is a totally different person. Hundred times more talented than I am. He was a genius, an artist, novelist, poet, painter and sparkling mind. I am plodding my way through life with much less. But I am grateful and happy especially since I have found this place. Harvard was not the right place for me, even though my years there were crucial for my life.

Vincent van Gogh always felt closer to me than Merton. His letters to Theo remain a real source of inspiration.

Peace and Love,
Henri

Henri offers suggestions about religious leadership to his friend Sister Connie Ostrander at the Benedictine monastery of St. Bede.

OCTOBER 11, 1985

Dear Connie,

Thanks so much for your good letter and Chapter address. I read both with much attention. Your chapter address is beautiful, wise, careful and clear-cut. It is clear from your words how much reform is needed; especially in the area of prayer, poverty and obedience.

A suggestion: speak much about Jesus. You focus much on the Spirit, which is good, but at this moment in the life of your community there is an obvious need to face the concreteness of the incarnation. Speak often about the life of Jesus. That is where the spiritual life starts. It makes us look at the poor, obedient and prayerful man of Nazareth. Also ask your community to read the life of the Saints: Charles de Foucauld, Marthe Robin, Jean Vianney, Francis of Assisi, etc.

And be sure to ask people always to prefer the poor, very concretely. Without being with the poor it is hard to see Jesus.

I admire your work. Be firm, loving and always focused on Jesus.

Love,
Henri

A letter to Jutta, a very loyal friend from his days at Harvard, about relationships between men and women.

OCTOBER 21, 1985

Dear Jutta,

Many thanks for your kind letter. The worst that can happen in our day is a hostility and separation between men and women. When the demon can make us believe that the two ways of which God made his Love known to us are to hate each other, we are being threatened in the center of our humanity. It is so important that we develop a deeply Christian perspective on being woman and being man. How can there ever be peace when the sacred ground from where life comes forth is being poisoned. Be sure to witness in your way to the reconciling love of God. I am very curious to see Mary Carney's pictures. Your pictures of the beautiful wood carving of the blind man are on my wall.

It would be great if you could help out a little when Peter [Weiskel, Henri's assistant] is gone, but I am afraid that you have already too much to do!

Love,
Henri

Henri's few years at Harvard Divinity School were not easy ones. He would remark that the environment was so competitive that it made friendship with other faculty difficult. An exception was James Luther Adams (1901– 1994), a retired Unitarian theologian who lived close to Henri on Harvard Square adjacent to the Harvard Divinity School.

Henri and Adams shared a friendship of mutual respect and interest. In this letter, we see that Henri is finding words to describe how being with handicapped people is focusing his attention on the heart and inspiring a new way of seeing. He has become absorbed by icons, most especially by the Rublev icon of Christ the Savior.

OCTOBER 30, 1985

Dear James,*

What a joy it was to receive your kind letter. I realize that the flood has made life quite hard for you, and I admire your vitality and unwavering good spirits in the midst of it all. This morning I was praying the 23rd Psalm and was struck by the words: "you will revive my drooping spirits." My spirits have an inclination to droop easily so I really need to pray the psalm often, but when I saw you last in your basement surrounded by your wet papers I was impressed to see that your spirits were so up! The Good Shepherd must truly guide you along the right path.

It was so good to read that you have been able to accomplish so much even though the flood has caused such a delay. I am very eager to read the book about Paul Tillich. I am even more eager to read about your own life. I hope you will publish the parts of your autobiography that are already finished. It must be especially interesting to write about Vatican II during the time of the synod.

---

* This letter is printed from the James Luther Adams Papers, by kind courtesy of the Special Collections Research Center, Syracuse University Libraries.

I hope that the synod will affirm the openness to "new conditions and new forms of life" about which John XXIII spoke. I just finished reading the biography of John XXIII by Peter Hebblethwaite.* A very remarkable book that helps to see the mysterious interplay between the Divine Spirit and the human spirits. Your own personal recollections of Vatican II will be very important. I hope to read them someday soon!†

I am doing very well here in France. The handicapped people have a special gift to bring you closer to the heart of God. Their poverty reveals the heart. They teach me that human beings distinguish themselves from the rest of creation not so much by the mind as by the heart. The ability to give and receive love is what makes us human. I have just finished a small book about intimacy, fecundity and ecstasy in the spiritual life. Much of what I have written is inspired by my life here among people who think so poorly but have such a great heart.

Right now I am working on some reflections about the Rublev Icon of Christ, the Savior. It is one of the most moving works of art I have ever seen. The more I pray with it and gaze at it the more I see. Sometimes it feels as if I never will find words to convey the deep emotions it evokes in me. I suffer from my inability to say what I see and feel. I guess we all do to some degree. We have to ask continuously forgiveness for not being able to say what we want to say. But I trust that a gentle and forgiving reader can hear beyond the words we say. I am more and more convinced that the best student is the one who is always willing to forgive his teacher for not being able to speak the full truth. Maybe that is one of the reasons that I finally felt I had to leave Harvard. I often felt "taken" by my word and accused of not saying it. How much do we have to pray before speaking about God! Prayer can create that fellowship of

---

* Peter Hebblethwaite, *John XXIII: Pope of the Council* (London: Chapman, 1984).

† The autobiography was published in 1995 as *Not Without Dust and Heat: A Memoir* (Chicago: Exploration Press, 1995).

the weak on which those who teach and study the divine mysteries can constantly forgive each other for not being able to know
God. Art is helping me. The works of Rublev, Rembrandt and van
Gogh have often given me ways to communicate the mystery of
God's presence among us, when words proved so inadequate. A
few weeks ago I was in the Louvre and saw Rembrandt's *Pilgrim of
Emmaus*. I stood there for half an hour and was so overwhelmed
by the ecstatic as well as intimate look of Jesus and the splendid
light on his hands breaking the bread that I felt as if I was present
at the celebration of the Eucharist. The many tourists and talk-
ative guides had vanished from my consciousness. I truly was in
church!

[. . .]

Thanks again for your very kind letter. It means so much to
me to have you as a friend. You know how I failed to become a real
part of the H.D.S. [Harvard Divinity School] faculty. Your kindness to me during my time at the Carriage House was a real gift
and gave me a sense of belonging to the school that I did not have
before. I hope and pray that we will stay in touch. Be sure of my
frequent prayers for you and your ongoing ministry in the service
of Our Lord.

Yours,
Henri

[. . .]

*Henri comforts Carol, his friend and administrative assistant, whose col-
league and friend has died.*

NOVEMBER 26, 1985

Dear Carol,

Many thanks for your kind letter. You have truly received a gift from Bonnie. Living in the presence. God is always where we are. Not in the past (with its disappointments) nor in the future (with its worries) but in the present where love can touch us. Death is easier to accept when we live our lives in love. Love is stronger than death and takes its "sting" away. I wish you could see this place here [L'Arche à Trosly]. Hopefully you can come in the future. There is so much that you will love here.

Thanks for the financial work. I will see around Christmas to whom to give some money. Peter [Weiskel] will be here for two weeks, so we can discuss that. I am curious what Egbert has to say about the prodigal son.* I very much want to write about it. I pray for you. Send my love to all in the family.

Peace,
Henri

As Henri's life was taking new turns in France, the AIDS "plague" was beginning to take the lives of men he knew and loved. Henri would become increasingly involved in AIDS ministry as the epidemic grew more acute throughout the 1990s.

Chris Glaser was one of Henri's students from Yale.

---

* This is a reference to a poster he has seen in the room of Simone Landrien, a new friend at L'Arche à Trosly, of a reproduction of Rembrandt's *Return of the Prodigal*, which will give birth to Henri's best-known work, *The Return of the Prodigal Son: A Story of Homecoming* (first released as *The Return of the Prodigal Son: A Meditation on Fathers, Brothers, and Sons*), published in 1992.

DECEMBER 20, 1985

Dear Chris,

How are you? I often think of you and pray for you. I know life is very hard for you during this plague of AIDS. I lost a dear friend in San Francisco last month. I was glad that we could see each other before his death (in August) and give him the Sacrament of the sick.

I hope and pray that this crisis will help us come to a new and deeper understanding of Human and Divine love. Some radical spiritual revolution may be asked for.

Keep in touch if you can. May Christ let his face shine upon you and fill you with joy and peace—

All is well with me. Busy praying, writing and thinking about my future.

Love,
Henri

PART II

1986–1989

A S THIS SECTION BEGINS, it is January 1986, and Henri is in Freiburg, Germany, to do some writing. He is turning fifty-four years old. Six months earlier, he made the difficult decision to leave his position at Harvard to explore a vocation with L'Arche. He is now living in L'Arche in Trosly-Breuil, France.

Henri felt good about the move. In a letter from March 8, 1986, he described L'Arche as a "real outgrowth from my search during the last years."* At L'Arche in Trosly-Breuil, he would meet Nathan Ball, a young Canadian working as an assistant.† They immediately struck up a deep, personal friendship. Ball, twenty-eight years old and a recent convert to Catholicism, had come to L'Arche with his girlfriend after the death of his handicapped brother. He was considering marriage and a vocation in L'Arche. This friendship would be one of the most significant of Henri's life.

In early 1986, Henri accepted a call to be pastor for L'Arche Daybreak in Richmond Hill, north of Toronto, Canada. He was soon immersed in the life of the community. He worked with Sue Mosteller, a sister of St. Joseph and longtime member of L'Arche, to establish a program to nourish and sustain the spiritual life of

---

* Letter to Connie Ostrander, March 8, 1986.

† At L'Arche, the people assisting handicapped people (core members) are called assistants.

core members and their assistants. He developed ecumenical litur-
gies and embraced the interfaith reality of L'Arche. Nathan would
join him to work as a part-time assistant for the community while
taking a divinity degree.

As a member of the community, Henri shared a house with assistants and handicapped people. He was asked to help with the
care of Adam Arnett, one of the most profoundly disabled of the
core members. Through Adam he started to experience the gift of
handicapped people for revealing God's love. In 1987, he wrote:

> *After many years of studying and teaching theology, it truly has
> been a blessed discovery that many of the broken people of L'Arche
> have revealed more about God's love to me than much of my study-
> ing and teaching ever did.* *

At L'Arche, Henri's focus turned from global issues to the teachings of Jesus. He would write a number of books on this theme,
including his popular *In the Name of Jesus: Reflections on Christian
Leadership* (New York: Crossroad, 1989) and another dedicated to
his nephew in the Netherlands concerning the growing seculariza-
tion of society, *Letters to Marc about Jesus: Spiritual Living in a Material World* (San Francisco: Harper and Row, 1988).†

Henri was also writing for journals such as *Sojourners, Commonweal* and *America*. He was becoming an increasingly sought after
speaker, making frequent trips throughout the United States, as
well as to Europe, the Soviet Union and Central America. He was
receiving upward of forty speaking invitations a month. Letters
from readers poured in. By 1989, he was inundated by close to fifty
letters a week.

The move from Harvard to L'Arche had been propitious.

---

* Letter to Father Paul Walsh, February 16, 1987.

† Published first in the Netherlands as *Brieven aan Marc: Over Jezus en de Zin van het
Leven* (Tielt: Lannoo, 1987).

Friendships with Nathan, Sue, Adam and others provided him with community and a sense that he had finally found his home. But within the safety of L'Arche he would encounter the most devastating emotional crisis of his life.

Over Christmas 1987, his friendship with Nathan broke down. Nathan asked that all contact between them stop. Nathan, who was in a romantic relationship at the time, began to find Henri's intensity too demanding. "Unable to bear the expectations we had put upon each other, we entered into a long period of silence," Nathan would recall.* Henri was desolate. He lost his self-esteem and the energy to continue working.

Reflecting on his experience at L'Arche, Henri wrote to a friend:

It seems that L'Arche leads us to the inner place where we most deeply experience our immense desire for communion and at the same time the total impossibility to see that desire fulfilled in the place where we live.†

The community sent him to a retreat center in Winnipeg for clergy needing spiritual and psychological help. He would stay for seven months of intensive therapy. The healing process included writing daily spiritual imperatives. They would later be published in 1996 as *The Inner Voice of Love: A Journey through Anguish to Freedom* (New York: Doubleday, 1996).

In the summer of 1988, Henri moved back to Daybreak on a part-time basis, intent to live his reconciliation with Nathan within the wider context of the community. In a letter to a friend from July 1988, he writes, "It will also be very hard for both of us, but we are committed to looking at our struggle as something greater than just the two of us. Please keep us in your prayers as we

---

* Nathan Ball, "A Covenant Friendship," in *Befriending Life: Encounters with Henri Nouwen*, ed. Beth Porter (New York: Doubleday, 2001), 96.

† Letter to Marcus, January 20, 1990.

try to live this struggle faithfully. It is very painful, but, hopeful also fruitful."*

By 1989, Henri was back full-time at Daybreak. His sense of belonging was reinforced by a serious injury in a road accident, after which the community gathered around him. He wrote, "Although the accident was not a minor one I feel very peaceful and happy at this moment and I have a good sense that the accident is like a new push by God to keep me moving in the direction I had chosen to go, that of loving God without reserve. So all is really well now, very well indeed . . ."†

In the months following the accident, he experienced debilitating fatigue, but his mood remained hopeful and his mind alive with new ideas for books. "Homecoming" would become a consistent theme in his speaking and writing. Henri had finally found his home.

As Part II begins, Henri is in Freiburg, the home of his German publisher, Verlag Herder. He is there for five weeks to do some writing. He writes to Nathan Ball, his new friend from Trosly.

JANUARY 23, 1986

Dear Nathan,

Your letter brings me much joy. Thanks so much for writing. I continue to be surprised how healing and comforting your words can be. It is such a blessing to be able to read your words encouraging me in my love for you and giving so much in return. I am so grateful to have a place in your heart and prayers. I feel united with you,

* Letter to Jeff Imbach, July 13, 1988.

† Letter to John and Aminda Baird, February 6, 1989.

and being alone here is a very different experience because of your friendship.

It is very good to be here. I live in the motherhouse of the Vincentian sisters* and I am treated as a Cardinal! The house is across from Herder Verlag, which makes it all very easy and handy.

After a lot of parties in honor of Hermann Herder's 60th birthday I have settled in a quiet rhythm of prayer and study and even a little bit of sport. I could not have done a better thing. I am putting up a hard struggle to get some ideas on paper, to enter deeper in the heart of God and to conquer my own loneliness. There are many demons but many angels as well! I am more and more convinced that I will be a better friend when I have dared to face my loneliness alone. There must be some hidden strengths which are only revealing themselves in the desert.

I am grateful that I can share with you my great, often agonizing, search for affection and deep friendship. It has been a life long struggle and it will probably always be with me, but having a dear friend to help me struggle faithfully and without fear makes all the difference.

I am sending you some cards from the museum in Freiburg which move me very much. They give me much consolation. I like you to have them so that our prayer together—even at a distance—can be deeper and stronger.

I am close to finishing a rather long piece on the Pentecost Icon of the Novgorod School.† It has been a true revelation to me. Yes, indeed, let us see what God gives to us during this time away.

---

* The Vincentian Sisters of Charity (VSC), a women's religious order, had their motherhouse in Freiburg, Germany.

† The article was published as "The Fullness of Divine Love: Reflections on a Russian Pentecost Icon," *Sojourners*, June 1986: 24–27. A revised version of this article was published in Henri's book *Behold the Beauty of the Lord: Praying with Icons* (Notre Dame, IN: Ave Maria Press, 1987). It was a reflection on Andrei Rublev's icon *The Descent of the Holy Spirit*, painted toward the end of the fifteenth century.

I pray that you will find the solitude and rest you need to grow strong in the Spirit. I pray that your life with the friends at Surgeon* will prove nurturing and hope giving. And I pray that Our Lord will show us ways to help each other in our desire to be faithful to his love.

Peace and Love,
Henri

FEBRUARY 10, 1986

Dear Nathan,

Your letter brought me much joy. Thanks so much for your loving friendship, your openness, your trust, your willingness to take risks with me.

I look forward to sharing with you in more detail my experiences here. I have been graced by a great sense of God's protection. Somehow it feels that God has sent some special angels to surround me with their wings and keep me from being burned by the destructive fires that often threaten me from within and without.

I marvel at the fact that great inner unrest, great feeling of confusion, inadequacy, neediness and primitive impulses can exist together with a sense that God has not left me alone and covers me with a cloud of love. I have to trust more what I "know" in my heart than what I feel.

I am very hopeful that Lent will bring special graces. Maybe I can drive out at least some demons with prayer and fasting!

I am so glad you are using my room. Please consider it as your

---

* Surgeon, where Nathan lived, is one of the L'Arche homes at L'Arche à Cuise, a sister community to L'Arche à Trosly.

own. It feels so good to me to know that our lives are connected and that we pray in the same places.

There are so many things I want to tell you and discuss with you. But maybe this paper is not the best form to tell it all. So we must be patient.

The work goes rather well. I finished the first draft of the icon book and wait for Peter's typed and edited version. Meanwhile I am on the phone with Doubleday a lot about the final pages of the "Lifesigns" book. Now I am starting a small text in Dutch in the hope to speak some words of hope to my nephew and his generation.* I have not written in Dutch for years, so it is going to be a new experience.

There is a chance that [Robert] Jonas will come here for a short visit.† That would be a real joy. But it is not certain yet. We might travel together back to Trosly. I will keep you informed.

Pray for me. Keep me close to God's heart and to yours. Ask God that I can be faithful and have the strength to keep the demons at a safe distance, to trust that God's love is more real than the affectations of the princes of this world and the courage to act on what I know is truthful even when I do not feel it.

I hold you very close in my prayers and thoughts. Trust in my deep and strong desire to be a friend for you who can give you joy and peace and a deep sense of being loved, and who wants to receive from you your tears as well as your smiles and loud laughter.

Love,
Henri

---

* Henri is referring to his book *Letters to Marc About Jesus: Spiritual Living in a Material World*, first published in Dutch as *Brieven aan Marc: Over Jezus en de Zin van het Leven* by his Belgian publisher Lannoo in 1987.

† Robert Jonas first met Henri as a spiritual directee, but this shifted to a friendship that lasted until Henri's death. A chronicle of this visit can be found in Henri's published diary of the time, *The Road to Daybreak: A Spiritual Journey* (Garden City, NY: Doubleday, 1988).

As Henri ventured out into "the old country," he didn't forget his friends in the United States. His friend Sister Connie continued to have challenges at St. Bede Monastery, and Henri repeats his wisdom for good Christian leadership: prayer, preference for the poor and avoidance of "gossip, backbiting and recriminations."

Henri shares the news that he has accepted a call to L'Arche Daybreak in Toronto.

MARCH 8, 1986

Dear Connie,

Thanks so much for your kind letter, which I found in L'Arche after I returned there from a five weeks stay in Freiburg, Germany.

I am doing very well. I enjoy being in Europe and getting a real feel for "the old country." I was in Ireland, Holland, Germany, and I will still go to England and Russia.

I have accepted a call from the L'Arche community in Daybreak, Toronto, to start there a small spiritual Centre for L'Arche in North America. I discussed this with my bishop, Cardinal [Adrianus] Simonis, who gave me his blessings. I look forward to going there. It feels like a real outgrowth from my search during the last years.

I am doing some writing in English and in Dutch. I am trying to write a small book in Dutch about Jesus. It feels very good to do it.

I do not expect to be in Cambridge [Massachusetts] for any length of time. Just to move! We probably have to wait a little before we can meet again. Maybe you can visit in Toronto someday soon.

I keep you in my prayers. You certainly have no easy task, but I hope you can continue to challenge your sisters to live the rule of Benedict, to pray unceasingly, to always choose the poor and to avoid all form of gossip, backbiting and recriminations. If that evokes hostility, there is no reason to be afraid. Carry your burden as Christ's burden and you will find it to be a light burden.

Most important is to live in constant communion with Jesus. When Jesus offers us the space to be together we can live together in peace and joy.

Send my love to all in the community.

Love and Peace,
Henri

P.S. Do not consult a graphologist! I wrote this letter in a train going from Amsterdam to Arnhem. A lot of shaking!

In this letter, Henri extends himself as a friend to Dennis O'Neill, a Catholic priest in Chicago, who has written about his anger at the Church and other institutions. Henri wrote the foreword to O'Neill's book Lazarus Interlude: A Story of God's Healing Love in a Moment of Ministry *(Notre Dame, IN: Ave Maria Press, 1983).*

APRIL 9, 1986

Dear Dennis,

Your letter is a great gift to me. Thank you, dear friend, for your openness, your honesty, your struggle, your love. You are a beautiful man and very deeply loved by God but also by me and those who know your heart. Your letter filled me with real joy because of its strong energy and deep connection.

I wished, like you, that we could talk. We sure will be able to soon.

What I pray for is that your capacity to love and share your love will be greater than your anger at the Church and other institutions that emerge in your mind as potential persecutors. Love your enemies with the same passion as you love your friends! Please write more about yourself, your emotions, your prayer, your love for God's people. I do want to know you, pray for you and support you in your vocation. I am doing well, although a little overwhelmed with small things that keep me away from the "only necessary thing." Please pray for me. Make me part of your heart. Write soon. I will write soon too.

Love,
Henri

Henri is writing from L'Arche in Trosly-Breuil to Senator Hatfield, who continues to battle false accusations of corruption.

APRIL 8, 1986

Dear Senator Hatfield,

Many thanks for your kind letter and your moving reflection of the crucified Lord. I recently was in Colmar and saw there the Isenheimer Altar.* I enclose two cards portraying the front piece of the Altar.

The suffering Christ was painted to comfort those who suffered from the pestilence. It was put in the chapel of the hospital where people came to die. The painter, Mathias Grünewald, did not simply want to offer hope by painting the rising Lord (he also painted that on another panel!), but he wanted to offer hope by showing that God truly had become God-with-us. Jesus has suf-

---

* The Isenheimer Altar is an altarpiece sculpted and painted by, respectively, the Germans Niclaus of Haguenau and Matthias Grünewald in 1512–1516. It is on display at the Unterlinden Museum at Colmar, France.

fered all our pains, and there is no human suffering that Jesus
has not suffered. In and through him all that humanity has suffered and will suffer is offered to the Father in a worthy sacrifice.
Jesus, who was without sin, has taken on himself all the sins by
humanity and has been crushed under its weight. There lies our
first hope. Not only on the resurrection but also on the solidarity
of the Son of God with all human suffering.

I am always struck that poor people are so attracted to images
of the suffering Christ. In Spain and Latin America Good Friday
often seems even more important than Easter. There is a certain
realism here. People are looking for strength to live their hard life
faithfully. They often find more consolation in knowing that God
is with them in the struggle, in the agony and even in the experience of being abandoned by God, than in the knowledge that finally life will prove stronger than death. For most people the most
burning question is: how to make it another day, another week,
another year. Looking at the crucified Jesus in his desolation they
can say: "But we are not alone, he is with us." There we come to
understand fully what it means that God is compassionate, that
God is a God who suffers with us.

Indeed, as you say so beautifully, thus we can live out in our
body the suffering of Jesus. Paul says so mysteriously: "It makes
me happy . . . to do what I can to make up all that has still to be
undergone by Christ" (Col. 1:24). There we become indeed "His
hands, his feet, his voice, his witness." Here is revealed to us the
deepest meaning of history: it is the full unfolding of the immense
suffering that God has suffered on the cross in Jesus Christ. This
also is the full unfolding of God's unfathomable love for us. Here
also you can catch a glimpse of the mystery of the Church as the
body of Christ. What we see happening in Nicaragua, Guatemala,
El Salvador, Ireland, South Africa, Iran and Iraq is much more
than a series of political tragedies that cause much human suffering. It is the manifestation of the immensity of God's pain for
our sake. It is a "new" way revealing how much Jesus suffered on

the cross. In his humanity we see the body suffering. I often see with my eyes of faith the body of Christ stretched out over our Globe crying out "God, my God, why have you forsaken us." What moves me most is that this vision fills me as much with hope as with anguish.

I am planning to be in Washington, DC, on May 15th and 16th. I very much hope that you will have a little time to meet. If another day fits you better, please let me know. I can juggle my dates a little.

It was great to have Jim [Towey] here.* He is fondly remembered by many. Maybe one day you too can visit in France or in Canada.

Please send my warm wishes to your wife, Antoinette. I keep you both close to my heart and the heart of God.

In his Peace and love,
Henri Nouwen

Henri writes to his friend Barb, who continues to care for troubled family members and struggle with guilt, anger and desolation.

MAY 15, 1986

Dear Barb,

Thanks so much for your letters. The mystery is that God does need us! God became a weak, broken, agonizing, lonely, rejected human being, so that we could be with God as we are with people who need us.

Do not focus so much on the powerful God "up there," but on the God with us. Keep your eyes fixed on Jesus always, and you will find comfort and consolation. God does not leave you alone.

---

* Towey was Senator Hatfield's adviser. He became good friends with Henri and played an instrumental role in connecting Henri and Hatfield.

He sent Jesus to you to live and feel fully your struggle. You are not alone in your anger, frustration and desolation. Look at the cross and be there as John and Mary.

Do not allow guilt feelings to take over. Guilt feelings do not come from the Spirit of Jesus. Just live your life day by day and try to say thanks whenever you can. Do not trust your feelings. Trust your knowledge that God loves you, Edmund, Robert and Andrew and act according to that knowledge.

I pray for you with fervor and love—know that you are loved and that the Lord is much nearer than you can feel—

Peace and Love,
Henri

Henri's friendship with Nathan continues to deepen, even as he travels extensively through Europe and the United States for various talks and meetings. He refers to the friendship as an anchor that allows him to be faithful "in all things." The letter is filled with interesting details about the variety of people he is meeting as well as an observation, born out of his friendship with Nathan, that the core of the spiritual struggle is having the courage to "let yourself be loved." It is a first glimpse of a theme about the nature of love, identity and God that would build to his seminal work Life of the Beloved: Spiritual Living in a Secular World, *published in 1992.*

MAY 19, 1986

Dear Nathan,

It is 7:15 A.M. I am sitting in a United Airline D.C. 10 getting ready to fly from Chicago to Boston. I think of you with great love and affection. You have been with me at many places and around many people since I left Paris. I have not allowed you to go far from me. Holding you close and telling you all I have felt and done has given me deep peace and a real sense of safety. Your love and faithful friendship has been my real anchor as I struggled to be faithful in all things.

The telephone calls were a real grace. God has given you an uncanny sense of knowing what I needed at the moment. Your love for me has given you a knowledge of me that nobody has ever had. I can't tell you how helpful you have been.

The journey turns out to be most of all a test of faith in Jesus. I am trying to know nothing but him and proclaim him at all times and at all places. It is such a joy to feel deeply the joy of speaking about Jesus to bankers, Senators, business people, priests. I know now how graced we are and how God has given us to each other to be his disciples.

It has been far from easy. At every step on the way there is a temptation. I see it now so much clearer. The clearer I see it, the more tempting moments I recognize! My unfaithfulness goes so deep: curiosity, fantasies, gossip, desire for attention and little indulgences. Often, very often, I had to stay very close to you to find the strength to move away from these temptations. But those are great rewards. The greatest is the experience that Jesus offers his presence, his affection and love.

I have given to all my close friends a copy of the *Icon* which I also gave to you. That has had a deep effect on my relationships. I could speak very directly about the deep affection of Jesus for John and for us and then could also express my own love for the people I stayed with, while staying truly faithful. Senator Hatfield was so grateful for the *Icon* that he showed it to all his staff members and spoke to them openly about the great love of Jesus.

One of the good things is my increasing desire to go to Daybreak. The more I travel, see people and am invited to do "important" things, the more I feel the need for a simple community, a home, a place where we can be together and pray. I am very eager to visit Daybreak and discuss many things with them. Please keep me very close to your heart during these days. I very much want also to prepare your coming so that you can really deeply experience being called there. You will be very close to me at every moment during my stay there.

I am a little nervous about my visit to Pittsburgh.* I do not know how to prepare for the commencement address. Should I just pray or should I write down a talk? How much should I trust that the Lord will give me words? Something in me says that I am entering into a new phase of life in which preparing speeches is a lack of faithfulness. I sense a desire to take greater risks with Jesus and be less concerned about how much praise I will receive. But I feel like entering into a new land.

Yesterday I spoke spontaneously during the Eucharist at the occasion of the 25th anniversary of the ordination of my priest-friend Bob Ferrigan. I just felt like getting up at the end of the Mass to say a few words. There were about sixty Chicago priests and five hundred people. I had nothing prepared, but as I spoke I realized that what I said I had learned from our friendship. I spoke about the courage to let yourself be loved. The response was very very strong. People felt that I had touched the core of their struggle. Thank you, dear friend. You were there with me. I now wonder if I should keep trusting myself and go to Pittsburgh without any prepared text. I probably will!

America is such a world in need of Jesus. Everybody asked me to speak about him: the Kennedy family, the Senators, the Young Presidents' Organization (people who made a million before they are thirty!) the priests, the bishops, the sisters, the students . . . Everybody! I am so glad that you go to study theology in Toronto. The church, the world need you to speak about Jesus, loudly, clearly, intelligently and with great zeal. Whether you become a priest or not, will marry or not, you are clearly called to proclaim the love of Jesus. You are very blessed! God holds you so close to his love. Jesus

---

* Henri gave the commencement speech at Pittsburgh Theological Seminary on May 22, 1986.

is so generous with you. Your life is such a gift. What you have done
to me is such a mysterious divine event that I cannot stop telling
you how much I love you and how grateful I am.

How much I wished that I could ask you about yourself, your
struggle, your retreat, your thoughts about Daybreak, your smiles
and tears. I am waiting to hear about all of that.

I call [Robert] Jonas every day. Sometimes two or three times.
It is a great help. He keeps close to my daily ups and downs and
reminds me of God's love with good words.

Send my love to Christine and all the people at the Surgeon.
Also special love to Mammie Vanier and to Jean [Vanier].

I love you and hold you close to my heart.

Henri

*In another deeply personal letter to Nathan, Henri reflects on his decision
to move to Daybreak and his conviction that it is where God wants him
to be.*

MAY 27, 1986

Dear Nathan,

It is Tuesday morning 27th of May 8 A.M. Within a few hours I will
be on my way to San Francisco. I just finished an hour of meditation and prayer. I was very distracted and a little anxious. I feel
very tired, mostly because of all the meetings I have had since I
came here [to the L'Arche Daybreak community in Richmond Hill,
Ontario] and the general feeling of "newness" and the lack of time
alone.

Although I am very tired and wished you were here, I feel very
good about my time here. As I told you on the phone, I have been
very well received and there is a real desire in the community to

grow stronger in the Spirit. Also your coming is a source of joy and hope to the community.

I am deeply convinced that our coming to Daybreak is the right thing. Jesus calls us there. I know it is not going to be easy and that I will have many moments of fear, anxiety, frustration and even despair, but I know that this is the place where God wants me to be. Jean [Vanier] wants me here, my bishop sends me here and you will be here with me, and I feel deeply in my heart that whatever struggle there will be, it will be a struggle to bring me closer to Jesus.

I very much want you to feel full of confidence and trust. I want to tell you again how strongly I feel that you have made all the right decisions. It is time for you to leave Trosly, it is time for you to prepare yourself explicitly and directly for a ministry in Jesus' name, it is time for you to be back in Canada and to deepen your relationship with L'Arche here.

I am also very, very glad that I can support you here. We can pray together, talk together about theology and life at L'Arche, sing together and listen together to Jesus who wants both of us to give ourselves completely to him. The readings during my days here (Mark 10:13–31) tell me all I have to know: become a child, let go of my wealth and trust that I will receive all I need and more than that. I want to give these readings also to you. If you have a little time, read them with me and dwell there a while. You will find joy and peace there.

There is still a very long road ahead for both of us. I realize that the road is first of all a road of faithfulness, prayer, simple service and a very clear commitment to continue on the direction we have chosen. Every day I feel the demons talking about other directions, back to the useful career, popularity, publicity, success and most of all to the sensual experiences.* But I now have a very

---

* In his journal from this time period he names these pleasures, writing "It seemed as if the city were tempting us with its sensuality: its many colors, movements, things to buy and people to look at" (*The Road to Daybreak: A Spiritual Journey* [Garden City, NY: Doubleday, 1988], 67). He continues, "Often such experiences

concrete idea how to struggle. Every minute offers a choice, what to think, what to say, what to do. It is amazing the clarity I have. But also amazing how strong the power is of the demon. But I know that together we can be strong and enjoy our little victories and ask forgiveness for our little defects.

I feel very sad that I cannot meet your father and mother. I really experience a real desire to know them and their "dreams." Please give them my warm greetings. I hope we both can be in Calgary [Alberta, Canada] together soon. I very much pray that your time together in Trosly will be full of joy and peace and a very happy conclusion of a very good time for you.

Keep me close, very close, in your prayers. The trip is far from over. San Francisco, Los Angeles, Madison, Chicago, Boston, London, Liverpool, Cork. Full of opportunities to proclaim the love of God, but also full of seductions and temptations.* So please, hold me very close, and give me some extra prayers! I pray for you each day and very often: little short prayers in between all that is going on.

Thanks so much for your support during my days in Pittsburgh. I felt your presence very much during the commencement address. I think it went well, and I trust that it will bear fruits.

Send my love to Christine and special greetings to all at the Surgeon—

I love you with the strong faithful love of Jesus.

I hold you very close to my heart and the heart of God.

I enjoy your friendship every moment of my day and feel very safe in it.

Love,
Henri

---

remain hidden and cause much shame and guilt. But by confessing to each other how easily we are seduced by the attractions of the world, we affirmed our true commitment and safeguarded that commitment with each other" (Ibid., 67).

* The details of Henri's trip are captured in *The Road to Daybreak*.

By September 1986, Henri has made the move to Daybreak in Richmond Hill, Ontario, just north of Toronto, Canada. He writes to his Dutch friend Jurjen Beumer, a Protestant minister who has begun work as a pastor in the city of Haarlem.

SEPTEMBER 10, 1986

Dear Jurjen,

Thanks so much for your wonderful letter, which I received a few days ago. I am in a situation in which it is impossible for me to find some quiet time to write you a long letter back. However, I am dictating this letter to you in English so that at least you have a word from me.

I am very, very glad that your first impressions of your new milieu are so positive.* It is really a joy for me that you have made this step and that you can start doing new things in new ways with new people. I hope and pray that you will be able to use all your creativity as a minister of God and will especially be able to keep the Lord Jesus in the center of your and your people's life. I am increasingly convinced of the importance of preaching the Name of the Lord Jesus as the rising Lord, the Lord who overcame the powers of death and came to set us free. The freedom that the Gospel offers is a different freedom from what the world can bring us, and it is so important for people today to really come to know and experience this freedom. I wish you much fervor and hope and much confidence in your new task.

Thanks so much for your beautiful article on Karl Barth and prayer.† I have read it with great interest and was deeply moved by

---

* Beumer had been appointed pastor and director of an inner-city mission, Sociaal Basis Pastoraat in the center of Haarlem, Netherlands.

† Jurjen Beumer, "Mens en Wereld zonder Masker: Karl Barth en het Gebed," in *Karl Barth: En Theologisch Portret*, ed. Jurjen Beumer and G. H. ter Schegget (Baarn: Ten Have, 1986), 38–51.

it. It is a beautiful piece of work, and I am jealous of the discipline and care with which you have written it. I am very honored that you have dedicated this article to me. It makes me feel deeply connected with you and your ministry, and it also is an invitation to me to continue my thinking and writing in the area of prayer.

It is really good to hear that the I.K.O.N. programme had so many good effects for you.* I am really happy that we did this work together, and I am grateful to you for making it possible. I obviously have not heard as much about it as you, but this is understandable considering my absence from Holland. What you write about "language" is very important, and I hope that in the future we can discuss this in more detail. It always will be a very important question about how we speak the mysteries of God in our lives.

Enclosed I send you a little book that was just published.† You are already familiar with the contents, but I thought you might just like to see it in this form.

Yours,
Henri

Henri writes to his friend Chris to express his sadness that their friendship "cannot blossom and deepen" and to explain what friendship means to him as a celibate priest.

---

* A Dutch TV program (*Interkerkelijke Omroep Nederland*) based in Hilversum.

† *Lifesigns: Intimacy, Fecundity, and Ecstasy in Christian Perspective* (Garden City, NY: Doubleday, 1986).

OCTOBER 22, 1986

Dear Chris,

Many thanks for your note. I am not angry but sad that our friendship cannot blossom and deepen. Somehow I am not able to let you know and understand my feelings about my vocation as a priest, my way of looking at celibacy and my desire to have a real solid affectionate friendship with you.

It seems that you treat me as an interesting visitor, a respected stranger or a good connection but have a very hard time to feel at ease around me and free enough to let me experience that you want to be friends. Maybe your distance simply means that I force myself on you and that there is not a mutuality that makes friendship possible. If that is the case, we have to be realistic and not be more for each other than good acquaintances.

I honestly do not want anything more or less than a good solid loving friendship. It is important for me to express to you at times my feelings and emotions and my affective struggles. There are few people to whom I let myself be known in that way, and when I am with you there is a certain hope that you will give me some extra space to be with you as a friend who does not have to hide much. But the last few times I felt so much distance and so much resistance to be with me where I am needy that I wondered if it would be wise for me to pursue our friendship. I do not want to be in pain every time I leave you. Nor do I want you to feel guilty or simply frustrated.

I love being a priest and I have a deep life-long commitment to live in the Church as a celibate priest. The older I become, the stronger my love is for Jesus and his church. Outside of an intimate connection with Jesus and his church my life cannot bear fruit. Celibacy is not easy, but it is a small price for the gift it offers. What I keep hoping for are friends who protect, support and care for my celibate choice while not withholding from me a nurturing affective friendship that allows me to shed some tears of

loneliness from time to time and return to the "battlefield" knowing that I have friends who support me.

Maybe this is not what you can understand and appreciate.
Your often made suggestion that maybe I should not be a celibate
priest is very disturbing to me and often deepens my sense of isola-
tion and loneliness. But it makes me more sad than angry. I realize
that you think and feel very differently about the church than I
do, and I respect your views. But for our friendship to grow stronger, deeper, freer and healthier, we have to find a way of loving each
other that nurtures both of us.

I didn't work on your manuscript mostly because I felt frustrated with our relationship and didn't know how to study it while
feeling at peace. But I do want to pick it up again and respond to
it as good as I can. Probably I need some more time to get to the
right "inner space."

Enclosed I am sending you some "things" that you might like
to have. I am most interested in your looking at the journal pieces
published in the N.O.R. [*New Oxford Review*]. These tell you a little
more about my spiritual struggles.

Send my warm love to George. I hope he is feeling well these
days, and I pray that your love for each other is growing deeper
and stronger.

Please write when you can. Be assured of my sincere desire to
be a faithful and honest friend. There are few days that I do not
pray for you.

Love,
Henri

Just one month into his new life as pastor for Daybreak, and Henri is feeling as busy as ever. In a rare moment for letter writing, he addresses his friend Barb, who continues to struggle with family problems.

NOVEMBER 5, 1986

Dear Barb,

Thanks so much for your letters. It is really good to hear from you, and I wish I had an opportunity to write you more often, but my life here at Daybreak is so full that it is hard to find a quiet time to write to friends. I hope you understand.

I am very glad that you had a good time in St. John's. It is so important for you to have a place where you can go to pray, be quiet and meet some very caring people. When you have such a place where your heart can be nurtured, it will also be easier to see Christ "in his distressing disguise." Only when Christ really is alive in your heart can you recognize him in your neighbor because it is the Christ in you who calls forth the Christ in other. I really feel that it is very important for you to have a regular discipline of prayer and spiritual reading. That and some caring friends such as Jutta will allow you to live through these very painful and difficult years and will prevent your heart from becoming bitter and resentful. Be sure to also pray to Mary, the mother of God. She can really touch you in a very special way and give you the kind of inner peace and joy that has great sustaining power. Mary so well knows the suffering of a mother in life. Being with her in prayer is a true grace.

Enclosed I am sending you a little icon to help you to give Mary this special place in your life. Thanks so much for your letter. Be sure that I always pray for you and for both of your sons.

Yours with love,
Henri

❧

Henri writes to Sister Connie Ostrander about the "descending road" of discipleship, encouraging her to be faithful in spite of the continued challenges she faces as a religious leader.

DECEMBER 17, 1986

Dear Connie,

Thanks so much for your good letter. I wish I were able to write you a long letter back in response, but it is really impossible at this moment considering all the work here.

I just want you to know that I keep you in my prayers and want to fully support you as you try to be faithful to your task and live a life of discipleship. It certainly is a descending road that Jesus asks you to follow, but it seems very important that you do not focus on results, accomplishments or success but first of all on the Lord, who wants you to be faithful even when darkness surrounds you. I deeply admire your flexibility and tenacity in the midst of all the struggles. You are a real example to me, and I am deeply convinced that you are being prepared for an even deeper journey into the heart of Jesus.

Meanwhile, I am doing well, enjoying my new life here at Daybreak, trying more and more to learn the ways of L'Arche. Please give my love to all the friends in the community and ask them to pray for me.

Yours,
Love,
Henri

Henri writes to his friends Sophie (née Albregts) and Jim Fitzgerald in Ireland. The Nouwen family had long-standing ties with the Albregts. In addition, Piet Kasteel, a good friend of Henri's parents, was at one time the ambassador for the Netherlands to Ireland, which led to frequent visits to the isle by Henri and the Nouwen family. Henri performed the marriage ceremony for Sophie and Jim in 1961 and kept in touch through letters and visits for the rest of his life.

Henri writes of his extreme fatigue as he enters his fourth month as L'Arche Daybreak.

JANUARY 1987

Dear Sophie and Jim,

Many thanks for your very good letter from Hong Kong. I was so glad to hear from you. I wished I could have written earlier, but I was so busy in Toronto that I had to wait for a quieter time. Now I am in Tegucigalpa (the capital of Honduras) to make a retreat with 50 L'Arche people and I have a little quiet time to write.

My life in Toronto is very good but also very tiring. The demands made of me are enormous and sometimes I wished I could be dead for just one week and then wake up completely rested! Fatigue continues to plague me, and I hope that I can find a better rhythm. But it always will be a struggle. My time with you and Leonie and Paddy were like a real oasis.* Ireland is such a relaxing place for me. Hopefully there will be another occasion for a visit.

The book *Lifesigns* that I started to write in your nice quiet guest room has been well received and widely read. I am very happy with it. If I haven't sent you a copy yet, let me know so I will send it

---

* Leonie "Loliet" Kiely-Albregts and Paddy Kiely are part of the Albregts clan. Henri married the couple in 1966.

immediately. Meanwhile my small book on Russian Icons just appeared. I will send you a copy soon.

I hope that Jim's wall goes well. Your good mood even under hard circumstances is a real inspiration to me. You know how to live what I preach about!

Peace and love,
Henri

Henri writes to John Eudes Bamberger, abbot of the Abbey of the Genesee, about finding a place to "stay" at Daybreak and his sense that everything in his life was leading him to L'Arche. He also writes of the increasing intensity of his struggles with his "demons" and his determination to remain faithful.

JANUARY 1987

Dear Father John Eudes,

Many thanks for your kind Christmas greetings and the fruitcake, which is being enjoyed by many. Life has been very good for me ever since I came to this community for and with mentally, and often physically, handicapped men and women.

I have truly found a home here and feel that the Lord has truly called me here. The [Genesee] Abbey, Yale, Latin America and Harvard were all very important parts of my journey towards L'Arche. It is for the first time that I have the feeling that I am here to stay. Thanks be to God.

Meanwhile, my struggles are no less than in the past. So I really need your prayers and the prayers of the community. If the spiritual life is a life in which one's problems and inner anguish are gradually and progressively overcome, my life is a complete failure. Often it seems that growing older means losing many of one's youthful resistances and leads to an increasing awareness of the dark forces in one's heart and to an always more naked confrontation with the demons. There is less and less in me that I can trust, and I depend more and more on the mercy of Jesus. Only by clinging to Him can I remain faithful. Please pray for me more than ever and hold me close to your heart and the heart of Our Lord.

Peace and love,
Henri

P.S. Send my warm greetings to all the brethren and ask them to pray for me and for all the poor people I am living with.

Ed Wojcicki was the editor of Catholic Times *newspaper. In 1986, Wojcicki began an Advent tradition of writing an open letter to Henri through his column, "Editor's Looking Glass." Henri, fatigued and experiencing periods of anguish, received the gesture with gratitude. He wrote Wojcicki to thank him, beginning a decade of mutual support for each other's writing.*

JAN. 2, 1987

Dear Ed Wojcicki,

Many thanks for your kind note and the very, very encouraging— heart-warming column. I cannot tell you how much your words meant to me. They came at the right time and touch my heart deeply. I am also very grateful to know that sharing my journal notes with others is being perceived as a gift and received as such.

I am very happy to be part of your "new tradition."* It is good

---

* The first column was entitled "Dear Henri: About Those Feelings," *Catholic Times,* November 30, 1986.

to be soul-brothers able to encourage each other on the road of faithfulness. It is indeed a narrow road, and we have to keep each other moving on it!

I love being at Daybreak. Very hard . . . but very good!

Thanks so much for your letter. Stay in touch—

Peace,
Henri

This is a letter of consolation for Jurjen Beumer on the death of his father.

JANUARY 10, 1987

Dear Jurjen,

Many thanks for your very kind letter. I am very moved by what you write about the death of your father. I am so happy that you had a good and cordial farewell. I realize how important that is for you, especially since you told me a little about the tensions in your relationship with your father. Somehow I am convinced that this is a very important moment in your life, a moment in which you are facing your own mortality in a new way and where your father will become a new companion in your own journey. I am deeply convinced that the death of those whom we love always is a death for us, that is to say, a death that calls us to deepen our own basic commitments and to develop a new freedom to proclaim what we most believe in. Mourning is a process in which you are, so to say, freed from old bonds but in which new bonds, more spiritual bonds, are being made.

I would like you to know that I pray for you especially in these days of grief and that I will pray for your father during my daily Eucharist. I have really experienced in the East [Eastern Orthodox hesychastic tradition] the importance of our connection with

those who have died, and I have discovered there the full meaning
of the community of saints.

I am very happy that your father was able to read the Barth
article about prayer. I am, indeed, very moved that you dedicated
that article to me and that that article became also the instrument
of reconciliation. I see this as a sign that your life and my life are
in a very mysterious way connected. For both of us who are still
on the journey, many new directions are still possible, and it is important that we dare to explore these directions without fear. That
sometimes seems a little scary, but God is a God of love, of perfect
love, and perfect love casteth out all fear.

I am very happy with your articles about Jean Vanier and
Pierre-Marie.* I am really impressed by your ability to write so well
and so concisely. I very much hope that you can also send me the
other articles. I am increasingly convinced of the importance of
your writing ministry. You have a real talent for bringing people
in touch with new levels of existence, and the fact that you are the
writer makes it more convincing.

Here all is well. I indeed wish you could visit this community.
In many ways it is very similar to the Trosly community, but in
other ways very different. Within a few months we hope to start
a small "spiritual center." It will be a smaller version of what La
Ferme† in Trosly is, but much more directly connected with the
different foyers [L'Arche houses]. I very much like the atmosphere
of this place. The people are warm. It is very supportive and very
creative. It looks as if, in the future, many new things will develop
here, and I am very glad to be a part of it.

I am not sure yet if I can make it to Holland this year. Life
here doesn't really allow me to be gone very often, but I trust that

---

* Abbé Pierre, Order of Friars Minor Capuchin, grand officier of the National Order
of Quebec (1912–2007), was a French Catholic priest, member of the Resistance
during World War II, and deputy of the Popular Republican Movement.

† La Ferme is a spiritual center in France connected to L'Arche à Trosly.

we will meet each other soon again either here or in Holland. I am very grateful that you continue to stay in touch and that our friendship can grow deeper and stronger.

Yours,
Henri Nouwen

In the late 1980s, Henri was attracting the attention of the evangelical community. Jeff Imbach, an evangelical minister and spiritual director from Alberta, Canada, wrote Henri in 1986 requesting assistance for a book he was writing on Christian medieval mysticism. This began an exchange of letters about writing, publishing and other topics that lasted a decade, the two often sending each other manuscripts for comment. Henri wrote the introduction for Imbach's first published book, The Recovery of Love: Christian Mysticism and the Addictive Society *(New York: Crossroad, 1992).*

Imbach had begun research on Christian mystics and had written to get Henri's opinion on the value of using stages or levels to describe the experience of God.

JANUARY 10, 1987

Dear Jeff,

Thank you so much for your wonderful letter, which I have read different times with great attention. I am writing you this note simply to express my appreciation for what you wrote, even though I am not in a position right now to give you a very articulate response. I am really overwhelmed by the work here and haven't had time to join you in the reading of Ruusbroeck.* I wish I could have

---

* Blessed John of Ruusbroeck (1293 or 1294–December 2, 1381) was one of the Flemish mystics. He wrote many books, including *The Sparkling Stone.*

read the same books you did, but that not being possible at this moment, I hope you will accept my limited response. First of all I'd like to thank you especially for the pages from *The Sparkling Stone*. I have read them at different times and also shared them with a few friends. These pages have proven to be very meaningful and in a very powerful way help us to come in touch with our inner restlessness in our search for God.

There are many things to write about, but I want simply to mention here that I have always considered the idea of levels or stages more something that reflects our limited way of reflecting on the experience of God than a description of how God works in us. For me, therefore, stages or levels are more after-thoughts of an experience that was in itself completely holistic. I really do not believe that God works in stages, but I do believe that when we start describing the immense experience of God's grace we usually use the concept of "level" as a way to come to terms with the immense richness of the experience we are trying to write about. Concepts such as "via purgativa," "via illuminativa" and "via unitiva"* are really not saying much about the hierarchical order. They seem to be more human attempts to describe an experience that includes many different aspects of God's presence in our lives. Thus, they say more about us than about God. I can very well understand your hesitation concerning creation spirituality. I haven't really read much by Matthew Fox or Meister Eckhart, but I have a similar question to yours.

I am leaving it at this for the moment. I certainly feel I should write you much more, but I simply do not have the opportunity just now. I am going to [L'Arche in] Honduras for two weeks on

---

* *Via purgativa* is Latin for "way of purgation." Together with the illuminative way (*via illuminativa*) and the unitive way (*via unitiva*) it is an important concept in traditional ascetical theology, which distinguishes various approaches and stages of the spiritual life (source: *Consecrated Phrases: A Latin Theological Dictionary: Latin Expressions Commonly Found in Theological Writings*, ed. James T. Bretzke, S.J. [Collegeville, MN: Liturgical Press, 2013], 256).

Tuesday, and hopefully I can find some quiet time for reflection there. In the meantime, I hope you have been able to get in touch with Dr. Dupré* and that he has been able to be of some help to you.

Greetings from Nathan. With best wishes,
Henri J. M. Nouwen

Henri writes a letter of encouragement to a parish priest who has started a program to welcome mentally handicapped people into his church.

FEBRUARY 16, 1987

Dear Father Paul Walsh,

It is a great joy for me to hear about your desire to develop within your parish a place of welcome for mentally handicapped people. This letter is simply meant to be a letter of encouragement.

For the largest part of my life I have been rather unaware of the great gift which handicapped people have to offer us. Since I have been living and working at L'Arche, I have become convinced that every Christian community that gives part of its energy to the care of people with a mental handicap will soon discover the special graces connected with that care. After many years of studying and teaching theology, it truly has been a blessed discovery that many of the broken people of L'Arche have revealed more about God's love to me than much of my studying and teaching ever did.

---

* Henri suggested that Imbach contact Louis Dupré, a Catholic philosopher and friend of Henri from Yale. Henri wrote the preface for Dupré's book *The Deeper Life: An Introduction to Christian Mysticism* (New York: Crossroad, 1981).

As I am trying to understand this better, I have come to real-ize that mentally handicapped people, first of all, teach me that "being" is more important than "doing." In our competitive world so much emphasis is given to doing that we forget that God first of all asks us simply to be with Him and with each other. Mentally handicapped people, who can "do" so little, can "be" so much.

During my time at L'Arche I have also learned that the heart is more important than the mind. The heart is the core of our being, and it is there where the gifts of trust, hope and love are being of-fered to us. Mentally handicapped people, who often cannot be as mindful as others, are uniquely gifted to bring us in touch with the treasures of the heart. In a world where so much attention is paid to analysis, discussion of issues and strategies for the future, the "poor in spirit" offer us the hopeful message that it is from the heart that true peace and joy flow.

Finally, I have come to see that people with a mental handicap have a unique gift to call us to community. Precisely because they are so dependent on others, they call us to live together, sharing our gifts, and form a sign of light in the midst of this world. I have been deeply impressed by how people from the most different cultures and socio-economic backgrounds, who other-wise would never have met, have started to live in community because of their common desire to live with and learn from men-tally handicapped people. In a world so filled with individual-ism and so preoccupied with stars and heroes, the call of the handicapped to form communities of love is truly a blessing from Heaven.

It is such a joy for me to know that you too have sensed the special gift that the handicapped people can offer to the Chris-tian community. By revealing to us that being is more impor-tant than doing, the heart is more important than the mind and community is more important than individual stardom, they are truly messengers of the Gospel and witnesses to the Lord who became poor for us. I pray fervently that you will continue meeting, praying and working together to let this new ministry come to maturity among you. I am very sorry that I wasn't able to visit you personally, but I hope that this letter will convince you of my true desire to encourage you and to be of service to you.

With warm greetings,
Sincerely yours,
Henri J. M. Nouwen

This is a letter to his friend Sister Connie Ostrander about the importance of Jesus in the religious life of the monastery.

APRIL 2, 1987

Dear Connie,

Many thanks for your letter. Yes, it is the Spirit of Jesus we need. Keep your eyes and the eyes of your sisters focused (fixed) on him. Words like "God" and "Spirit" so easily tempt us to overlook the "word became flesh and dwelled among us." Your special task as superior is to keep Jesus, the crucified and risen Lord, in the heart of your people and in the center of your community. Keep speaking about him and keep his words calling you and your sisters to faithfulness.

I am so glad to read that you feel "effortless" about leading the community. I am so grateful for the many graces you are receiving.

Here all is well. I will be here for a long time. At least three years, but I hope much longer. It is a very hard life for me, but it is the life God is calling me to live. It will probably take me at least three years to make this my true home. There still are many "pulls" in different directions, but I have to let go of it and trust in the life with the little ones.

Keep me in your prayers. Be joyful and full of love.

Love,
Henri

Henri comments on a paper Imbach has sent him on another Christian mystic, Hadewijch. *Henri also thanks Imbach for his prayers "to protect my deepest inner self." With a spiritual director's heart, Imbach has sensed that Henri continues to struggle with finding time to care for himself.*

APRIL 6, 1987

Dear Jeff,

Thanks so much for your very kind letter and your second paper on Hadewijch. Your paper is really beautiful and makes a statement that couldn't be made more clearly and succinctly. Your sentence "Where we have stressed single-minded commitment, Hadewijch stresses love's desire for transforming union with God," really speaks volumes and opens up a very important message for the Evangelical community. I really think that you are discovering a way of speaking to contemporary Christians with a voice of the past that is so seldom heard. The whole emphasis on embracing love, rather than letting go of our idolatries is so needed in the world that even in spiritual matters wants to be successful.

Thanks so much for offering to pray to protect my deepest

---

* Hadewijch was a thirteenth-century poet and mystic, probably living in what is now known as Belgium. Her writings include visions, prose letters and poetry. Hadewijch was one of the most important direct influences on John of Ruusbroeck.

inner self. You really touch me deeply by this offer, and I gladly
accept it and feel very much supported by you. It is, indeed, very
hard and often seemingly impossible to keep the door of the "portable cell" sufficiently closed.* Even at Daybreak, where so many
people support me spiritually, this is much harder than I thought,
so your prayers are extremely important for me. Thanks so much
for being in touch. I look forward to seeing your next reflections.

With warm greetings,
Yours,
Henri

*Henri writes to encourage Jeff Imbach to persevere with his writings on
medieval mystics for a contemporary audience.*

APRIL 24, 1987

Dear Jeff,

Many thanks for your very good letter. I quite well understand
that it is not always easy to connect Hadewijch and Ruusbroeck
with contemporary issues. It sometimes might indeed feel a little
too contrived, but I do like to encourage you to continue working
on the mystical themes since I really feel that there is the real treasure for you. Your meditations about the revelation of error mixed
with truth, about the history of spirituality as the context for see-

---

* "Portable cell" refers to silence. Henri wrote about this in his book *The Way of the
Heart: Desert Spirituality and Contemporary Ministry* (New York: Seabury Press, 1981):
"It is a good discipline to wonder in each new situation if people wouldn't be better
served by our silence than by our words. But having acknowledged this, a more
important message from the desert is that silence is above all a quality of the heart
that can stay with us even in our conversation with others. It is a portable cell we
carry with us wherever we go. From it we speak to those in need and to it we return
after our words have borne fruit" (p. 65).

ing the larger tradition of Christianity, which also embraces sensuality, and about re-thinking the meaning of being "born again" are very valuable contributions to the evangelical community. I enjoyed very much reading them, and I do truly believe that they are touching very important places in the evangelical soul.

But I do have somewhat of a problem here. I would regret seeing you primarily as a critical voice in the evangelical community. Your criticism is good, valuable and helpful, but, like all criticism, it tends to be more evaluative than nurturing, and I feel that it is precisely people like Hadewijch and Ruusbroeck who can prevent you from becoming primarily a voice that points to the weaknesses in the evangelical community. Your great challenge is to offer perspectives to evangelicals which lead them deeper into the mystery of the Incarnation and offer ways to live as people of the Resurrection. I, therefore, hope that you continue to look for those treasures in the medieval mystics that can be offered as a source of spiritual deepening to evangelical people. Your sentence, "We need to have the courage to explore again the high reaches of those phrases (such as 'born again') and see how those high reaches were described by others in the Christian tradition before us," really speaks to me, and I feel that is where you best describe your own task. I really hope and pray that you will persevere in this beautiful and extremely blessed work.

With warm greetings and much love,
Henri

Paul is a theologian writing a book about Père Thomas Philippe, a Dominican priest. He is struggling with Père Thomas's difficult personality and abrasive relationship style and has written to Henri for support on how to continue.

APRIL 28, 1987

Dear Paul,

You may have wondered why it took me so long to write in response to the very open and honest letter that you wrote me in
February. The reason for the delay has been that I was somewhat
at a loss as to how to really be a good friend to you and offer you
the kind of support you not only need, but also fully deserve. I
have thought of you often in these past few months, and I have
prayed for you and asked the Lord to give you that inner light and
inner freedom that would enable you to do your work well without
becoming oppressed by anguish-filled relationships.

I am really not surprised that you write how difficult your relationship with Father Thomas is. I have seen and experienced the
power of his thoughts and visions, and I quite well understand
how strong your desire is to have a normal, easy and open friendship with him, but it seems that precisely that which attracts you
so much in him is also the reason that makes this free and easy
relationship so difficult. I can very well feel your great desire to
discuss with him freely some of the questions you have about his
thinking and to write about him with his full support and sympathy. Somehow it seems that that desire is probably never going to
be completely fulfilled. Sometimes it seems that we have to accept
the fact that different human beings fulfill different needs and
that no one human being can fulfill all our needs. I love to be in
your house; I love to sit around the table and chat with you and
your family and be an easy-going friend for you, but I am certainly
not the kind of person you ever would want to write a book about.
Father Thomas is a totally different person. It is hard to get him
to your home, to feel relaxed and to ask him what you would like
to ask. But he is precisely the man worthy of writing a book about
because his deep spiritual vision is of unique importance for the
Church.

Many years ago I was deeply attracted to the writing of Father

Thomas. His writings and his thoughts deeply, deeply impressed me and evoked in me a deep desire to get to know him better, but when I read about his relationships with people during his life, I found out that he was a quite aloof person who had a hard time really feeling at ease with people in a casual way. It is a real paradox that those who often write so movingly about the heart and the spirituality of the heart are not always able to be the kind of people that we would like them to be for us.

What do I try to say with all of this? First of all, I want you to trust in my real friendship for you and my real support. Certain things that Father Thomas cannot offer you, I can offer you, and secondly, I really do believe it is worthwhile continuing and completing the work you have started even when the personal relationship with Father Thomas never will be ideal. I think you have very important things to say and to write, and I trust that what you say and write will bear fruit in the life of others. Do not let the value of that depend on how you feel about Father Thomas or how Father Thomas feels about you. I think you can really trust that Father Thomas will never speak against you. He is a truly holy man and, despite his obvious shortcomings, a man who has no other desire than to let his knowledge bear fruit in the life of many people. You certainly are a person who can help him with that, even though he cannot be directly involved in it. Finally, I want to suggest to you that you spend every day some time praying for him. I am convinced that the more you pray for him, the more it will become clear what the unique quality of your relationship with him is. I also feel that through simple contemplative prayer you will become more and more in touch with your own vocation as a theologian and writer.

The fact is that much of the suffering taking place in the Church is the result of tensions among those who love the Lord. Ever since the conflict between Paul and Peter, and Paul and Barnabas, much pain within the Church has been the result of conflict among the disciples of Jesus. To live that kind of conflict well is one of the hardest aspects of the Christian life. The only way to find our way through it is unceasing prayer. I really don't see any other way. I hope you agree.

Be sure of my friendship, my love, my support and my great desire to see you filled with the Lord's spirit and full of good energy. I do not know when we will be able to see each other again, but I trust that there will be time soon for us to share our thoughts and feelings.

With warm greetings and much love,
Yours,
Henri Nouwen

It has been a year since Henri's arrival at L'Arche Daybreak, and although he remains convinced of his vocation there, his friendship with Nathan Ball has started to deteriorate. Nathan has asked for space, and Henri is struggling to find "the most creative way of being friends." He writes to his friend Jeff Imbach, who is also a family friend of Nathan, for prayers.

SEPTEMBER 29, 1987

Dear Jeff,

I find myself thinking about you often and wondering how you are doing. It would be good to hear from you again.

I had a very intense summer in England trying to deal directly with some of my emotional struggles.* It was a good and very healing time even though there is still a lot of "work" to be done in the years to come. I feel very committed to being at L'Arche and

---

* Henri frequently stayed and wrote at Brook Place, a Christian ecumenical center in Chertsey run by his friends Patricia and Bart Gavigan.

especially at Daybreak, and I hope that this year will be a year of deepening my love for Jesus, who brought me here.

Please keep me and Nathan very much in your prayers. We are still struggling to find the most creative way of being friends. At times it is a hard and painful struggle, but we are both trying to face it openly and in faith. The fact of your affection both for Nathan and for me makes it very important that you keep us both in your prayers.

Please let me know how you are doing personally as well as in your studies. I hope that you will continue the work that you started so creatively last year.

Much love,
Henri

Wayne Muller is a therapist, United Church of Christ minister, community advocate, and author. While a student at Harvard Divinity School in 1983, he had taken one of Henri's courses, and they would often meet outside of class to discuss areas of mutual interest. With Henri's influence and help, Muller followed in Henri's footsteps to Peru, living with the same family and attending the same language school as Henri did during his Latin American sojourn.

Muller had written to Henri about his disenchantment with parish ministry.

NOVEMBER 5, 1987

Dear Wayne,

What a wonderful gift your letter is! It is so good to hear from you and to be aware that you have not forgotten about me. Thanks for giving me such a good impression of what is on your mind lately.

I very much understand the struggle you are experiencing with the church, and I am really happy that you are developing a clear understanding of your vocation in light of the limitations of parish ministry.

One thing I would like to ask you is to keep faithful to a life of prayer. Without prayer, confession, anger and frustrations may become unbearable for you, but when in prayer you connect them with the struggle of Jesus himself, I trust that your vocation will deepen. It is so important to be in the world and really in it, but without being of it, and that is only possible when you live a life of prayer. I also would like you to stay faithful to the church, even when you see its tendency to be self-indulgent. In the long run, living in Christ without being connected with the church is impossible. I have seen this over and over again. The church continues to be the place where Christ calls us to faithfulness and from where Christ sends us out into the world.

I am very excited about the project you are developing with Christine. It sounds very creative and important. I'd like to be of as much support to you in this respect in any way I can.

Life at L'Arche is really good for me. It is hard and demanding and often more intense than I would like it to be, but it is really the place where God calls me to be. Enclosed I send you a paper about ministry that I wrote recently. I thought you might like to see it. Please give my love to Christine.

Love,
Henri

P.S. Regretfully, I will not be able to come to the Episcopal Convention to participate in a conference on parish life. I really need to stay here.

Henri writes in response to Jeff Imbach's article about sexuality and religious leaders.

NOVEMBER 5, 1987

Dear Jeff,

Thanks so much for your good letter and your article on the Gordon MacDonald case.* I am very, very impressed by what you wrote. Your nine pages about the subject are extremely valuable to me and I think will be for many people. Be sure to continue thinking in this area. Your vision about how to respond to unfulfilled longing is of extreme importance for the development of a contemporary asceticism. It will be important for you to describe in the future some of the concrete disciplines that are necessary to let the unfulfilled longing bring us closer to God, but what you have done so far is already an important step.

I am very familiar with the idea of sexuality being a powerful giant which we have to keep in control. Your vision of sexuality as a gift of God that calls us closer to Him is a vision that the church really needs to hear more and more. A new and more mature vision about faithfulness might develop from it.

Thanks so much for your letter and the writing you sent me. Please pray for me and for Nathan in these days. I very much need your on-going support and prayer as we continue to struggle with our relationship. Stay in touch.

Love,
Henri

---

* Gordon MacDonald was an evangelical pastor who had an extramarital affair.

Henri responds to a letter from his friend Lee Udell, a hospital chaplain, who has written with questions about end-of-life care for people with severe handicaps. He challenges Henri for romanticizing the spiritual gifts of his friend Adam rather than addressing his very real, concrete pain. Lee also pushes Henri to think about how he represents himself in his published writing.*

Henri responds with thoughts about how life with Adam and other core members at L'Arche is affecting him.

NOVEMBER 10, 1987

Dear Lee,

Thanks so much for your good letter. I really appreciate your honest, direct and challenging words. There are many important questions which I won't be able to respond to well in this letter. There are many, many things that I would like to write to you, but the main thing I want to say is that the way I am receiving from Adam is a spiritual way, which, in a certain sense, transcends the emotional, the physical and the intellectual. It is very hard for me to articulate exactly what a handicapped man like Adam is offering me, but in a very profound way I do believe that he has become for me a very concrete representation of the suffering Christ. His emptiness and his complete dependency have given me a deeper spiritual knowledge of Christ's descending way than anything I have ever read or heard. I really feel deeply that Adam is extremely precious in God's eyes and that in a very profound sense he was sent to us for our healing and salvation.

---

* Udell had written, "I think you are overly critical of Henri Nouwen. I have known you for some years now. I have never found you to be the competitive, self-serving person you describe. There may be a portion of you like this, but not the majority of you. I cannot believe that most of your generous spirit and talk of the spiritual life springs from egoism and a desire to be popular and to be well-published."

One of the most remarkable things Adam has done for us is to bring us together in a community of love and to help us to discover God's presence among us in a completely new way. We really do not talk much about these things, and I am not trying to "use" Adam for my own spiritual ends, but I realize something is happening because of him which has a very profound significance, not only for me as an individual, but for all who live in this community and, indirectly, for society and the Church. As far as I am concerned, there is so much purification still to take place. I understand your remark that my talking of the spiritual life does not just spring from egotism or a desire to be popular, but since I am here I have really discovered how much more inner purification I have to live, how God calls me to follow him radically on the way to the cross and the resurrection.

I very much hope that we can talk about this more in the future. Hopefully I will find words to say better what I write you in this letter, but I hope that you realize that I have taken your questions to heart and keep thinking about them.

Yours,
Henri

Henri writes to his friend Brock about his emotional state.

He is living in a retreat center for clergy in Winnipeg, where he has been sent by the Daybreak community to recuperate from emotional and physical exhaustion.

DECEMBER 27, 1987

Dear Brock,

Thanks so much for your wonderful letter, for all your words of support and love and for your poem "Word Clown." I really need your prayers and support at this time because I find myself in a very hard place. During the past few months so much physical and emotional fatigue has built up in me that the community decided to give me a month of rest, but you know how during periods of rest sometimes the demons are very active. I am particularly mourning because of a broken friendship and am still not able to find the strength to let the mourning set me free. It is so hard to let go of someone you really care for deeply and to recognize that you are not the person who can offer the support and love that he needs.

So I really ask you to help me live this period of rest and mourning in a way that is healing for me but also fruitful for others. You quote rightly, "Blessed are those who mourn, for they shall be comforted." I really have to meditate on these words more than ever and how hard it is to "let go."

Be sure of my love and friendship for you. May the joy and peace of Jesus fill your mind and heart.

Yours,
Henri

Henri received numerous letters from people anxious to get clarification on Church teachings. In this letter, Henri writes to a man about proselytizing and the universal quality of God's love.

DECEMBER 28, 1987

Dear John,

Thanks so much for your letter which you wrote in September. Regretfully, I wasn't able to respond earlier since it took a long time to arrive.

It is hard for me to answer the many questions which you

raised because they are very complicated, but maybe I can just share with you my own faith. I have always found much strength in the words of Jesus, "When I will be lifted up, I will draw all people to me" (Gospel of John). I am deeply convinced that Jesus came for all people and that He took on human flesh so that all human flesh could be destined for resurrection. I, therefore, believe that all human beings are embraced by God's love and are called to enjoy the fruits of Christ's redemption. For me, this implies two very important things. First of all, that nobody, whether Buddhist, Christian or Muslim is automatically excluded from the saving work of Jesus. Everyone who is born in the flesh that God Himself took on can be led to the glory of God even when he does not explicitly know about Jesus or the story of the Gospels. Secondly, I firmly believe that anyone who has been given the privilege of knowing Jesus and the Christian message has a unique vocation to proclaim Jesus to the world and be a living witness of the risen Christ.

I am convinced that anyone who has been touched deeply by Jesus will discover eventually in himself a call to share the love of Jesus with others, not to force anyone into becoming a Christian or manipulate anyone into Baptism, but to be a living sign of the love that has been discovered through Jesus and that needs to be made known. The desire to proclaim Jesus belongs to the essence of knowing Him and loving Him. This proclamation can take place in very different ways. It doesn't always have to be by words. Everyone has his different vocation; some will proclaim the Gospel by a simple faithfulness to those close to them. Not everyone is called to the same task, and, once we know Jesus, we will gradually discover what our particular way of proclaiming the Gospel is. I do think however, that it is wrong to believe that we are called to save the world by trying with all our will-power to make other people accept Jesus or Baptism. That would be a taking on of a divine role that doesn't belong to us. Only God saves and God's Spirit blows where it wants, even among those who do not know Jesus and never will know explicitly about Him. I think this is quite orthodox thinking and not at all heretical or liberal. It is very important for you to pray quietly and to discover in which way Jesus calls you to proclaim the Good News, and, when you discover this call, you will also find there can't be any compulsiveness or obsessiveness to your vocation. It is not so much a "must" as a "may" that characterizes the Christian witness.

Thanks so much for your good, kind letter. I really will include you in my prayers, and I really hope that you will find an increasing peace and joy in your heart.

With warm greetings,
Yours,
Henri J. M. Nouwen

Henri writes to a woman who works with the elderly and is experiencing burnout.

MARCH 10, 1988

Dear Dolores,

Many, many thanks for your very wonderful letter in response to the article I wrote on Adam.* I very much appreciate the many things you write.

One thing that seems crucial to me is that even when you live a very intense type of service, you keep at least one hour a day free for prayer. My sense is that, if we are no longer centered by Jesus in prayer, it becomes harder and harder to experience Him

---

* Around this time, Henri began to publish articles about his friend Adam and his experiences at L'Arche in several journals, including "The Peace That Is Not of This World," published in *Weavings* magazine in March 1988.

in the people we work with. I really appreciate the work you are
doing with the elderly and admire your great dedication, but, if
you want to do it long term and remain faithful in it, I think it is
very important that you "spoil" yourself—spend some good time
with Jesus and Him alone. This is the way to prevent burn-out
and to remain always joyful even when you see so much suffering and pain. Somehow the marketplace and the soul have to stay
together.

I also hope you will find someone who can give you some support in your spiritual life. It is always so wonderful to have a fellow
Christian with whom you can pray and talk about your work and
who prays also for you.

Thanks so much again for your good letter.

With warm greetings,
Yours,
Henri

Sister Marcia (Monica) Hobart is a diocesan anchoress living in the United*
States. She wrote Henri a letter of appreciation after reading Genesee
Diary. *They exchanged letters for the next twenty years.*

MARCH 15, 1988

Dear Monica,

Your letter is a real blessing. Indeed, this is a very hard time for me.
Our Lord is pruning me, purifying me, simplifying me. I have to
let go of so much so that Jesus can become my only desire. It seems

---

* In Christianity, an anchoress is a woman who chooses to withdraw from the world
to lead a life of solitude, prayer and asceticism. The word *anchoress* comes from the
Greek "anachōreō" meaning to withdraw.

so impossible, but with God everything is possible. Please keep me in your prayers during these months of trial and hope. I pray for you and ask Our Lord to keep you faithful in your vocation. May the Mother of Jesus guide you always closer to her Son.

It was so good to meet you and be assured of your prayers.

Peace,
Henri

Henri writes to a minister who is considering a call to be the leader, for an elected term, of the United Church of Canada.

At the time of this letter, written from Winnipeg, Henri was in his fourth month of intensive therapy.

APRIL 5, 1988

Dear Gordon,

Thanks so much for your very beautiful letter. It was a real gift to me. Your warm friendship towards me and your opening your heart to me, I experience as a really special blessing. I very much would like to just spend time with you during these months of decision-making, and I feel sad that it is unlikely that I can be in Toronto in the coming months. I want you to know first of all, that I keep you very much in my prayers and think about you often. I pray especially that the Spirit of God will guide you in your decision on whether or not to accept the nomination for Moderator of the United Church of Canada. I must confess there is something in me that says that it would be good for you to accept the nomination and at least give your church a chance to consider you as their future Moderator and enter into a discernment process about that. I am saying this because I wonder if the Lord will not give you a special state of grace in which the new task will call forth in you spiritual gifts that you obviously have, but that have not yet been fully brought into the open. In other words, I have an intuition that you might discover God's unique presence in your life and your unique spiritual and pastoral gifts when you would be asked to act as Moderator. Maybe for some people it is true that accepting a very difficult but spiritually challenging position is God's way of calling them to sanctity. I wonder if this might be the case with you.

Meanwhile, I very much would love to talk with you about it more if that is good for you. Therefore, I am adding my phone number here in Winnipeg so that we could at least have a long conversation by phone. I am mostly at home and would love to talk with you. Be sure, meanwhile, that I am going to spend some extra time in prayer, asking God to guide you in this very important decision.

Love and many prayers,
Henri

Henri offers words of consolation to a friend in Germany who is suffering from depression. He shares his own struggles as well as his insights born of his recent experience that one must go into the pain in order to discover God's unconditional love.

APRIL 14, 1988

Dear Michael,

What a joy it was to receive your long and warm letter! So good to hear from you and to be brought up to date. You can be sure that I have thought of you and prayed for you and Marlene and wondered how things were going. I now am so glad to hear that you finished your studies and have started your own independent practice and with such good results. I am also hoping very much that Marlene will soon be accepted in medical school. I can see how good that would be for her as well as for you. Most of all, I am very, very happy to hear that you will be married in the Church on August 13th. I obviously would love to be there, but at this moment I am really unable to say if this would be possible. In the case I could take my vacation during August, I certainly would make it a priority to be at your Church wedding because my friendship with you is very important for me and I believe that it is a friendship for life. I, therefore, find it important that I share special moments of your life. So be sure of my desire to be there. Whether things will work out that way, I cannot know for certain at this time.

I may already have told you that since December I have been living in Winnipeg to recover from physical and emotional exhaustion that overwhelmed me. Around Christmas I realized that I could no longer function at Daybreak. I needed a long break to pray, to think, to get some good spiritual guidance and to do some quiet writing. There was a lot of anxiety and fear in my heart, and I knew that I could no longer run away from it, but had to live it through. Fortunately, the Lord gave me two very good people to help me in the process of healing, and now I feel that I am on the way to recovery and hope to be able to return to Daybreak in the near future. But as you may realize, there are still many uncertain factors and I have to be patient so that I will not return before I am really ready. That is also the main reason why I am not sure if I can come to Europe in August.

What you wrote about depression and hopelessness is something that I can understand better now than ever before. During the past few months I have also experienced the pain of depression and hopelessness, but I am glad that I can write you that by living it through with the help of some capable spiritual guides, I have come to new hope and new joy. The depression and hopelessness that you and I both know about are clearly rooted in very early life experiences, experiences that took place long before we could speak or think. It is the primal experience of feeling not safe and not unconditionally loved. Somehow, we got the message that love needs to be earned and that we are only worth loving if we prove this to others, and thus, whatever we do and whatever we accomplish in life, we continue to wonder if people truly love us and if God is really there for us with His unconditional love. I think that you and I are both challenged to enter into that fearful primal place and to discover there that God does love us fully and unconditionally; even though our parents might not have been able to let us truly experience that early love, I think that it is important that at one point in our life we are able to forgive our parents, since they are also wounded and limited people, and to truly trust that their wounded and broken love was in fact, a reflection of the total and unconditional love of God.

I am so glad that Marlene is there for you and is offering you such a wonderful, faithful love, but I also realize that Marlene will not be able to take that depression and hopelessness totally away from you. I think all she can do is offer you the safe context within which you can find the courage to enter that deep place of hopelessness and depression and discover that beyond your hopelessness and depression there is a God who offers you unconditional love and maybe there will be a time when you will need some special spiritual and emotional support to enter that place. But I want to tell you that I am very hopeful when I think about you, and I trust that a deep healing is really possible. I have even greater hope because of the presence of Marlene in your life.

Well, these are some words of love and friendship for you, and I hope you receive them as a sign of my commitment to you. Be sure that I pray for you and for Marlene and that I very much hope that we will see each other again soon.

Much love,
Henri

❦

Henri's friend Jim Forest has remarried. He and his new wife, Nancy, who are living in Holland, have recently converted to the Russian Orthodox Church.

Henri writes from Daybreak, where he is visiting for a week.

MAY 4, 1988

Dear Jim and Nancy,

Thanks so much for your letters and for your words of encouragement sent to me and to Connie [Connie Ellis, Henri's administrative assistant]. It was really good to know about your concern and your personal interest in my life. It obviously was a really great surprise for me to read that you both had joined the Orthodox Church. I have been sorting out my own response to your decision, and I discover that my main response is that I feel very sad that the Catholic Church in Holland has not been able to provide you with a "friendly spiritual life and sacramentally-centered home."

It increasingly fills me with great sorrow that the Church in Holland has become for so many people a sterile place where deep spiritual life doesn't seem to be encouraged or nurtured. I really do have a sense that the main reason for your move is precisely to find a welcoming spiritual home, and I am not surprised that the beauty, warmth and spiritual depth of the Orthodox Church has attracted you so much. I guess at some point I had hoped that it would have been possible for you to stay in the Roman Catholic Church and bring some of the Orthodox spirituality there, but I guess it is too much to ask of starving people to offer food to the hungry.

I certainly hope to be able to continue to stay in touch with you as you enter more deeply into the life and spirit of the Orthodox Church. A very close friend of mine, John Garvey, who writes a column in *Commonweal*, also recently took the same step as you have taken. I will send him your newsletter of April 18th, in which

I am sure he will be very interested. As you can see from the introduction that he wrote for *Circles of Love*,* which I enclose, he finds much strength in the spiritual writers of the Orthodox Church.† I must also say that I myself have found the spiritual writings, especially of 19th-century Russian Orthodox mystics, an increasingly great source for my own spiritual development. Maybe I might even say that the older I become, the more I can really hear well the power and strength of that spiritual tradition.

I deeply hope that you will both be true bridge-builders between the Orthodox Church and the Roman Catholic Church. Somehow I find it very mysterious that, because of the Bolshevik Revolution, so many Orthodox Christians came to Western Europe and are now becoming a formidable spiritual force. Wherever I see renewal in the Roman Catholic Church, I see icons and I see literature from Russian Orthodox sources. Maybe the Orthodox Church came to the West in order to help the Roman Church to renew itself.

As far as I am concerned, I am still struggling but doing a little better. I am presently at Daybreak for a week to visit people here and renew my contact with the community, and I hope and pray that I will soon be strong enough to return here permanently. I love L'Arche and I love Daybreak and have a strong desire to continue my ministry here.

Be sure to keep me in your prayers because there is still a lot of healing to be done and I need to rely more than ever on God's gentle grace.

With much love and warm greetings,
Yours,
Henri

---

* *Circles of Love: Daily Readings with Henri J. M. Nouwen* (Springfield, IL: Templegate, 1988).

† See letter to Garvey, December 20, 1978.

⚜

Henri writes to his friend Robert J. Wicks, a spiritual writer and professor of pastoral counseling at Loyola College in Maryland. He shares his hope that he can return to Daybreak "before too long" and identifies his recent experience as a "deep spiritual crisis."

MAY 19, 1988

Dear Bob,

Thanks so much for your good letter. I really appreciate your staying in touch and your support during this time of my life. I have still not returned to Daybreak and it might take me a few more months before I am able to do so, but I am gradually discovering some new inner strength, and I hope very much that I will be able to continue my ministry with the L'Arche community before too long.

It means a lot to me that you keep in touch and that you are willing to support me with your prayers. If anything holds me up, it is the prayers of friends and I rely on them. What I am experiencing is a really deep spiritual crisis in which I realize that God wants all of my heart, not simply a part of it. It seems as if He wants to test my faithfulness and my commitment in a new way. He is really asking me to let go of everything that does not bring me closer to Him. He calls me to a more generous prayer life and to a more fearless ministry. This year is a kind of desert year to purify my heart. It is painful, but also full of grace.

Meanwhile, I hope that your summer will be good and creative and, most of all, prayerful. I am very interested in your new book. I am even curious to know which psychological perils you have in mind. I am so used to reading about the spiritual perils of psychological intimacy, that I am very curious to know more about the psychological perils of spiritual intimacy. Enclosed I send you a little book just published, as a sign of my friendship and love.*

With warm greetings,
Yours,
Henri

✦✦✦

Henri writes another letter to his friends Jim and Nancy Forest, expressing sadness about their decision to join the Russian Orthodox Church.

MAY 26, 1988

Dear Jim and Nancy,

Your letters are a real gift to me. I can't tell you how deeply grateful I am to both of you for taking the time and energy to let me understand better your decision to become members of the Russian Orthodox Church. Your letters are a real expression of deep friendship and give me much hope and much joy. They also, obviously, cause me some pain since I so much would have hoped that the Church of Thomas Merton and Dorothy Day would have been able to hold you, nurture you and lead you to an ever deeper communion with God—Father, Son and Spirit—and an ever greater love for Mary, the mother of Jesus, and an ever greater sense of being enveloped by the mystery of the Divine Presence.

I so much love the Catholic Church and its great spiritual treasures that it causes me pain and even anguish at times to see dear friends unable to find there the fulfilment of their deepest desires,

---

* Henri is probably referring to *The Road to Daybreak: A Spiritual Journey* (Garden City, NY: Doubleday, 1988), his published diary about his resignation from Harvard to discern a vocation with L'Arche.

but I realize how much all that you write to me comes from the center of your hearts and is a true expression of your fervent desire to serve God and God's people. I very much would have liked to sit down and write to you a very long letter responding to the different points you make. I also would have liked very much to give you a deeper insight into why I am so deeply in love with the Catholic Church even now. I very much hope that in the future I will be able to do so, but my present physical and emotional fatigue and my need to live a more hidden life make it impossible for me to do what I most want to do. But I know you will understand.

I just want you to know most of all how deeply grateful I am to you and how much your letters have deepened my love for both of you. I very much hope that the near future will allow us to be together again. I do not know yet when that will be, but I trust that the time for it will not be too far away.

Meanwhile, I have shared your letters with a few of my intimate friends who are struggling with similar questions as you are and for whom your letters are extremely significant.

Let us stay in touch. I certainly will write you again soon.

With warm greetings and much love,
Yours,
Henri

Ed Wojcicki, his friend and editor of the Catholic Times, *is at a crossroads. Henri writes with very concrete suggestions about how to live this time of decision making and discernment.*

JULY 13, 1988

Dear Ed,

Many thanks for your very good letter. I very much understand you when you say that you find yourself at another crossroad in life. I would very much like to encourage you to take that very seriously and ask the Lord fervently to show you where He is calling you. When I was at Harvard, I also had that very deep feeling that God was calling me to something new, and I was even afraid to pray because God might give me too clear an answer. But as I prayed, I found that God did, indeed, have something new in mind for me, and I am deeply grateful that I listened to His voice, even though I was led to places I would rather not go.

You certainly have the strength to overcome cynicism and become a model of hope. The simple fact that you raise that question makes me aware of your real search and the fact that God is calling you to something new. Try to take little steps in the direction of your inner call (a regular hour of silent prayer, talks with people who can truly listen to you, reading books that help you sharpen your own inner vocation, visits to places and people where some of your dream is lived out). Be sure never to let your life go flat. Always know that God is calling you to ever greater things.

Maybe one day you will have an opportunity to come and visit us for a few days, and then we could talk more about your vocation. I am certainly very open to that.

Thanks again for writing. Be sure to stay in touch.
With warm greetings,
Yours,
Henri

✦

Henri is regaining energy after nearly seven months in Winnipeg. He writes to his friend Jeff Imbach about a recent visit to Daybreak. As mentioned earlier, he describes how he and Nathan hope to live their struggle in the wider context of the community. The remainder of the letter consists of Henri's response to a proposed presentation on Orthodox spirituality to an evangelical audience.

JULY 13, 1988

Dear Jeff,

Thanks so much for your good letters, which I received today. I am presently at Daybreak for a week. Last week I was in Montreal to attend a L'Arche gathering and I decided, on the spur of the moment, to return to Daybreak to see how it would be back here. Last night I had a meeting with Nathan in which we were able to talk together and think together about the possibility of both of us living in the same community. Nathan was very gentle and caring and showed great willingness to struggle with me in finding a new way of expressing our care for each other. It is clear that this will require a lot of "withholding" and will also be very hard for both of us, but we are committed to looking at our struggle as something greater than just the two of us. Please keep us in your prayers as we try to live this struggle faithfully. It is very painful, but, hopeful, also fruitful.

As far as the session on Orthodox Spirituality is concerned, I just have a few thoughts you might like to be aware of:

1. I see the great value of the Jesus Prayer, but I do not think it can really be discussed outside of the context of the liturgy. If you separate the Jesus Prayer from the liturgy, it becomes a mantra, which, in a way, it is, but

it is more than that. The Jesus Prayer should never be separated from the larger context of the liturgical life of the Orthodox Church. You could say, in a way, that the Jesus Prayer is a continuation and deepening of what takes place in the sacred liturgy (the Eucharistic liturgy).

2. I do think that much of the spirit of Orthodox Spirituality is found in its music. I, therefore, think it would be very important to present some of the music of the liturgy as part of the session on Orthodox Spirituality.

3. Orthodox Spirituality is intimately connected with iconography. Very few people know the deeper meaning of icons, and I, therefore, think it would be very interesting for an audience to understand better the meaning of icons.

I have a feeling that, when we focus on the liturgy, the music and the iconography, we will probably have a better way of seeing how Evangelical people can discover the value of Orthodox Spirituality for their own life of prayer. Personally, I think that the way we present this type of thing is very important. I would like to stay away as much as possible from analysis and argument, and to present Orthodox Spirituality as an experience into which we all can enter to some degree.

As far as hesychasm is concerned, I have tried to translate its meaning in contemporary terms in my little book, *The Way of the Heart*.* There I discuss solitude, silence and prayer (fuge, tace, quiesce) as three core elements of hesychasm. I found increasingly that these three themes are very easily heard and understood by Evangelical people.

I will send you a few books that might be helpful in preparation

---

* *The Way of the Heart: Desert Spirituality and Contemporary Ministry* (New York: Seabury Press, 1981).

for the session we are thinking about. They may or may not be helpful, but I would like you to be aware of them.

Warm greetings,
Yours,
Henri

Sue Mosteller, a Catholic Sister of St. Joseph, was a long-term member of L'Arche Daybreak and a catalyst for calling Henri to Daybreak as pastor. She played a pivotal role in helping Henri and Nathan repair their broken friendship and would continue to be a trusted friend, intellectual partner and wise counsel for the rest of Henri's life.

Henri writes this letter to Sue as they both prepare to leave Winnipeg for a trip to France together. He expresses that he is feeling weak and apprehensive about the future. Reflecting on his week at Daybreak with Nathan, he contemplates his feelings of uselessness and emptiness as a means for God to enter his life more fully.

JULY 25, 1988

Dear Sue,

Time is going fast, and within a few days we will be on our way to Paris. Something seems to be coming to an end. Last night I packed my boxes and suitcases and emptied my little room. I know that this is a time of leaving even though I am still very apprehensive about the future. I feel so weak and vulnerable! It seems that only a complete trust in Jesus' guidance in all of this can make it possible for me to move beyond my anguish. Going to Marthe's* place gives me much hope and confidence because the strength I need has to be given to me. The fruitfulness of her life that was so

---

* The trip included a visit to the home of Marthe Robin (1902–1981), a French Roman Catholic mystic who was bedridden for more than five decades.

visibly weak, powerless and even completely "useless" has to give me the inner knowledge that God wants my life to be fruitful too even though I feel so empty.

As I mentioned to you on the phone, the week after Daybreak was a very hard week interiorly. I do not know yet what it all means. Most of all I think God does not want to give me any chance to rely on my own emotional resources and won't give me any consolation based on the "old ways." Well, no wishes, but much hope, no big plans, but trust, no great desires, but much love, no knowledge of the future, but a lot of empty space for God to walk in! There is a deep sense of uselessness, but maybe that is the kind of soil God needs to sow his seed!

I have been praying for you and will pray with special fervor for you during this week. I am very glad that you finished your paper. That must be a real relief to you. It is important to let it go now, even when it is not perfect. It certainly is very good! I am also very glad that you are going to Nominingue [Quebec]. It feels very good to me that we both are part of the renewal.* You will find there very good people with much love in their hearts and a great desire to be close to God and God's little people. I hope you have a chance to tell them how deeply connected I feel with all of them, how much I miss being there, how grateful I am for their friendship and how strong my hope is that they will grow in the knowledge of the Father's mercy and love. Your presence there can truly deepen and strengthen, widen and enrich the knowledge of God's loving presence that I tried to offer in the first days of the renewal.

See you in the plane!

Love,
Henri

---

* Henri is referring to a gathering of members of North American L'Arche communities called a L'Arche Renewal. He participated the previous month, giving talks on the theme of "returning" based on Rembrandt's painting *The Return of the Prodigal Son*. The talks were edited by Sue Mosteller as *Home Tonight: Further Reflections on the Parable of the Prodigal Son* (New York: Doubleday, 2009).

P.S. Thanks so much for the good wine on my anniversary. Also for your encouraging letter by Priority Mail. Real gifts!

Henri writes to his friend Jim Antal and Cindy Shannon, who are responding to their reading of the recently translated book Letters to Marc About Jesus.

AUGUST 4, 1988

Dear Cindy and Jim,

Thanks so much for your kind response to *Letters to Marc.** The personal relationship with Jesus is the core of the spiritual life, the way to a life in uninterrupted communion with the Divine life of Father, Son and Spirit. It is so sad to see so much human suffering coming from broken relationships and so little experience of the healing love of God. What else should theology be about than the knowledge of God's infinite love!

I so much would like to see Luke and play with him. Give him my love.

Enclosed some sunflowers for him.

Love,
Henri

P.S. I am in France on retreat. Hope to be back in Daybreak on September 2. Thanks so much for your friendship and support.

---

* This is a translation of *Brieven aan Marc: Over Jezus en de Zin van het Leven* (Tielt: Lannoo, 1987), published in 1988 by Harper and Row as *Letters to Marc About Jesus: Spiritual Living in a Material World.*

Peter Weiskel was Henri's teaching and administrative assistant at Harvard University. In 1984, he accompanied Henri to Guatemala to visit John Vesey, an American priest who, following the murder of Father Stan Rother, took over as pastor in Rother's parish.* Weiskel's photographs were part of the book Love in a Fearful Land: A Guatemalan Story *(Notre Dame, IN: Ave Maria Press, 1985) that Henri published about this trip. While Henri's assistant, Weiskel helped with a number of manuscripts, including* The Road to Daybreak, A Spirituality of Peacemaking[†] *and many other publications.*

Weiskel is now working as a hydrologist and is married to Kate. Henri writes about working in a milieu that may not support his spiritual life.

AUGUST 17, 1988

Dear Peter,

After writing this postcard to you and Kate, I read your story again and was again as moved as when I read it the first time. So well written and so concise and convincing![‡]

Meanwhile I also read Dale Vree's story and the stories of John Cort, Jim Forest, Thomas Howard and John Michael Talbot. What a remarkable variety of journeys! They all had the effect on me of making me deeply grateful for being a Catholic. But I have to keep reading these stories to also again and again become a Catholic.

---

* Stanley Francis Rother was an American Catholic priest and missionary to Guatemala. He was murdered on July 28, 1981, by one of the death squads that operated at that time with the connivance of the Guatemalan Army. On June 23, 2015, the Congregation of the Causes of Saints of the Holy See officially recognized Rother as a martyr, a critical stage before canonization.

† As mentioned earlier, this book remained unpublished until 2005 when it was released as *Peacework: Prayer, Resistance, Community* (Maryknoll, NY: Orbis, 1995).

‡ Weiskel contributed a chapter on his conversion to Catholicism to Dan O'Neill's book *The New Catholics: Contemporary Converts Tell Their Stories* (New York: Crossroad, 1987).

The Eucharist is such a gift indeed! I wished I had the language and the spiritual power to convince my fellow Catholics in Holland of that. I tried in my book *Letters to Marc*, but it seems to speak more to Dutch-speaking Belgians than to the Dutch!

Meanwhile I like to encourage you to deepen your love for the Eucharist and to have a disciplined prayer life, as you are now living in a milieu that is much less supportive of your spiritual journey. It is important for you to stay faithful and nurture the gifts you have received. It seems as if you, who do not belong to the world, are now sent into the world. So "do not model your behavior on the contemporary world, but let the renewing of your mind transform you, so that you may discern for yourselves what is the will of God—what is good and acceptable and mature" (Romans 12:2).

I keep you in my prayers and hope that we can soon meet again.

Love,
Henri

P.S. In the light of the "New Catholics" Dan Wakefield's book becomes even more interesting.* It seems as if there is still a long spiritual journey ahead of him. Pray for him as he reaches deeper into the mystery of Christ's Incarnation.

---

* Henri is referring to Wakefield's book *Returning: A Spiritual Journey* (Garden City, NY: Doubleday), published in 1988. Henri and Wakefield had been exchanging letters and ideas since 1983. One such letter is included in this volume; see letter from October 25, 1990.

Henri responds to a reader who had a negative reaction to his book on icons, Behold the Beauty of the Lord.*

SEPTEMBER 13, 1988

Dear Mr. Smith,

Many thanks for your letter in response to *Behold the Beauty of the Lord.* I really feel sad that you had such a negative response to it. I had hoped that you would have been able to read the book in a way that it would have given you some spiritual nurture.

I am sorry that you felt so irritated by the expressions "God of God" and "Mother of humanity." Before I published the text I had some very good Orthodox friends with good theological knowledge read it. They made some very helpful remarks which are integrated in the text but did not mention the two expressions as not being Orthodox. When I speak about Mary as the Mother for humanity, I simply mean that Mary is our mother and the mother of all people whom Jesus came to save. I obviously do not want to suggest that Mary is the mother of the children of the devil.

Meanwhile, I am very saddened by the angry tone of your letter. I think it is so important that we as Christians try to understand one another and be gentle with one another. If I had received your remarks before publication, I might have been able to phrase some sentences somewhat differently to avoid all possible misinterpretation. But I also feel that it is important that fellow Christians read it with a heart that is open to be touched by the mystery of God, even when that mystery is expressed in a somewhat different

---

* *Behold the Beauty of the Lord: Praying with Icons* (Notre Dame, IN: Ave Maria Press, 1987).

way from what they are used to. Most important of all, we Christians are trying to support each other as we witness for Jesus and his mother.

I will reflect seriously on your remarks and see if, in a future edition, I could make the changes that you indirectly suggest. May the Lord fill your heart with peace and joy and may we both continue to work for deeper unity among us in Christ.

Henri Nouwen

This is a letter to a Canadian Anglican minister in south Australia who is having a conflict with fellow ministers at her parish about where to put emphasis—on speaking about injustice or about Jesus.

SEPTEMBER 23, 1988

Dear Ann,

Many thanks for your very warm letter telling me about the way you have been living your ministry since we met here in Toronto. I so much appreciate that you share with me your struggles to be faithful in such a difficult and often painful situation. I really regret that we don't have the opportunity to quietly be together and explore what God is doing in your life and how the Spirit is guiding you.

Meanwhile, I just want to let you know that I really want to support you in your desire to be a minister who truly speaks in the Name of Jesus and who wants to give her life to proclaiming the crucified and risen Lord. It is hard for me to know how to offer you concrete help while you are living so many frustrations and so many experiences of rejection and of not being fully welcomed. It is an honor for me that you let me into this experience because it allows me to really pray for you and to hold you very close to my heart and to the heart of God.

I would very much like to recommend that you try to spend at least one hour a day in contemplative prayer during which you can pour out your wounded heart to God and let Jesus really touch you with His healing love. Without such a period of intimacy with Jesus, I cannot see how it would be possible for you not to become resentful and really angry, but the more you unite your heart with the heart of Jesus, the more I think you will be able to discern where to give in and where to hold on.

I am very happy to hear that you have your own prayer and praise service on Sunday nights. I feel that there you can really live out some of your dreams about ministry, and maybe it is in these small groups that you also will be more fruitful for the moment. It is so important to have people who pray with you and with whom you can share your deeper love for Jesus.

Meanwhile, I would not put too much energy into trying to change Stephen. I don't say you are trying to, but obviously he is in a very different place from you. It is very important that you continue to really be yourself in whatever you say from the pulpit because preaching means to witness to what you have seen, heard and touched yourself. On the other hand, I do not think that a direct confrontation with Stephen would be fruitful. He has to discover your own heart indirectly and gradually. Be sure to pray for him and to ask God to show you the ways to work well with him.

If you live through this very trying period, I think you will eventually be brought to a new place where you can experience some new freedom. In everything, continue to really work for the Lord, and if your inner pain becomes too great and your heart too tortured, don't hesitate to ask to be put in a position where your ministry can be less restricted.

Thanks so much for writing and please write again. Be sure

that I will respond to your needs the best I can. Enclosed is a little book that may give you some support.*

With much love and prayers,
Yours,
Henri

Henri writes to his friend Cynthia, who continues to struggle with feelings of abandonment and rejection after her husband's infidelity and the collapse of her marriage.

OCTOBER 8, 1988

Dear Cynthia,

It was a real joy to hear from you. You have been very much in my thoughts and prayers during the past month, and I have kept you close to my heart and to the heart of God.

It is very important for me to let you know that I really care deeply for you, that I love you and that I want to be faithful to our friendship whatever happens. You have suffered immensely over the past years, and you have experienced pain so deep that it made you feel very isolated and alone. I am very deeply aware of that, and I want you to know that in no way do I feel hurt by your silence and inability to write to me for some time. I understand well how hard it has been for you to write and how the experience of abandonment and rejection that you felt so acutely has made it very

---

* It is not known which book Nouwen sent; it may have been *The Way of the Heart: Desert Spirituality and Contemporary Ministry* (New York: Seabury Press, 1981), a treatise on solitude, silence and prayer. At the time of penning this letter, he would have been at work on *In the Name of Jesus: Reflections on Christian Leadership* (New York: Crossroad, 1989).

hard for you to trust fully in the permanence of friendship or the lasting quality of love.

I am saying all this because so much of your experience has also been part of my own journey. Reading your letter, I was deeply struck and somewhat overwhelmed by the similarity of our struggles, especially your feeling of being invisible and worthless— something I have lived myself so deeply. I realize how hard it is to take back the power that you have given to Ronald. It is, indeed, a slow and hard process. In a way, you have to be given back to yourself and rediscover your own beauty, your own goodness, the gift that you are for others.

I have been wondering in which way I could be of real support to you in these difficult times, and I have decided to send you the reflections I wrote during my own period of spiritual struggle.* As you can see, for me also it started with the break-up of a very life-giving relationship, a break-up which caused in me many of the same struggles you are going through. I, too, still have a long way to go, but the comments I am sending you might give you an idea of the direction in which I am moving, and in many ways I hope they will also speak to your own situation.

Although these comments are put together as if they are a book manuscript, I have not shared them with many people, but I want you to have them because I feel that in this way I can be of more support to you. Thanks so much for your letter, for your ongoing friendship and for sharing your struggle with me.

Just to keep you up on the externals, after six months in Winnipeg, I have now returned to the Daybreak community as of September 8th. Between now and Christmas I will spend three weeks a month at Daybreak and one week back in Winnipeg. I am very

---

* These are the spiritual imperatives that he wrote for himself while in Winnipeg that would eventually be published, with the encouragement of his friends, as *The Inner Voice of Love: A Journey Through Anguish to Freedom* (New York: Doubleday, 1996).

aware that although I have made some real spiritual progress, I still have to be very careful in order not to return to the old place of self-rejection. I am trying very hard to live a life that is more contained and more prayerful than my life in the past. In this way, I am really trying to claim more fully God's love for me, and to be more in touch with my own center.

Well, be sure to stay in touch. I would love to hear from you again. Hopefully your letter and this response is the beginning of some good, ongoing contact.

Much love,
Henri

Henri writes to Anita, a pastoral care leader in the Christian inner healing movement, who formed a ministry around reorienting people with same-sex attraction.

Henri responds to a letter in which Anita suggests that he might not be taking the correct approach to healing himself.

OCTOBER 11, 1988

Dear Anita,

Thank you for your note of June 28th. It was not an easy note to read. Your statement that my vision of God is askew, that the emotional imagery of my heart is also askew and I simply need to become available for healing, feels really quite distant and makes me feel somewhat condemned. It simply sounded like: "You know there must be other healing available for you; why don't you get your act together and accept the healing that is there for you." If you had any idea of what I have been struggling with over the past eight months and how I have been trying to really enter into the furnace of God's love and give up everything else in order to really let God heal me, you probably never would have written these words.

But, on the other hand, I know that you don't want to hurt me and that you do care for me. So I hope that you also can be patient and trust that God will do His work when His time comes. It quite easily might take another ten or twenty years until the deepest wounds in me are healed. It might even be that God wants to teach me how to live with them as a way to participate in the suffering of Jesus. I really don't know, but, healing or no healing, I trust that God is greater than my heart and that He desires to show me His love.

The visit of Alex in Winnipeg was a real blessing. His faithfulness to me, his kindness, his simplicity and his deep prayer have given me much hope. I really plan to stay in close touch with him in the years ahead because I have a feeling that God has put him in my way so that I can be faithful. I don't think I am ready yet to pray with you and Alex together. That feels quite scary to me. I would be too afraid of being told that I am not praying right or not living up to your expectations. So maybe we have to be very, very gentle and patient with each other. Please continue to pray for me and recommend me in the prayers of your community.

Yours in Christ,
Henri

Henri writes to Sue Mosteller on the eve of a trip she is making to L'Arche in Trosly-Breuil.

OCTOBER 15, 1988

Dear Sue,

Just a few words to send you on your way. The last month, our final month together at the Dayspring,* has indeed been a month of many graces. Marthe [Robin] is indeed guiding us and holds us safe. I am so grateful to you for the countless ways you support me and help me deepen my vocation. The Dayspring is a safe place, a sacred place, a place where Jesus is calling us ever closer to his heart and to the heart of the poor.

I know now that my struggle and pain will not diminish quickly or easily. They may become long-term companions to show me the narrow road. I am willing to keep them around if it is necessary. But I also keep praying to be able to travel on without them!

I am very glad that you will be with Jean [Vanier]. I hope you have some peaceful time with him and can pray with him for the Dayspring and our life together there.

I will pray very much for you during the coming two weeks. I hope that you can remain in a spirit of prayer as you are moving among so many people. Guard your heart and surround it with the images of the Dayspring Chapel. Somehow we have to come to that unceasing prayer about which St. Paul spoke. I guess all depends on where our heart dwells. It must be possible to "dwell in the house of the Lord all the days of our life."

May Mary and Joseph, St. Francis, St. Thérèse and Marthe travel with you and whisper good words in your ears.

Send my love to all the friends, especially to Mammie [Jean Vanier's mother]. I will miss you a lot but will survive!

Love,
Henri

---

* The Dayspring is the spiritual center that Henri and Sue began for the Daybreak community.

Henri writes to Sister Claire Marie de Jesus, a Dominican nun and good friend of Nathan Ball. Sister Claire and Henri met at L'Arche in Trosly-Breuil. Henri and Sue visited Sister Claire at her monastery in Langeac while they were in France together in the summer. Henri writes with an update about his activities since the visit.

OCTOBER 18, 1988

Dear Sister Claire,

It has been quite a little while since we spent such good hours together, and I have been thinking often about you, keeping you very close in my prayers. It was a real grace that we could be together and share our great love for Jesus and our desire to be faithful to His call. For both of us, it is obviously a struggle, but a real good one. Both Sue and I were extremely moved by our day at Langeac, and we have prayed often for you and your community since we were there.

There are many things I would like to tell you simply to keep you informed of my own ongoing journey and to help you to pray for me more concretely. After our very beautiful time at Châteauneuf-de-Galaure and our good visit with you and Pamela, we had a very lovely visit at Taizé and then returned to Trosly. Sue returned from there to Toronto, and I went to England and after that to Holland. My time in England and Holland was very difficult because people who are very close to me were in such different places from where I am at this moment. A very good friend of mine in England and his wife could not offer friendship to me at this time, and my family in Holland were not able to connect with my own spiritual journey, so I felt really lonely in both countries. But on the other hand, I realized that the Lord was asking me to let go of those attachments that prevented me from entering more deeply into L'Arche. It was very important for me to experience a lot of pain that did not seem to be the wrong kind of pain, but pain that showed me where God is calling me. Just before returning to Toronto, I spent some time with Père Thomas and Jean Vanier and both confirmed me deeply in my great desire to follow Jesus more radically in L'Arche.

On the 8th of September I returned to Daybreak, and I have been living in the community here since that time. I am really very glad to be back here and to make this more and more my home. As you will understand, it is not an easy, simple thing to do so because the pain around my relationship with Nathan is still very real and very deep. But I feel very deeply that it is important for both Nathan and me to live our struggle together in this community. We have talked together a few times, and we are both deeply committed to let the pain that came from our relationship bear fruit. I don't really know how Nathan is living it, but my impression is that for him there is more peace and inner tranquillity than for me. I am still quite anxious, I still have real attacks of anguish and sleeping is still a real problem. But I am quite, quite aware that this pain is given to me to purify my heart, to deepen my love for Jesus and to give Him every inch of my being. Whereas in the past the anguish seemed quite disruptive and often paralyzing, now I experience it a little more as a severe companion who wants to show me the narrow road. Once I have found that road and walk safely on it, the anguish might leave me, but right now I am trying simply to accept what the Lord gives me and trust that He knows when, how and where to give me new peace and new joy.

I return every month for a week in Winnipeg to continue receiving spiritual direction from my guides in Winnipeg. This is very important for me, and it gives me a sense of safety as I continue to enter more fully into the heart of Jesus. These weeks away from Daybreak also give me the opportunity to spend long hours in prayer and that is a real gift.

I am, of course, still worrying about how I will live the coming Christmas as Christmas now carries so many painful memories because of the fact that last year Christmas was the time when the break in the friendship occurred, but I trust that when December comes around the Lord will give me the grace to know how to live it.

I thank God for your dedication and your love. Especially I am grateful that you are committed to praying for me. I know that the Lord is asking constantly new things of me and I can only continue to say "yes" if I know that your community holds me tight in your prayers and points me ever more to the heart of Jesus. It would be wonderful to hear from you again and to know what you are living and how you are living it. I am very aware of your own real struggles and pain, and I want to assure you that I lift them up to the Lord constantly in my prayers.

I would also like to tell you that the Dayspring is becoming more and more a house of prayer. Sue and I spend many hours there in the presence of the Blessed Sacrament, and quite often people join us in prayer there. Also, the Eucharist is really a source of great joy for many people of our community. This week they have started to build ramps to allow wheelchairs to enter directly into the chapel. We are also building a new sacristy and a new vestibule. It is all very tiny and intimate, nothing like your great church, but in its simplicity and hiddenness it is a very blessed place. Both Sue and I feel very graced to be able to call people there to pray. Please ask your community to continue to pray for the Dayspring. We hope it will become a place where many people of L'Arche will hear the call of Jesus to follow Him more radically and to dedicate themselves more fully to the poor.

Well, this is some of the news from Daybreak. I hope it finds you in good spirits. Drop me a line when you have time.

With many prayers and much love,
Yours,
Henri

Sister Annice Callahan, a nun with the Society of the Sacred Heart, was
a professor of pastoral theology at Regis College, a Jesuit college in the To-
ronto School of Theology, University of Toronto. Henri was an occasional
guest lecturer in her classes after his move to L'Arche Daybreak.

Henri provides feedback on an article Callahan has written comparing
him with Ann Belford Ulanov, a professor of psychiatry and religion and
a Jungian psychoanalyst. He clarifies a common misunderstanding of the
"wounded healer" concept.

OCTOBER 31, 1988

Dear Annice,

I just finished reading your article, "Receptivity: Ann Belford
Ulanov in dialogue with Henri Nouwen." I really appreciated the
article very much and I would like to help you with it with the following remarks:

1. What I most miss in the article is an introduction of Ula-
    nov and Nouwen. Somehow I would like to know why
    you chose these two people and why you decided to com-
    pare them. Who are they? Do you know them both? Are
    they both having a significant influence on your think-
    ing? What are their professions? What kind of life are
    they living? How are they connected with you and with
    each other? All these questions suggest that as a reader, I
    really have a need to know who these two people are and
    why you chose them for your discussion on Receptivity. I
    have a need to know these two people more in order to be
    truly interested in a comparison between them. I feel you
    have to write a somewhat personal introduction about
    your relationship with these two people that situates the
    article better.

2. On page 10, you write, "Nouwen would agree that we minister best out of our needs and our wants [sic]." This is incorrect. It does not really represent my thinking. My opinion is not that we minister best out of our needs and wounds, but that we minister best when we have recognized our own needs and have attended to our own wounds. Our needs and wounds can only be a source of our ministry when they have been acknowledged and given appropriate attention. When we would minister to others out of our own needs and wounds, we would do harm to them. It is very important for us that we recognize how our needs and wounds can be a great source of our suffering and call us to an ever fuller surrender to God's first love, the love that can fulfill all our needs and heal all our wounds. As long as our needs are raw needs and our wounds are open wounds, we will inflict wounds on others and create needs in others without realizing it.

Well, these are some points that might be of help to you as you work on this.

With warm greetings,
Henri

Henri writes to a Dutch friend who was one of the many people who helped him through his depression. He writes of "doing a lot better" and identifies his struggle as spiritual. He is beginning to articulate his experience as a "coming home" and as a preparing of himself as a space where God can dwell.

NOVEMBER 17, 1988

Dear Hans,

Many thanks for your kind letter. It is so good to hear from you. I am doing a lot better than when I last wrote you. After a long period of healing away from my community I have now returned to Daybreak and am glad to be again part of the daily routine here. Most of my struggle was of a spiritual nature. It was a struggle to give all of my heart to God and not to allow myself to be dissipated by the many attractions of the world. I had very good spiritual directors who helped me to "come home" and to let God truly dwell in me.

It is indeed, a great joy to belong to the Lord and to really live in intimate communion with Him. I have discovered that God hears my prayers and sends His Spirit to me if I keep crying out to Him.

You are very right when you say that the struggle is not just a personal struggle but is a struggle between the powers of light and the powers of darkness. Jesus is already the victor, as you say, and that conviction should allow me to be engaged in the struggle in a very confident way.

Thanks so much for your friendship, your prayers, your support and your faithfulness. It means so much to me that you pray for me and continue to lift me up into the presence of God. Thanks for your encouragement and your words of consolation and comfort. Thanks for your love.

Dear brother, may the Lord bless you and give you much peace as you minister to me.

Yours,
Henri

✿

*Henri writes to his Quaker friends John and Aminda Baird. He developed
a deep friendship with John in the 1980s at Pendle Hill (as noted earlier, a
Quaker retreat center run, at the time, by Parker Palmer). They remained
very close through the exchange of letters.*

*Henri writes to encourage his friends in their difficult decision to move
to a new state. He also updates them on an accident he had in late January in which he was hit by the mirror of a passing van while walking on a
highway. He would write about this near-death experience in* Beyond the
Mirror: Reflections on Death and Life *(New York: Crossroad, 1990).*

The letter is written from the hospital, ten days after the accident.

FEBRUARY 6, 1989

Dear John and Aminda,

Thanks so much for your very good letter. I really understand how
hard your decision to move to North Carolina must be, even when
you are quite convinced that this is the direction God wants you
to go. It certainly is like dying to good and familiar things. I admire your willingness to listen to God's call and to move into new
directions even when you are facing so many insecurities and uncertainties. I know that the coming weeks will be hard and painful, but I trust that you can stand in your pain and discover there
the deep love of God. Moves such as these are always an occasion
to come to know in a new way God's love for you. It is a love that
transcends all human affection and bonds.

I am really grateful for your very great faithfulness to me over
the past years. It has really meant, and still means, so much to me. I
can't tell you how often I have dreamed of simply being with you, listening to your songs and talking with you about God's presence in
our lives. I trust that one day this will happen. As you know, the past
year has been a very, very hard one for me, but also a year in which
God has called me deeper and deeper to His heart. I don't know if I

ever wrote you, but a very deep and nurturing friendship came to a sudden end, and that threw me into an incredible anguish. The anguish was such that I had to leave the community and look for some spiritual guidance. For six months I struggled very hard, asking God to heal my heart and to help me to give myself completely to His love. Many good things happened in that time, even though they were painful, often excruciating. But I have grown a lot and discovered more and more the mystery that God chose to become one of us. In September I returned to my community and have been living there, feeling more and more convinced that L'Arche is truly the place where I belong, and that Daybreak is my home.

Ten days ago, while hitch-hiking, I was struck by a car, broke six ribs and had my spleen removed. I am still in hospital recuperating from this accident. Although the accident was not a minor one, I feel very peaceful and happy at this moment and I have a good sense that the accident is like a new push by God to keep me moving in the direction I had chosen to go, that of loving God without reserve. So all is really well now, very well indeed, and when I think back to the time I was with you at Pendle Hill, I realize how much I have moved since that time. How good it would be if we could sit together and talk about it all!

Thanks so much for being such a good friend. Give my love and hugs to Matthew. I wish I could see him. Please keep singing and writing songs.

Love,
Henri

Henri responds to a young man who has self-doubt and self-criticism about his experience as an assistant in one of the homes of L'Arche in France.
He continues to recuperate in the hospital from his accident.

Dear Brian,

It was a really wonderful surprise to receive your very kind and deeply personal letter. I am very grateful for your openness to me in response to reading *The Road to Daybreak*. As I reflected on your letter, I realized there are so many things I would like to talk to you about, and I am not sure if I am fully able to express myself in this letter, but I will try.

At one place in your letter you write, "It almost horrifies me to know that I am incapable of loving those people for who they are and no longer for what they bring me. I feel incapable of that and that frightens me." As I reflect on your struggle, I simply want to ask you to be very, very compassionate with yourself. The older we become, the more we realize how limited we are in our ability to love, how impure our hearts are and how complex our motivations are. And there is a real temptation to want to look inside of ourselves and clean it all out and become people with a pure heart, unstained intentions and unconditional love. Such an attempt is doomed to failure and leads us to ever greater despair. The more we look into ourselves and try to figure ourselves out, the more we become entangled in our own imperfections. Indeed, we cannot save ourselves. Only Jesus can save us. That is why it is so important to remove your inner eye away from the complexities of your own broken heart towards the pure but broken heart of Jesus. Looking at Him and His immense mercy will give you the ability to accept your own imperfections and to really let yourself be cared for by the mercy and love of Jesus.

I remember how Thomas Merton once wrote, "God is mercy in mercy in mercy." This means that the more we come to know ourselves, the more we come to know God's mercy, which is beyond the mercy we know. Letting go of the desire to be perfect lovers and allowing God to love our people through us, that is the great spiritual call that is given to you and to me. There in the pure heart of God, embraced by His unconditional love, you will find the true joy and peace your heart is longing for.

I think you did remarkably beautiful work in Compiègne. I think you really gave a lot of yourself to handicapped people and they have received so much from you. Don't second-guess your motivations or the value of what you did there. Just be grateful for the opportunity you have had to be a source of joy and peace to others. If it is true that you are weak and ignorant, it is only to be able to boast it so that the strength of Jesus can be revealed to you. Don't worry about recharging your spiritual batteries with the help of handicapped people. Let them love you. Let them support you. It may be that receiving is more difficult than giving. It is very important that you receive healing and joy and peace from those people with whom you live and for whom you care. So be thankful with yourself. Know that I hold you close in my prayer and in my care.

Ten days ago I was hit by a car while walking on the street. I broke six of my ribs and my spleen was removed by operation, so I am writing you from the hospital, where I am enjoying some quiet peaceful time that I otherwise would not have had! So I have special time to pray for you and to hold you close to Jesus.

Thanks again for your very good letter. Please pray for me.

With many warm greetings,
Yours,
Henri J. M. Nouwen

Henri writes to a reader who has written with questions about loneliness and the meaning of life.

Dear Michael,

Thanks so much for your kind letter and the article, "In de Handen van Rovers." I am deeply grateful to you for sending me these reflections. I look forward to reading the article in the near future. I may even have some special time for it as I am presently in the hospital. Two weeks ago I was hit by the mirror of a passing car, broke six ribs and had my spleen removed. I am gradually recovering from these injuries and just well enough again to do some reading.

As far as loneliness and the meaning of life are concerned, my brush with death really helped me to come to a deeper inner understanding of these questions. It is not that I have new words or new articulations, but I do have a very new sense of the presence of God in my life, and of being held very safe. During the hours that I thought I might die, I felt very peaceful and had a very deep knowledge that ultimately I am not alone and that my life had a very deep meaning, especially when I would be able to give it away.

Thank you for your lovely letter, for your great care and for the article.

With warm greetings,
Yours,
Henri J. M. Nouwen

Henri writes to a spiritual writer and teacher who is grieving for the breakdown of his marriage.
He is out of the hospital but convalescing at L'Arche Daybreak.

Dear Holden,

Thanks so much for your very personal, warm, and moving letter. I am very grateful that you shared the great pain you are suffering. I wish there were an opportunity for us to simply be together and be able to comfort and support each other. I very much trust that the pain you are suffering now is the pain in which you are faced with the most difficult choice of your life. It is a choice to be faithful to your God, and in a very special way also faithful to Brenda, who no longer is able to be with you.

I know from my own experience of separation how you have to choose hour by hour and minute by minute for this faithfulness. It is a faithfulness of the heart. I very much want to support you in this, and I promise you my deep, deep prayer, my friendship and my care. Somehow I trust that the spiritual journey which you have shared with so many people is now being deepened to the place where the deepest sorrow and the deepest joy touch each other.

I am deeply grateful for your response to the manuscript that I shared with you. Feel free to share it with anyone to whom you think it can be of real help, but keep it in a small circle, and encourage people to write me their responses if they care to do so.*

Sorry that I am late with this response, but a month ago I was hit by a passing car while hitch-hiking. Six ribs were broken, my spleen had to be removed and I had to stay more than three weeks in hospital. It was a very precious and blessed experience, but not without a lot of pain. God was very close and my community and

---

* Henri is likely referring to the spiritual imperatives that he wrote during his stay in Winnipeg that would eventually be published as *The Inner Voice of Love: A Journey Through Anguish to Freedom* (New York: Doubleday, 1996).

friends extremely loving. I am now back home, but it will probably take a few more months to be fully restored.

Yours,
Henri

❀

Henri met Frank Alton, a Protestant minister, in Lima, Peru.
  Henri writes to Frank about burnout in ministry and its connection to receiving the love of Jesus.

MARCH 7, 1989

Dear Frank,

Thanks so much for your wonderful letter of February 15th. I really appreciated all the things you wrote in response to *The Road to Daybreak*, and I very much feel that someday we should sit down together to talk about the many issues you raise. The question of receiving the love of Christ is really very important. I personally feel more and more that sometimes it is harder for us to fully receive love than to give it. I am more and more convinced that we will find the peace and joy of Christ when we let Him truly enter into the deepest places of our heart, especially those places where we are afraid, insecure and self-rejecting. Somehow, true ministry is letting other people drink from the water that overflows from your fountain. Burn-out seems to happen when you let people drink your fountain dry and, so, have nothing left to give. You are very right when you say that burn-out quite often is the result of not going far enough in our love for Christ and depending too much on our own resources. I think you touch here a really important area that is crucial for the way we live our lives faithfully.

Meanwhile, I am doing quite well. I am still most of the day in my bedroom and have to be careful not to do too much, but, if all goes well, I will be back in shape around Easter. Thanks again for your letter.

Yours,
Henri

Rose Marciano Lucey was a peace activist and cofounder of the Christian Family Movement. After the death of her son John, she became active in AIDS ministry. Henri met Rose and her husband, Dan Lucey, while he was at Harvard. Henri wrote the foreword for her book Roots and Wings: Dreamers and Doers of the Christian Family Movement *(San Jose, CA: Resource Publications, 1987).*

In a telephone conversation with Rose, Henri has heard of her plan to give a lecture about religion and addiction. He writes of his misgivings about her plan.

MARCH 13, 1989

Dear Rose,

Since our last telephone conversation, I have been thinking a lot about your plan to give a lecture about addiction to religiosity. I have thought a lot about this, and increasingly I felt uncomfortable and felt a strong need to write you about my feelings.

I very much understand, appreciate and affirm the criticism that you increasingly feel towards the Church, and I also know from my own history how some of the things you are planning to speak about can, indeed, be marked as oppressive, manipulative and fear-invoking. I also realize that many things have happened in your own life, past and present, that allow you to speak with strong conviction and with much persuasion.

But I beg you to be very, very careful here. There is such an immense need in people's hearts to hear about the love of God, and to hear from people who have suffered much that love is stronger than fear, that life is stronger than death, and that hope is stronger than despair. Wherever I meet people, I see this enormous need to hear about the love which they can claim beyond all the experiences of betrayal, broken relationships, and tragic loss. I have come to know you as a person with enormous gifts to affirm people, to deepen their awareness that they are safely held even in the midst of an enormous amount of pain, and to give them a sense that they can be a light in the world even when there is so much darkness around them. You are one of the most transparent women I know, and right through all your pain and suffering there is always this light, this smile, this word of hope. You are in a period of your life in which you are faced with a real choice to not let your incredible anguish and pain obscure the great light that is within you.

I am really worried that your speaking about addiction to religiosity will get a willing ear, but not lead people to the place where they most need to go. I have seen this happening in my own country. Everyone is increasingly coming up with horror stories about the Church in the '40s and '50s, stories about the Church encouraging people to have children when they really couldn't welcome them well, about the Church making people afraid of hell and damnation, the Church creating scrupulosity and rigidity in their daily life, and while all these things may be true, the memory of them and the recalling of them does not offer the life and the light that is so desperately searched for by many people. I also feel that sometimes we have forgotten that we were part of a culture that was quite different from the contemporary culture. It wasn't all oppression and manipulation. I can't even think about my vocation to the priesthood without gratefully remembering the great love for Jesus and Mary that my parents instilled in me. Sure, there was fear and there were power games, but most of all there were men and women of great faith and incredible spiritual depth to whom we owe so much.

Well, dear friend, my love for you is very deep and very strong, and I know how crucial this time of your life is. You have a voice that will be heard far and wide, and I really pray fervently that every word you speak will be hope-giving, life-giving and love-giving. Most of all, I hope that through your work people will re-discover Jesus as a faithful companion on their journey, and be encouraged to go to Him and find with Him all the consolation and comfort they need. This letter comes out of the depths of my heart and is written with much love. My recent illness has really convinced me of the importance of not judging or condemning, not even our own past, and of looking at people with immense compassion and love in the way Jesus looked at the adulterous woman and made her discover her own goodness through the eyes of Jesus and thus find the strength to "sin no more." You told me on the phone that you felt that I had become soft, and you obviously meant something positive in that. I, indeed, want to be softer, not condemning or judging, but being more and more compassionate. It is out of this desire that I am writing you, and I hope that we can work together to make people see the immense, inexhaustible love of God.

With much love,
Yours,
Henri

Henri writes to George, a deacon of the Catholic Church, who feels rejected and is questioning his vocation.

MARCH 17, 1989

Dear George,

Thanks so much for your very kind and personal letter. What you write about your vocation really speaks deeply to me. It is obviously hard to know what your experience of having been "dumped" truly means, but I hope you are willing to hold on to the reality of your ordination to the Diaconate, even when you feel in total darkness. I hope that you are able to trust that the call of Jesus to follow Him in a special way—a call that has been affirmed by the Church—is real and will bear fruit if you are faithful to it. It might take many years before you will fully know the deeper meaning of your call, and your period of dryness and darkness may be a real part of the way to deeper understanding of God's unique love for you.

I'd like to tell you that it is only now, thirty years after my ordination, that I am starting to understand to what I am really called, and starting to claim more fully and directly the mission that God has given me. The past thirty years have not been useless or fruitless but filled with obscurities and ambiguities, and with a lot of spiritual wandering, but I have always been able to hold on to the truth of my ordination, especially during moments when many of the people around me questioned its value and even, at times, encourage me to move in different directions. I am intensely grateful for the grace God has given me to remain faithful to my call, even though I haven't always lived faithfully, and the long years of dryness are now revealed to me as the time needed to prepare myself for a more radical commitment to Jesus.

So, dear brother, live with hope and courage and confidence, and trust that the seeds that have been sown in your heart will bear fruit in ways quite beyond your own expectations. Thanks so much again for your very good letter. Be sure of my prayers and love.

Yours,
Henri Nouwen

Henri writes to Ken, who cannot find a publisher for his book on the spiritual life.

APRIL 24, 1989

Dear Ken,

It is good to hear from you again. It certainly has been a long time since we have been in touch. I really don't know very well how to respond to your letter in which you express your frustrations with publishers. I wish I could give you a helpful answer. The main thing I want to say to you is to keep your inner freedom in the midst of all of it. Somehow the many things you write about in your books speak about that freedom and show ways to acquire it. I so much wish that in the midst of the disappointments and frustrations and feelings of betrayal, you can continue to keep your heart free from bitterness and resentment, because all these very negative feelings eventually will enslave you and take your most precious gift away.

I promise to really pray for you, that you find more and more inner peace, and I really trust that your writing will find its way to the people who need to read it and be nurtured by it. I trust that the more you find inner peace, the easier it also will become to find the kind of people who can show you the right support and encouragement.

I certainly hope that you will find new energy to write your fourth book. You certainly are a writer, and you definitely have great gifts there, so don't let anyone take them away from you.

Meanwhile, try to spend some real time in daily prayer. It will purify your heart and make you more receptive to the deeper voice of God's love. Thanks so much for writing.

Sincerely yours,
Henri

Fred Rogers, the creator and host of the children's television program Mis-
ter Rogers' Neighborhood, befriended Henri in 1984. The two men shared
a friendship of letters and visits for the next twelve years. Fred has written
Henri about some criticism he has received and how it has hurt him.

APRIL 25, 1989

Dear Fred,*

I have just returned from Europe where I received permission from
my Bishop to stay at L'Arche. I am now back here hoping to settle
more definitely and find a new rhythm of life that is a little more
livable than what I have had in the past.

I read the article you sent me and can very well understand
how much that must have hurt you. It must be really painful to
be confronted with a total misunderstanding of your mission and
your spiritual intentions. It is these little persecutions within the
church that hurt the most. I simply hope that you are not too surprised by them. They come and will keep coming precisely when
you do something significant for the Kingdom.

It has always struck me that the real pain comes often from the
people from whom we expected real support. It was Jesus' experience and the experience of all the great visionaries in the Church,
and it continues to be the experience of many who are committed
to Jesus.

I don't think it makes much sense to argue with the writer of
this article. He speaks from a very different plane and will not
be open to your explanations. Some of the criticisms we simply
have to suffer and see as invitations to enter deeper into the heart
of Jesus. I won't send you some of the reviews I get of my books,
but some are not very different from the tone of this piece. So I

---

* Letter to Fred Rogers by kind courtesy of The Fred Rogers Company.

certainly feel a unique solidarity with you. Let us pray for each other, that we remain faithful and not become bitter and that we continue to return to the center where we can find the joy and peace that is not of this world.

Thanks so much for staying in touch with me.

Much love,
Henri Nouwen

Henri writes to his friend Walter Gaffney, who is struggling with depression and self-rejection.

APRIL 25, 1989

Dear Walt,

It is so good to hear from you again! I just returned from Europe, where I received permission from my Archbishop to make Daybreak my permanent home. Considering my life, this is as permanent as I have ever been. So now I really have to start thinking long term, and this gives me a good occasion to express to you my great hope that we will see each other soon again. I do really feel from your letter that it would be wonderful if we could strengthen and deepen our friendship.

I don't really think you choose mediocrity, but I do think that your darkest side may be tempted to think about your life that way. You are one of the most vital and alive people I know, and I think your life has just begun (mine too!). I really hope that you continue to claim your great spiritual gifts and continue to say things that are hope-giving and life-giving to the many people who cross your path, and I know there are many. I am more and more convinced how important it is that, in the midst of the incredibly depressing events in the Church, and in the world, we continue to believe and hope, and don't allow ourselves to be dragged into the darkness that surrounds us on all sides. Somehow we have to keep choosing very consciously to live towards the light, even when sometimes darkness seems to be so much easier to choose for.

I am really excited about staying in touch with you, and I wish you could just come for a few days and get to know our community and have a sense of what L'Arche is all about. I really think it is important for me also to share with you in more detail what has happened to me since I left Yale.

Sincerely,
Henri

Henri writes to Raymond, a student who had recently visited Daybreak from Marquette University and who is questioning his belief in God and his suitability for life at L'Arche.

APRIL 25, 1989

Dear Raymond,

Thanks so much for your good letter with the questions you raised. I really appreciate your asking these questions. They obviously don't have a very simple answer. I really do believe that a person doesn't have to be a Christian or even believe in God in order to live well in a L'Arche community, but I do feel that it is important that such a person have an open heart and an open mind to the spiritual reality that surrounds him or her. My feeling about you is that you are really a very open and respectful person and that the fact that at this moment of your life you cannot affirm God as the center of your life does not mean that you cannot be a really caring and very creative member of a L'Arche community.

As far as your first question is concerned, yes, I do think that even when you struggle with the notion of God and have a hard time accepting some of the teachings you have been brought up with, you can still live a life that is spiritually profound and very authentic. In fact, I even think that at times we have to dare to let go of the God of our youth in order to find a more silent, and maybe even a more hidden, God. I am not sure if this is what will happen to you, but I do trust that faithfulness to a true spiritual way of living will lead you to the place where you will know your deepest vocation in life.

Your most difficult question to answer is the question of whether an atheist can have an intimate, fruitful and joyful life. If by an atheist you mean someone who continues to fight the existence of God, I think it is hard to remain joyful because you end up being so defensive, and therefore so unfree. But if you simply cannot affirm God at this moment of your life but remain open for the mystery of existence and even open to a God who can reach your heart deeply, then joy and peace can be really part of your life even when you have very little answer to the question about God. There is a form of atheism that becomes very dark and unfruitful, but there is also a form of atheism in which you remain open to the mystery of existence and open to discover in new ways that God is love. And to the degree you remain open, searching and willing to listen carefully, I think your life can be full of joy and peace. Often the search is more important than the answer, the quest is more important than the finding.

Meanwhile, I really want to assure you of my personal interest in you and in your journey. I pray for you, think of you and I was very, very glad that you came with the Marquette students to Daybreak.

With warm greetings,
Yours,
Henri Nouwen

❧

Henri writes to his friend Lawrence, whose wife doesn't want another child.

MAY 9, 1989

Dear Lawrence,

Thanks so much for your good letter. I am so glad to hear from you again. It certainly has been a long time.

I am sorry that you are still suffering so much inner pain and that there are still so many struggles in your heart. I can quite well understand your deep desire for another child, but I also realize that it has to be a desire that comes from both you and Joyce, and that you have to be really ready for it in a very deep spiritual and emotional way. I can quite well understand your feelings of aloneness and your desire to run, while knowing that there is no place to run to. At least, stay faithful to your heart and to your family. God has given you a lot, even in the midst of your pain and suffering, and I have been very much impressed with the way you have lived it over the past years. Don't make any hasty decisions. Let the Spirit work in you. If you and Joyce keep praying together and calling God to show you the way, I am sure that gradually you will see more clearly the direction in which to move.

It seems so important that you stay very close to your own heart and to the heart of God. If it is not time for another child yet, then maybe it is a sign that God calls you to a life of greater surrender and deeper inner peace. Be sure that I pray for you and Joyce in these times of uncertainty, that you will discover the depths of God's love. Thanks so much for staying in touch.

Peace,
Henri

❀

Dr. Wunibald Müller is a German pastoral theologian, psychotherapist and author. He helped establish the spiritual center Recollectio-Haus in Münsterschwarzach, Germany, with the Benedictine monk and spiritual writer Anselm Grün.

Henri writes in response to Müller's proposal for a spiritual therapeutic center for priests and religious in Germany.

MAY 18, 1989

Dear Wunibald,

Many thanks for your kind letter. I regret very much that I didn't get a chance to contact you while I was in Freiburg. I was quite ill there due to the injuries suffered in the car accident, and spent most of my time in bed. I had really wanted very much to spend some good time with you, but it seemed that I would have been unwise to do more than I was really able to do.

With great interest, I read your proposal for a spiritual therapeutic center for priests and religious. I like very much what you write, and I can quite well understand that in Germany a real need for such a center exists. My main concern would be that the word "spiritual" be more central than the word "therapeutic." I have come to know the center of formation, Southdown, close to Toronto, quite well. It is a beautiful place with fabulous facilities, but when I personally had to choose where to go in time of crisis, I felt the psycho-therapeutic approach was so dominant that I wasn't sure I would be guided in the spirit to discover how God was guiding my life in the midst of the crisis. I am obviously very positive towards therapeutic support for priests and religious, but I have an increasing sense that the most important crisis of our time is spiritual, and that we need places where people can grow stronger in the spirit and be able to integrate the emotional struggles in their spiritual journey.

I really want to support you in any possible respect in this project, and I also hope that you can, at some point, have the time to make extensive visits to the centers which already exist in the United States and England.

Much love,
Henri

Henri writes to his Jewish friend Fred Bratman. They had met when Bratman, a journalist in New Haven, was assigned to write a profile of Henri at Yale. In the course of the interview, Henri was able to detect Bratman's uncertainty about his vocation, and that was the beginning of a deep friendship. Henri would eventually write Life of the Beloved: Spiritual Living in a Secular World *(New York: Crossroad, 1992) for Fred in response to his questions about the spiritual life for non-Christians.*

Here, Henri is answering a questionnaire about the books that have most influenced him.*

JUNE 16, 1989

Dear Fred,

Let me try to respond to your inquiry about which book has most influenced me. The more I think about it, the more I realize that I can't come up with any particular book. First of all, I am not a real book reader and I don't have memories of any one major book except for the Bible which has profoundly influenced my life and thinking. So I first want to say that, indeed, the Bible is the basis of my life, a book that I read every day and that has an increasing

---

* Henri's response was published in *The Reader's Companion: A Book Lover's Guide to the Most Important Books in Every Field of Knowledge*, eds. Fred Bratman and Scott Lewis (New York: Hyperion, 1994).

influence on me. I perceive the Bible more and more as the Word of God that deeply transforms my inner life and continues to deepen, broaden and strengthen my spirit. I trust the Word of the Bible, and I want that Word to become, more and more, flesh in me. Maybe the question for me is not so much to read the Bible often but to let the Bible read me and reveal me to myself. If you would ask which book of the Bible has most influenced me it is, without any doubt, the Gospel of Saint John. There I have found the most intimate connections with my life, and there I continue to find an inexhaustible source for life, for love and for hope.

Besides the Bible, I have no other books to mention. What I do have to mention are writers, and the three writers who have, without any doubt, influenced me very much are John Henry Newman, Thomas Merton and Vincent Van Gogh. John Henry Newman was the most important writer during my time in the seminary. His sermons always impressed me very deeply. His *Apologia pro Vita Sua* and his *Idea of a University* also had a great impact on me. And finally, his distinction between real and notional assent set me on the mystical path.

Thomas Merton's works taken together had a profound influence on my thinking, especially his ability to bring concrete burning issues of the day in connection with the spiritual search affected me very much. I like very much his *Seeds of Contemplation*, his *Conjectures of a Guilty Bystander*, his *Sign of Jonas*, his *Zen and the Birds of Appetite*, and many others. More than any one of these books, it is his spirit and his way of approaching life that has influenced me deeply.

Then there is Vincent van Gogh. His *Letters to Theo* has had a major impact on my life, not one or two of them, but all of them together, especially in the context of his paintings, which have increasingly affected my deeper emotional life. Although Vincent van Gogh is certainly not a religious writer in the traditional sense of the word, for me he was a man whose spirit touched my spirit very deeply and who brought me in touch with some aspects of the spiritual life that no formal spiritual writer ever did.

Besides these three authors, there is one more influence that I'd like to mention; that is the influence of the Hesychastic tradition. It is the spiritual tradition of the Eastern Church. These are the writings of the Desert Fathers, the early monks of Mount Sinai, the monks who lived in the 10th century on Mount Athos and the many monks who wrote in 19th-century Russia. The *Philokalia** and the book *The Art of Prayer* [an Orthodox anthology] are probably the most important expressions of this tradition.

Well, I hope that this is somewhat of an answer to your question. Feel free to let me know if you want to know other things. I will gladly continue to respond. It was good to talk to you by phone again. Let's stay in touch.

With warm greetings,
Yours,
Henri

Henri writes to his friend Barb about her reactions to the draft of an article he has written about his road accident in which he describes his near-death experience.

---

* A collection of texts written between the fourth and fifteenth centuries by spiritual masters of the Eastern Orthodox hesychastic tradition.

Dear Barb,

Many thanks for your very kind response to "A Glimpse Beyond the Mirror."* I really appreciate your taking the time to respond so generously. Let me try to answer a few of your questions.

As far as the article itself is concerned, there were, of course, many, many more things that happened. Indeed, my father and my sister visited me, and many members of the community. In an epilogue that I am writing now, I mention this, but the main purpose of my story was to share my very vivid spiritual experience.

I can understand your difficulty with my desire to die and be with Jesus, but I do feel that indeed the desire was very real, and that I felt very intimately that my death would not take me away from those who are close to me, but bring me into closer unity with them. I have always been impressed by how close I am to a lot of people who have died long ago, but still have a very active influence on my life, an influence that is deeper and more lasting than when I had known them in the flesh. I once met Thomas Merton, for instance, and it was not a very life-giving meeting, but since his death I have developed a real closeness to him and cannot think of him as other than a close companion in my journey. As far as my family members are concerned, I, of course, never wish them to be dead so that I could be closer to them spiritually, but, on the other hand, those I have loved deeply continue to have a bond with me after death and in some aspects a different bond from that I had with them during their life. It seems in a way that their spirit can speak more directly to my spirit. With those who have died, I have a great freedom in my relationship. I don't have any more

---

* "A Glimpse Behind the Mirror: Reflections on Death and Life," *Weavings, a Journal of the Christian Spiritual Life* (November–December 1989), 13–23. An expanded version of this article was published as *Beyond the Mirror: Reflections on Death and Life* (New York: Crossroad, 1990).

to be afraid that I hurt them. I can unburden my heart to them and trust that they will connect my concerns with the heart of God. So, while I in no way desire or hope for the death of anyone, to the contrary, I love life and those who are alive, there is a great mystery that a bond of love continues and even deepens after they have died.

Well, I hope these little thoughts are of some support to you. Thanks so much for your wonderful letter. Be sure of my prayers and love.

With warm greetings,
Yours,
Henri

Henri writes to Ed Wojcicki about power.

JUNE 23, 1989

Dear Ed,

Thanks so much for your very kind response to *In the Name of Jesus*. I really appreciate what you say about power and love, and I agree that I need to do a lot more work on it to avoid falling into over-simplification.

I continue to be impressed with how Jesus continues to stay away from Power. Even when it is offered to him constantly, he radically says "No" to the Satan who offers him different forms of power. During His ministry, he stays away from accepting any form of political power, but, indeed, His love for people was so powerful that the dead came to life and the sick were healed. But the power of love is obviously a power that comes from Jesus' deep rootedness in His Father; whereas the power he keeps declining is the power that is found in the identity that people give us. Maybe it all boils down to that power that comes from our deep connectedness with God is life-giving and healing; whereas the power that comes of our need for affirmation and success in the human community leads easily to manipulative and destructive behavior. I, personally, have no difficulties with people having political, economic or social power, as long as their identity remains rooted in the relations with God. Very concretely, that often means a willingness to let go of power when holding on to power asks for a moral or spiritual compromise. In the political world, I have often seen how concerns for re-election were so dominant that you could hardly see how a senator or representative could truly speak from his [or her] center.

Well, these are just some quick responses to your good letter. I am excited about your plan to write a book about cynicism and desire for hope. Cynicism is truly a very important subject to deal with at this moment.

My health is better, but not totally restored yet. Next week I am going to Vancouver for a week of rest, and I hope to get another few weeks in the summer. Keep me in your prayers and stay in touch.

Yours,
Henri

Henri writes to his friend Cynthia, who continues to suffer from the breakdown of her marriage due to an affair by her husband.

JULY 11, 1989

Dear Cynthia,

Thanks so much for your letter. I am so grateful to hear from you again, even though there was so much pain in your letter and so much struggle. I am really grateful that you wrote it all to me and did not hide the deeper pains of your soul. I understand fully how hard it is to continue to trust in the loving God who will respond to your deepest needs. But I do believe that you have that vitality in you that allows you to return again and again to the reality of God's presence in your life, and to the truth that Jesus came into this world to take our sadness away and to help us discover that where we feel most poor and often most lost, God is closest.

There are many things I would like to talk to you about and it is hard for me to put them in a letter, but one thing I want to ask you is to not allow the dark forces of your soul to draw you into a deep pit. When you give too much attention to the voices of despair, you will find yourself quickly moving downwards into depression. Don't trust those voices, but continue to give special attention to the voice that speaks of hope, the same voice that said to Jesus, "You are my beloved son. On you my favor rests." Trust deeply that you are God's favored daughter, and try to speak and act and even think out of that knowledge, even when you don't always feel it.

One very concrete suggestion I have is to spend every morning a half-hour simply speaking in your heart a sacred text, e.g., Psalm 23, Psalm 131, Chapter 13 of Corinthians about love, the prayer of St. Francis—"Make me an instrument of your peace . . ." or other passages that speak to you. Let these sacred words enter deeply into your consciousness and try to live from that place during the day. As you find yourself drawn back into the darkness during the day, use a very simple word to call yourself back, e.g., "Lord Jesus Christ have mercy on me." A human being is the result of his thoughts, Buddha said. Therefore, it is important that you do every possible thing to think the thoughts of God so that you can always enter more deeply into His peace. As you know, God dwells within you, and it is these simple prayers that bring you in touch with that inner holy place where God dwells.

I think of you often and pray for you. I am deeply convinced that within you there is an enormous vitality and strength that will help you not to go into depression, but to claim yourself as a woman deeply loved and deeply lovable. Try to forgive Ronald. I know it is hard. He left you not because you are not lovable, but because of his own limitations and struggles and inability to give you what you most needed. Don't blame him, nor blame yourself. Try to really trust that underneath all the anguish and loneliness of your life you are really deeply loved and safely held.

With much love,
Yours,
Henri

Henri writes to his friend Walter Gaffney, who has started a new business but continues to suffer from bouts of ennui.

JULY 11, 1989

Dear Walt,

So good to hear from you! Thanks so much for writing. I am obviously intrigued by the small business you are going to start. I certainly wish you all possible success, and I certainly hope it will be fun for you. I pray for you especially that your mind and heart will be more united because your mind sees so clearly all the good things you have been given, but your Irish heart is still resisting receiving that and being joyful about it. But, from knowing you, I know that you have this great ability to bounce back, staying vital and fighting off ennui. I also hope that you stay close to Jesus in the midst of everything. Jesus is, as you know, much more than a story. He is a source of life and is truly able to touch you deeply so that you can go beyond the failure-success syndrome. I really believe that it is possible for you to develop a simple life of prayer that can give you that "holy indifference." By that, I mean the place where you feel so truly safe and so well held that the ups and downs of your life aren't able to distress you or excite you. I have personally found much help in spending every day a little time just repeating in my mind a sacred text such as the prayer of St. Francis, "Make me an instrument of your peace . . ." When I let these words enter deeply into my consciousness, something new in me happens and I am moved beyond the places where exultation or depression dwell.

Thanks so much for encouraging me to keep writing. That means a lot to me. Frankly, I have been and am still tempted to give it up, but I know it is a temptation. I am still not doing as well as I want. I suffer from immense fatigue and at times become quite depressed because of it. The past few days I have had to practically stay in bed because of lack of energy, but I hope and pray that I will find my strength back in the future and will be able to continue to do some creative thinking and writing. Life at L'Arche has been very demanding and tiring. I very much love to be here and I consider it a true vocation, but I haven't found the right rhythm and find myself often on the verge of exhaustion. So keep me in your prayers.

I would very much love to see you again, but August is not a good time. I will be away most of that month in Europe, and, when I come back, I have to face a lot of extra work, especially around the 20th Anniversary of our community. The best thing seems to be to just wait and see when a good time comes up. Sometimes I even think that it might be nicer for me to come to you so that I can be away for a while from the busy life here, but let's see what is best and be in touch at the end of August.

With much love,
Yours,
Henri

Sister Marcia, Henri's friend the anchoress, has moved. He writes to offer his prayers as she settles into her new home and struggles with loneliness and feelings of separation.

JULY 17, 1989

Dear Marcia,

Thanks so much for your very kind letter. I really keep you in my prayers as you try to settle out there in Oregon. From your letter, it is clear that the real settling will be to settle more and more deeply into the heart of Jesus. Only there will you be able to live the loneliness and the experience of being separated. It will, indeed, take a long time to let your understanding descend fully into your heart, but I trust that with a faithful life of contemplation and hopefully, with a good spiritual guide, God will lead you to that place of deep belonging where you can find peace and joy.

Enclosed is a little story I wrote about my recent illness.* I thought you might like to see it.

With warm wishes and many prayers,
Yours,
Henri

Writing to his Dutch friend Jurjen, who wished to make Henri's work better known in Holland, Henri clarifies his ideas about the relationship be-

---

* He is referring to his article "A Glimpse Behind the Mirror: Reflections on Death and Life."

tween the first commandment, to love God, and the second commandment,
to love your neighbor.

Dear Jurjen,

Thanks so much for your very good letter. What you write about
love is extremely important, and I would very much like to respond
to it. I am deeply impressed by the quote of Saint Teresa of Ávila
which you included in your letter.* It is a very powerful expression
of the truth that we can only love people well if we make our love
of God our primary concern. I have very much experienced what
Teresa writes about. I have been so enamored of certain people and
so deeply impressed by their beauty and goodness that my love for
them, instead of being a way to God, got in the way of my desire to
love God without reserve. The longer I live and struggle with these
issues, the more it is becoming clear to me that the first commandment truly is the first. We are called to love God with our whole
heart, whole mind and whole soul, and only when we have given
all our love to God can we truly discover our neighbor and love
him or her as we love ourselves.

The second commandment truly is equal to the first, but it also
is the second commandment. If we were to say that the first commandment is to love your neighbor with your whole heart, your
whole mind and your whole soul and the second commandment

---

* The quote (in Dutch) included in Beumer's letter was from *Teresa of Ávila: The
Book of My Life.* English translation: "Here is one benefit I derived from my vision
of Christ. Before he appeared to me, I had this troubling tendency to become very
attached to anyone I thought liked me. As soon as I began to detect that someone
had fond feelings for me and I myself found them attractive, I would start thinking
about them all the time and recalling every detail of our encounters. I had no
intention of forsaking God, but I was very happy whenever I got to see these people.
I loved to think about them and reflect on all the positive qualities I perceived in
them. This habit was becoming a serious problem and leading my soul astray."
(From *Teresa of Ávila: The Book of My Life,* translated by Mirabai Starr [New Seeds,
2008]: chapter XXXVII, 1).

is to love God as you love yourself, our whole relational life would end up in chaos. I experienced that deeply myself and I see it in many well-intentioned people around me. Indeed, when you quote the words "ubi caritas, Deus ibi est," you would suggest that love between people leads to the love of God, but you have to be very careful here. This is only true when love is not simply affection or friendship or eros, but true charity and charity is precisely loving our neighbors because of our love for God. Loving our neighbors, as Jesus calls us to do, means to give love without wanting anything in return—"If you love those who love you, what thanks can you expect?" The mystery of the love for our neighbors is precisely that we can love him or her so freely that we can be detached from every form of human reward and this is only possible if we are deeply anchored in the love of God.

All the great saints in history about whom I have read have been people who were so passionately in love with God that they were completely free to love other people in a deep, affective way without any strings attached. True charity is gratuitous love, a love that gives gratuitously and receives gratuitously. It is following the first commandment that asks us to give everything we have to God that makes the second commandment truly possible.

I am writing this so elaborately to you because I think that we are touching here the source of much of the suffering in our contemporary society. We have such a need for love that we often expect from our fellow human beings something that only God can give, and then we quickly end up being angry, resentful, lustful and sometimes even very violent. As soon as the first commandment is no longer truly the first our society moves to the edge of self-destruction.

I am grateful that you say that you too have experienced relational pain. Maybe this is a time for you to explore more deeply in your heart how to make the love of God your primary concern. I am truly calling you to the mystical life. As long as we remain on the level of the moral life, we cannot fully grasp the mystery of love that is revealed to us through Jesus.

I also want to respond more briefly to your critical note about my writing. I very much appreciate that note and I understand very well what you are talking about, but I want you to at least consider the fact that I wrote more about social issues of our society when I was at Harvard than now when I am living among handicapped people. It seems that the closer I come to the poor and broken people of our world, the greater my desire is to speak directly about God and the less I feel impelled to deal with the burning issues of our day. This doesn't mean that I am not any more interested in these issues; in fact, I am more interested in them than ever, but somehow the way I enter into these issues has shifted. Presently I am very much directly involved in the life of handicapped people and I am becoming more and more involved in the struggles of people who have AIDS as well as people who live with great inner anguish and pain. Somehow these people are calling me to be more and more God-centered and seem to ask me less to help them solve their problems than to reveal to them God's immense and intimate love for them. So I really feel that the society and its pain are closer to me than ever but that I live more in it and am more connected with it than before and therefore write and think about it in a new way. There is a strange paradox that I wrote more about poverty, oppression and exploitation as a professor at the university and less about these issues since I am closer to the reality of poverty, oppression and exploitation. I don't have any big explanations for this movement but I notice it in my own heart and I have seen similar movements in people like Jean Vanier and Mother Teresa. It is a great mystery that the closer you come to the poor, the more you want to write about God.

Well, I hope that this is somewhat of a response to your remarks and helps you also to understand better where I am in this respect.

Thank you so much for your friendship and support. I very much appreciated the article you wrote in *TROUW* [a Dutch periodical]. The way you are making me a little more known in Holland fills me with gratitude and hope but most important of all is your friendship and your personal interest in my life, and I am deeply grateful for that.

Meanwhile, I am not yet ready to seriously consider a conference around my person. I feel I am just discovering many new directions in my life and that I need a lot of solitude and quiet time to deepen the direction in which God is calling me. Maybe in a few years I would be more ready to share of my adventures with God with others. Right now it seems that God wants me to really stay home more and live a more hidden life.

> With warm greetings,
> Yours,
> Henri Nouwen

❦

Mary is a Catholic lay woman who reached out to Henri after reading his books. They corresponded on an annual basis.

Henri writes to console Mary after the death of her friend Ruth.

SEPTEMBER 15, 1989

Dear Mary,

Thanks so much for writing me and telling me about Ruth's death. It really meant a lot to me that you were willing to share this struggle and pain with me, especially that you were willing to let me know not only about your grief, but also about the deep faith with which you live it.

I am becoming more and more aware how profound the call is to love God with our whole mind, our whole heart, and our whole soul. Only then will it be possible to let go of people we deeply love without being deeply wounded by the loss. It is such a great mystery that God calls us to love one another and, at the same time, calls us to love Him with our whole being. Increasingly I come to see that grief, in the most spiritual sense, is the way to enter more fully into the heart of God, and there remain deeply connected with the source of love, the same love that allowed us to be so close to our friends. The risk of loving is always great because everyone you deeply love will also become a source of grief and pain for you at times during their life or by their death. Grief, when lived in faith and great trust, can lead us ever closer to the heart of God where we can find the deepest consolation and comfort. Be sure that I pray for you in this time of grief.

Thanks for your notes on *Seeds of Hope*.* It really means a lot to me that you paid so much attention to it.

Peace,
Henri

Henri responds to a reader who, after reading Henri's 1979 book Clowning in Rome,† *has questions about the value of Church to those who are spiritual but not religious.*

---

* Henri is referring to the first Henri Nouwen reader, edited by Robert Durback and entitled *Seeds of Hope: A Henri Nouwen Reader* (New York: Bantam Books, 1989).

† *Clowning in Rome: Reflections on Solitude, Celibacy, Prayer, and Contemplation* (Garden City, New York: Image Books, 1979).

Dear Seth,

Thanks so much for your very good letter and for your kind words about *Clowning in Rome*. I appreciate the honesty with which you write about the Church. I wish I could write you a very long letter in response to what you write but at least I want to say to you that the mystical life, the life of communion with God, is indeed the heart of all spirituality. You are right that all the great saints have found this God, but I also want to say that all the mystics I have read such as John of the Cross, Teresa of Àvila, Thomas à Kempis, Meister Eckhart were all people deeply connected with the Church.

The Church, as you say so clearly can be in the way of God, but it never will cease to be also the way to God. This is the hard paradox of the religious life. When we give up the Church completely, we will end up by losing God. In many ways, we are in the same situation Jesus was in during his life. He strongly criticized the religious leaders of his time, but continued to say that people should listen to their words without following their example. While Jesus was very critical of the religious institutions of his time, he never suggested that people could do without them. And this is even true today. I just spent a month in France and I was deeply impressed by the beautiful new spiritual life that is developing in the French Church. But the French Church also is a Church full of conflict and a Church in which there are many hardened hearts among the clergy, as well as lay people.

It has always struck me that the great Saints such as St. Francis and the contemporary "saints" such as Mother Teresa and Jean Vanier continue to say that we have to remain faithful to the Church even in the midst of all conflicts. Without sound doctrine about who God is as Father, Son and Holy Spirit, without some external structure, it will be impossible to live a faithful spiritual life. Doctrines and structures are basically nothing but the fences around the garden where we can meet God. They are to keep us connected with the truth so that we can enter freely in communion with the One who wants to share His love with us.

Well, these are just some reflections I have and they are obviously very tentative, but I simply wanted you to know that I never would have been able to write *Clowning in Rome* if I had not been deeply connected with the Church.

Again, thanks for writing and for your openness and directness. Enclosed I send you one of my later books that you might like to read. It means a lot me that you are interested in what I am trying to express in words.

Sincerely yours,
Henri Nouwen

Maurice L. Monette, a Catholic priest, met Henri at the Center for Concern, a social justice agency in Washington, DC, in 1983. Henri had just returned from his visit to Nicaragua. Monette helped organize Henri's subsequent multi-city tour "An Interrupted Journey" to raise awareness of the impact of the CIA-sponsored contra war in Nicaragua. The two men remained good friends over the years.

In 1989, Monette informed Henri that he was leaving the priesthood to marry a man. Henri writes to make an impassioned plea for Maurice to continue his priestly vocation.

NOVEMBER 10, 1989

Dear Maurice,

Just a note to let you know that I am thinking of you and praying for you. Somehow you are very much on my mind and I am increasingly aware of how crucial this is going to be for your future. I am not sure in which way I can be of good support to you or which way I can continue to call you to deepen and strengthen your priestly vocation. I very deeply believe in your great gifts, not only as an educator and as a man of great intelligence, but also as someone who can speak in the name of Jesus and whose voice can be heard by many people who are searching desperately for a love that holds them safe. During the past year I have come in touch with so many people who are screaming from the center of their being with an immense desire for a deep sense of belonging and a deep experience of inner safety and security.

I really believe that it is the unique vocation of the Church to respond to that scream and to that desire, and that the Church has within itself all the treasures, especially the treasures of the mystical tradition, that are needed to give people new courage, new hope, and a true experience of love. I am, of course very aware of the loneliness and pain that exist in the Church, and especially that of many priests and that for many people the Church has, in fact, become an unsafe place where the voice of love can hardly be heard. Still, I believe deeply that outside of the Church things won't be easier and that within the Church there are many people and resources that allow us to live our priesthood in a way that doesn't dry up, but gives us nurture.

I so much want to keep you in the Church and in the priest-hood, not simply because you started there, but because I feel that you have something to offer now that the Church needs and that many people are asking for. I also realize that staying in the Church asks a lot of sacrifice and a lot of willingness to let go of the fulfilment of desires that seem to be so evident and pressing. But, if my own experience has any validity, I have come to realize that underneath my deep experience of loneliness and my deep need for affection there is a place where I can experience an unlimited love that precedes the many limited forms of love that offer themselves to me.

I realize by now that in order to survive well in the Church we have to live a mystical life, and we have to live it together somewhere in community and with a lot of support. Somehow I feel that the time has come for people like you and me and others who live in similar situations to call each other to a new way of faithfulness and a new way of communion that allows us to live in the Church without feeling oppressed by the Church. I keep wondering if there are ways in which we can become truly messengers of God's love in a world so screaming for love.

Well, these are just some things I wanted to send your way. I just returned from San Francisco after a two-day retreat with Eknath Easwaran,* one of whose books I sent you, and a day with some priests who work in the AIDS ministry. I learned a lot and have a lot to talk to you about.

Meanwhile, I have made a decision to spend the next few months exclusively in writing. I would have liked to be able to do it here in our community, but that has proven to be impossible, and so I am leaving for L'Arche in France on the 25th of November for a few months. I hope to get some real writing done there and to return with some new energy and new insights.

Be sure of my deep affection for you and my great desire to stay in touch with you.

With warm greetings,
Yours,
Love,
Henri

---

* Eknath Easwaran (1910–1999), originally from Kerala, India, was an American-based spiritual teacher and author of books on meditation.

Henri writes again to Maurice to express his deep hope that Maurice will remain a priest, assuring him of his unconditional love for Maurice, no matter what decision he makes.

Maurice would eventually leave the priesthood, a story he tells in his book Confessions of a Gay Married Priest: A Spiritual Journey *(The Vallarta Institute, 2013). As promised, Henri maintained and grew his friendship with Maurice and his husband, Jeff, exchanging visits and telephone calls. Henri's affection continued even after he died: three days after, Maurice received a philodendron Henri had sent him for his fiftieth birthday.*

NOVEMBER 22, 1989

Dear Maurice,

It is always very good to talk with you on the phone, and I am really grateful for your openness to me and your willingness to share with me your ongoing spiritual journey. It is very important for me to be able to be somewhat of a different voice amongst the many voices you are hearing these days. I fully understand how important it is for you to hear people's affirmative responses to your thoughts of leaving the priesthood, and I know how important it is for you to discover how people really desire to give you their love and friendship and affirmation. You are a very beautiful and loving presence and I am very happy that many people help to affirm that in time of change and transition.

You know how much I love you and how important your friendship with me is. At the same time, there is a deep sadness and grief in me when I see you moving away from your priesthood and from the Church. It is not a superficial sadness or simply a regret, but it is a deep cry that comes from one who so much wants you to live a fulfilled and holy life.

The assassination of the Jesuit priests, their cook and her little girl has deeply affected me and also again made me aware of the crucial importance of their witness.* Somehow, I feel that their dedicated commitment is the best that the Church has to give to the world. When Pedro Arupe spoke at the last general Chapter of the Jesuits, he predicted that the Jesuits' commitment to peace and justice would cost many lives.† His prediction has come true in a more dramatic way than we could have expected. When I participated in a service in memory of these martyrs, I felt an incredible and new deep sense of what it means to be part of the Church and that somehow their Martyrdom will bear fruit not only for the people of Salvador, but also for the purification of the Church. I am writing you all this not to manipulate your emotions and feelings, but to simply express to you my deep conviction that, even in the midst of all the lack of understanding and lack of creative response to the such crying needs of many people, the Church is still an incredible source of hope and new life and courage. I am confident that the Church will continue to carry the Gospel from one generation to the next through its saints, its martyrs, and its courageous spokespeople.

I so much want you to stay in the Church and continue to be a voice that can be heard and responded to. I know that you can continue to do many good things for many people, but outside the Church your voice will not carry so far or be able to represent so many people. You so much want to continue your priestly ministry even when you leave the priesthood, but I find that difficult to fully understand. Somehow your priesthood is intimately connected with your ordination in the Church, and your bonds with the priesthood of Jesus who has commissioned you through the

---

* On November 16, 1989, six Jesuits, along with their housekeeper and her daughter (Elba and Celina Ramos), were murdered at the Jesuit University of Central America. The killings occurred in the context of the civil war that ravaged El Salvador in the 1980s.

† Pedro Arrupe, S.J. (1907–1991), was a Spanish Jesuit priest who served as the twenty-eighth superior general (1965–1983) of the Society of Jesus.

Church to offer Him as food and drink to His people. Every time I celebrate the Eucharist, I feel that enormous connection with Jesus and through Jesus with his people all over the world, and I continue to hope that you do not let go of that so precious connection.

I want to assure you that my friendship with you is in no way conditional on your choices. I love you and I will continue to love you whatever your decision, even when it will cost me much pain. But I want you to hear my voice among the many other voices that surround you. It is a voice that comes out of love and affection and deep friendship. I know there are countless practical questions concerning celibacy, community support, and a viable ministry. I don't really have concrete answers for these questions, but I somehow believe that the answers will come when your basic choices are clear.

Thank you for letting me speak to you this way. Thank you for giving me the freedom to express my own pain around your journey. That means a lot to me and deepens my friendship and love for you.

On Saturday I am off to France until the end of February. It will be a time of praying and writing. It will be a time of solitude. You will be very much with me during these months and I pray that we will be able to be in touch somewhat. Pray for me, that I will be able to write well and say things that are good for my community, for the Church, and for the world in which I live.

Much love,
Henri

Marcus was an assistant at L'Arche Daybreak. He was going through a difficult struggle with depression and loneliness. This is the first of many cards Henri sends to his friend from Trosly-Breuil, France, where he was staying for four months.

DECEMBER 16, 1989

Dear Marcus,

Thank you for your faithfulness in the midst of all the disorder, wilderness, depression and anguish. I know it so well! I will ask Père Thomas to pray for you. I will see him in one hour.

I hope you like this card. It is such a powerful portrait by van Gogh.* Beauty given to a hard painful life! This simple poor boy has become world known because the poor van Gogh painted him. I believe that our poor lives become beautiful and life giving when we are willing to pose quietly for God. When you look long at the face, you see much anguish and much pain, but in some strange mysterious way it offers consolation and comfort.

I pray for you, think of you and hold you close to my heart and the heart of God.

Much love,
Henri

---

* This letter was written on a postcard of Vincent van Gogh's painting *Young Man with a Cap (Armand Roulin)*, 1888, Private Collection, Zürich, Switzerland (F536).

PART III

1990–1996

I N HIS FINAL SIX years Henri's hectic schedule continued, but his restless search for home and belonging subsided. The L'Arche Daybreak community had become his anchor and place of refuge.

The demands on Henri's time, however, continued to grow. Almost every week brought a new speaking engagement. More and more visitors came to Daybreak for retreats. He was in demand for weddings and funerals. He was being interviewed by television and documentary producers in Canada, the United States and Holland. In 1992, he appeared on the American evangelical television program *Hour of Power*. In 1994, he taught a course on spirituality with members of Daybreak at Regis College, University of Toronto. He also traveled extensively, including two trips to Ukraine to lead youth retreats. The Daybreak community eventually had to form a committee to help Henri limit his engagements.

In addition to his full calendar, Henri was dedicating more and more of his time to writing. He published eleven new books in this period, including *Life of the Beloved: Spiritual Living in a Secular World* and his most popular work, *The Return of the Prodigal Son: A Meditation on Fathers, Brothers, and Sons* (later released as *The Return of the Prodigal Son: A Story of Homecoming*). Three more books would be published posthumously, and a fourth, a meditation about the trapeze as a metaphor for the spiritual life, was nascent in multiple notebooks and reams of paper at the time of his death.

Henri continued to respond to world events. This was the time of the Gulf War and the AIDS crisis. Henri corresponded with social justice activists such as John Dear and attended peace rallies in Washington, DC. He gave talks on death and dying at an AIDS conference in Chicago, and accompanied many men and their families through their illness.

Yet even with all these activities, travels and demands, Henri's personal life was more peaceful. His friendship with Nathan was restored, and the two continued to work together at Daybreak, making several trips together and keeping in touch when apart with long letters and phone calls. He never transcended his struggles with intimacy and feelings of rejection, but accepted them as "gateways to the unlimited love of God."*

In the years following his breakdown, Henri began to grapple with his complex relationship with his aging father. In *The Return of the Prodigal Son*, a meditation on Rembrandt van Rijn's depiction of the parable, he explored the themes of unconditional love and forgiveness.

> *The return to the "Father from whom all fatherhood takes its name" allows me to let my dad be no less than the good, loving, but limited human being he is, and to let my heavenly Father be the God whose unlimited, unconditional love melts away all resentments and anger and makes me free to love beyond the need to please or find approval.*[†]

Henri visited Europe frequently during this period. It was during a trip to Freiburg in 1991 that Henri saw the trapeze artists the

---

* From Henri's introduction to Dennis O'Neill, *Lazarus Interlude: A Story of God's Healing Love in a Moment of Ministry* (Notre Dame, IN: Ave Maria Press, 1983), 10.

† *The Return of the Prodigal Son: A Meditation on Fathers, Brothers, and Sons* (New York: Doubleday, 1992), 78.

Flying Rodleighs for the first time and was instantly captivated. He introduced himself to the troupe and a friendship ensued. He would visit them on four subsequent occasions. In the art of the trapeze, Henri saw the full drama of the spiritual life play out: we learn to risk loving fully because God is there to catch us. Within this security we can become truly free. He began to form the idea of a book that would speak to a broader audience by incorporating this arresting illustration of the immensity of God's love and the human place within it.

In his final year, Henri was involved in the planning of a new spirituality center at Daybreak, where he would transition to senior pastor and have an apartment of his own. He hoped to slow the pace of his life and apply himself more to his writing. He had moved beyond many of his fears and compulsions. In a letter from this period he wrote:

*I have moved from the intense anguish to a place of more inner rest. I am glad to tell you this because I really want you to know that we can truly grow into a deeper knowledge of being loved with an everlasting love and feel safe in that knowledge.**

He had just completed a sabbatical year and was en route to Russia to make a documentary about the Prodigal Son when he collapsed in his hotel room in Holland. He was rushed to the hospital. Word went out to his family and close friends, but by the time they got to his bedside the worst seemed to be over; he began to recover, and they started making plans for his discharge. He hoped to be able to go to Russia after all. In the early morning of September 21, 1996, alone in his hospital room, he had a massive cardiac arrest and died. He was sixty-four.

---

* Letter to Jean, September 13, 1991.

This chapter begins with a series of letters to his friend at Daybreak who continued to struggle with depression.

JANUARY 2, 1990

Dear Marcus,

May this card bring you a great peace. As you start the new decade I pray for you and ask Jesus to hold you very close to him, whatever will happen in your life or the life of our changing world.

Somehow I sense that great things can happen and will happen when we are very clear and level headed about our commitment to a life with God in and through Jesus.

This beautiful sculpture is very dear to me.[*] It expresses the great interiority of Jesus. Jesus is sitting on a donkey on his way into Jerusalem. People acclaim him but he knows already the journey he has to make to fulfill his vocation.

There is deep peace, deep communion with the Father and great compassion in his face—

I think of you, pray for you and love you—
Henri

---

[*] This letter was written on an art card illustrated with a photograph of the sculpture *Christus auf dem Palmesel* (Christ on a Donkey), a wooden carving from the fourteenth century, which is housed in the Augustiner Museum in Freiburg, Germany.

Dear Marcus,

After a day in Paris with Lon who also lives "Chez Mammie"* I can send you this card of Rodin.† I saw the "real thing" and was overwhelmed by its splendid sensuality. For Rodin the body is everything. All his sculptures sing praise to the beauty of the human body. I read the story of Rodin's life and saw his agony as well as ecstasy. Camille Claudel, sister of Paul Claudel, lost her mind when he rejected her. So much beauty and such enormous agony, pain and suffering. Both Michelangelo and Rodin had to pay heavily for their talents.

Spirit and Body cannot be separated. That is what the incarnation and resurrection is all about. But what a struggle! Some destroyed their bodies through self-castigation, others through unrestricted sensuality. Jesus loved the whole person body, mind and soul. But how to purify our passions while remaining passionate? I feel we need to keep thinking about these things. There remains so much hidden pain in so many hearts.

[the letter continues the next day]

---

* During his year at L'Arche in Trosly-Breuil, Henri shared a house with a number of people, including Jean Vanier's mother, Pauline "Mammie" Vanier.

† The image on the card was Auguste Rodin's sculpture *Le Baiser* (The Kiss), 1886, which hangs in the Musée Rodin in Paris.

JANUARY 20, 1990

Dear Marcus,

Just got your "Four Blue Spruce" card and your good—and pain filled letter. I am grateful you keep writing me in the midst of your pain.

There is something about L'Arche that makes us suffer immensely. I never suffered so much and intensely as since I came to Daybreak. You know it. Somehow L'Arche opens up our deepest hungers, our deepest loneliness and our deepest sensitivities. I never have felt so at home and so lonely at the same time. I never have felt so abandoned and so supported at the same time. I never felt such a need for love while being so surrounded by loving people. It seems that L'Arche leads us to the inner place where we most deeply experience our immense desire for communion and at the same time the total impossibility to see that desire fulfilled in the place where we live. In L'Arche—at least for me—the extremes touch each other. Loneliness and joy; depression and ecstasy, communion and alienation.

I write this to you, because I love you so much. I would love to hold you and let all the sorrows of your heart melt away, but I know that when we meet again we won't be able to do much more than be together and speak words of understanding while the space between us remains open and empty. A space only for God to fill. It is good to be aware of the great mystery of which we are part. It is the mystery of a yearning creation, groaning for its full freedom. Rodin's kiss doesn't tell the truth of life. It speaks about a desire that cannot be fulfilled between people. Rodin's tragic life makes that so tragically clear.

How then to live it all day by day? I hope and pray that you will hold on to a daily time alone with God, a time when you can bring all your yearning before God and let him touch you there.

Leonard Cohen prays in his book *Book of Mercy*:

Blessed are you who has given each man a shield of Loneliness so that he cannot forget you. You are the truth of loneliness, and only your name addresses it. Strengthen my loneliness that I may be healed in your name, which is beyond all consolations that are uttered on this earth. Only in your name I can stand in the rush of time, only when this loneliness is yours can I lift my sins toward your mercy.*

Having thus been in the presence of God, I think you have to try to "step over" it in your daily actions. I think in part you are doing this already. I just want to say how important it is to not make your depressions the main subject of your thoughts, words and actions but to live "beyond your depression" in the freedom you cannot yet feel but which is more real than your loneliness. I am sure that the handicapped people can be a real encouragement for you in this regard.

I am also glad that Sam is there for you. See him as often as you can, and spend some good time outside the community involving yourself with people and things that can give you real life. Often art, good books and good conversations can give much new life. I have discovered that the larger our view in life is, the better can we live our moments of depression. Once I stood looking in the Grand Canyon, and when I saw the billions of years carved in stone in front of me I felt as if the heaviness of heart left me. Somehow I felt very small and very significant at the same time and my introspection in my own pain was turned into adoration. You too need a Grand Canyon, whatever way it comes to you!

> Be sure of my love, my care, my prayers and my firm friendship—
> May Jesus hold you very safe in his embrace—
> Love,
> Henri

Henri writes to his Daybreak friend Lorenzo about trees, time and distractions.

JANUARY 28, 1990

Dear Lorenzo,

Many warm greetings from the Forest of Compiègne. I just came back from a walk in the forest, and I was impressed by the many trees who were there long before I came along and will be there long after I have gone. Their beauty and age give me peace and trust. So many things that distract us will soon be forgotten. They ask me to be quiet, to pray, to trust and to wait. Not easy for me!

I think of you with much love and affection and pray for you. I will be so glad to see you again.

> Love,
> Henri

✤

Henri writes again to his friend Marcus. This time it is on a series of three cards. He uses nature and artistic imagery to offer consolation and counsel about how to walk through depression.

Dear Marcus,

When I saw these cards I thought of you.* I felt deeply that these cards express the beauty of your sadness. They express waiting, expectation, restful trust that the sun will break through and show clearly the beauty of the land. But the mist has its own beauty. It calls us to prayer, to interiority, to trust.

As you can see: there is a path, but you must accept that at this moment you cannot see far ahead of you. But you don't have to! One day, when you least expect it all will look so different!

I hold you close in my love and prayers. Try to rest in Jesus' love. He loves you so much. Be sure of my deep desire to be very faithful to you.

Love, much love,
Henri

Thanks so much for your letter of January 17th. I read it and reread it prayerfully. There is so much hope in your struggle, so much new life to be born.

Somewhere you are called to a new fruitfulness. I wonder if God is not calling you to embrace your singleness in a new way.

---

* The first card was a photograph by Eva Rubinstein of a country road shrouded in mist entitled *Maine*, 1978. The second, a photograph by Frank Horvat, *Sechuan, China*, 1985, consisted of a view of a lake encircled by mountains and fog. The third card, another photograph by Rubinstein, *Lazienki Park*, was of an elegant bridge spanning a mist-filled pond with majestic trees on either side.

Maybe he is calling you to a life of committed celibacy in order to give you a new fruitfulness! This thought just came to me, and I simply give it to you with love and tenderness.

"Depression" can also be grief, or a mourning about what could not be. You may have come to a time in your life of new deep choices, which ask for much dying—in order to give much life.

Henri

JANUARY 29, 1990 (CONTINUED)

There is a bridge there. You are walking on it. There is another side. Trust it!

Some trees are weeping. Others are reaching up to heaven. You stand in between these trees.

Be sure all will be well, very well indeed.

Love,
Henri

Henri writes to his friend Jutta about waiting, patience and trust.

JANUARY 29, 1990

Dear Jutta,

Be at peace, pray every day, knock on the door. It will be opened. Behind the door there is a whole new world waiting to be discovered by you.

Be patient, very patient. God loves you, not for what you do, but for who you are. He wants to touch you in your waiting, your solitude, your silence. Be faithful, trust. Maybe this is the time to read "The Song of Songs" in the Old Testament. It will teach you much about Jesus.

I am growing slowly. I need much patience too!
Be sure of my love and prayers.

Love,
Henri

Henri writes to a Canadian theology student who had written with multiple questions about themes in his writing. He responds with an important clarification about how we see God and how God sees us.

FEBRUARY 22, 1990

Dear Anna,

Thanks so much for your kind letter. I would really like to help you. Right now, however, it is hard to spend much time responding to your different questions, but I am sending you a copy of the book *Seeds of Hope*, where you might find responses to some of your questions.

The main thought I would like to give you at this point is simply that we cannot see God in others or in the world, but the God in us sees God in others and the world. The deeper our communion with God is, the more we will discover Him in all that we see. That is why Jesus says those who are happy are those who have eyes to see and ears to hear. The mystery of the spiritual life is that heart speaks to heart, spirit speaks to spirit, God speaks to God, and that we are lifted up into the inner communion that takes place within God.

Thanks so much for writing me. Much luck with your thesis!

Sincerely,
Henri Nouwen

Henri's friend Jurjen Beumer regularly sent him articles from the Dutch press. Here he reflects on articles by a priest and a theologian, concerned by what he perceives as an angry, critical attitude toward the Church.

MARCH 12, 1990

Dear Jurjen,

Many, many thanks for your very kind letter and for the articles and song you enclosed with it. I was very glad to read your positive memories of our time together. For me also your visit was very important, and I am glad that our friendship could grow deeper and stronger. I am deeply convinced that in times of inner pain God always sends us to people who hold us faithful and reveal to us in a new way the mystery of God's love. I very much hope and pray that in the future we can continue to support and help each other.

Thanks so much for your very kind and very encouraging review of the Icon Book. I am truly grateful that you have given it some special attention. I am really happy with the part that *TROUW* published.

With great interest, I read Jan van Hooydonk's article on Sjef Donders* and Sjirk Altena's on Eugen Drewermann.† I have read both pieces with great attention, and I would simply like to share with you my concerns about the tone of both articles, even more than about their concrete content. Reading both articles, I sensed

---

* Father Joseph "Sjef" Donders (d. 2013) was a Dutch priest and prolific author who served for many years in Kenya as a member of the Missionaries of Africa before settling in the United States.

† Eugen Drewermann is a German theologian and former Roman Catholic priest. In 1989, Drewermann published *Kleriker: Psychogramm eines Ideals* (Clergy: Psychology of an Ideal) (Olten, Switzerland: Walter-Verlag, 1989), which led to his silencing at the behest of then-Cardinal Joseph Ratzinger (later Pope Benedict XVI).

an undertone of anger and bitterness, not only towards the Church but even towards God. It is hard for me to articulate my emotions well, but I feel a real personal sadness when I think about Donders, and especially about Eugen Drewermann. It seems to me that they are both speaking from a space that would lead to increasing frustration and an increasing sense of inner discontent which does not allow the Spirit of God to really transform their deeper selves. I miss a spirit of joy and peace in the midst of all the conflicts that are really there, and I am quite overwhelmed by the heavy-handed generalizations with which they speak about the Church and the life of the Spirit.

I did read Paul Knitter's book about the question of whether Jesus is the way or a way, and I found the book very interesting and important, but certainly not a book that gives the question the spiritual depth that it really requires.[*] Something very simplistic happens when people say that Jesus is not the way, but a way, and I wonder often whether that statement doesn't come from a fear that Christianity is oppressive and manipulative, instead of from an experience of Jesus as a Savior of the world.

I just finished reading Harvey Cox's new book, *Many Mansions*, and I was deeply impressed by the way Harvey speaks of the importance of Jesus in the dialogue of Moslems, Buddhists, Hindus and Jews.[†] The gentleness of Harvey Cox and his great conviction that people from all religions want to hear in a very deep way the voice of Jesus is so different from the somewhat harsh statements that Donders makes in his conversation with Hooydonk. Much more than Donders, it is Eugen Drewermann who raises many, many questions in my mind and in my heart. While I was in Germany, I

---

[*] Henri may be referring to Knitter's book *No Other Name?: A Critical Survey of Christian Attitudes Toward the World Religions* (Maryknoll, NY: Orbis, 1985).

[†] Harvey Cox, *Many Mansions: A Christian's Encounter with Other Faiths* (Boston: Beacon Press, 1988).

became very much aware of the great importance of his writings in the German religious scene, and I took some of his books with me to become more familiar with his thinking. Again, it is not just simply his opinions that concern me, but it is the angry, bitter, sarcastic and cynical tone that disturbs me. What he writes about the Church and the priests and ministers shows so little tenderness, so little forgiveness, so little humour, that it scares me by its heavy-handedness and its authoritarian style. When he writes that the Church does not offer any contribution to relieving those who suffer in life, I wonder from which interior place he makes such a statement. I am really terribly afraid that his writing will lead to a very negative response from Church leaders and that this response will only pour oil on the fire of his anger and will, in the long run, harm him, his readers and also those whom he is trying to call to something new. There is so much ego, so much self-will; there is so much drivenness and compulsiveness in what he writes that it almost seems as if he would not be able to really hear well those who would enter into dialogue with him. I am also really concerned about the strong "faith" in psychoanalysis. I am very convinced of the valuable contribution of psychoanalysis to the spiritual life, but the way Eugen Drewermann re-interprets the Christian message from a psychoanalytic perspective really strikes me as a new dogmatism that is as intolerant as any Church dogmatism in the past.

I am writing all this to you, not so much to criticize Donders or Drewermann, but to express my deep feeling that someone should start speaking words of hope and healing in this world, whether in the Church or outside of it. And I have a sense that we are constantly being seduced into focusing all our attention on the obvious weakness and limitations of the churches. There is such a need for words of compassion, forgiveness, healing, and new life that I feel increasingly sad that some of our greatest minds are spending their time and energy in being angry and disappointed with the spiritual communities of which they are part.

Meanwhile. I hope you received my two little books *Beyond the Mirror** and *Walk with Jesus,*† and also the book, *Van Gogh and God.*‡ If you haven't received them yet, they will arrive soon. I especially hope that the Van Gogh book will give you much inspiration and new vision.

Thanks so much for all your friendship and your support, and the many ways in which you witness for the Gospel of Jesus.

With warm wishes,
Yours,
Henri

Henri's breakdown in 1988 and his slow recovery started to bear fruit in the 1990s. His spiritual vision began to focus on claiming his identity as the Beloved Child of God. Here, writing to his friend Jutta at the outset of Holy Week, he urges her to do the same.

PALM SUNDAY, APRIL 8, 1990

For Jutta

Jesus suffered and died for our sake. He suffered and died, not in despair, not as the rejected one, but as the Beloved Child of God. From the moment he heard the voice that said: "You are my Beloved on you my favor rests," he lived his life and suffered his pain under the Blessing of his Father. He knew that even when everyone would run away from him, his Father would never leave him alone.

---

* *Beyond the Mirror: Reflections on Death and Life* (New York: Crossroad, 1990).

† *Walk with Jesus: Stations of the Cross* (Maryknoll, NY: Orbis, 1990).

‡ Cliff Edwards, *Van Gogh and God: A Creative Spiritual Quest* (Chicago: Loyola University Press, 1989).

For us, the greatest temptation is to lose touch with the Blessing. We are the Beloved Sons and Daughters of God. When we live our suffering under the blessing even the greatest pain, yes even death, will lead us deeper into the forgiving and life giving heart of God. But when we think we are not loved, when we reflect on ourselves as being under the curse, when we say or think "I am not good," our suffering will lead us to despair and our death cannot give life.

As we enter Holy Week, let us trust, with a deep trust that we are God's Beloved Children and have been richly blessed so we can live our struggles, pains and suffering under the Blessing and thus be brought always closer to a life in and with the crucified and risen Lord.

Henri Nouwen

The theme of claiming one's identity as God's Beloved appears again in a letter to his friend Ann in Australia, who was struggling with challenges to her ministry.

MAY 24, 1990

Dear Ann,

Your letter which reveals so much pain and suffering has been with me now a few days, and I'd like to write and give you some hope, courage, and confidence. You have been through some very hard times, and I realize that your heart feels very heavy and that it is very hard for you to be in touch with your own goodness and strength, and your own great gifts. I am glad that you did decide to ask for some professional help, and I pray that in the coming weeks and months you will find that depression will lift and you

will see things in a new light, and that your heart will be somewhat healed.

At this particular moment, I would like to ask you not to focus
too much on the ways in which you have been misunderstood, not
appreciated or treated unjustly. Although this certainly has happened and has caused you a lot of hurt, I do think that God is
calling you to a deeper place where you can step beyond these understandable complaints. Somewhere you have to hear again very
clearly the blessing of God that says, "You are my beloved daughter; on you my favor rests." When you can hear that voice speaking
gently in your heart, it might be possible to let go of some of the
hurts that are now causing you so much pain.

Be sure of my love and my friendship. I certainly would love to
see you again when you are back in Canada. Enclosed I send you a
copy of a little book I wrote about my experience with God after a
serious accident.* I hope it brings you some comfort and consolation.

With warm greetings,
Yours,
Henri

Henri writes to a young man who is anxious about his future.

AUGUST 27, 1990

Dear Peter,

How good it was to hear from you! Thanks so much for taking the
time and energy to write me such a nice long letter. I know how

---

* *Beyond the Mirror: Reflections on Death and Life* (New York: Crossroad, 1990).

busy you are at Madonna House,* and I appreciate that you are giving me some of your time there.

Let me simply say that it was really good to meet you and that I feel deeply grateful to God for bringing us together. You are a wonderful person, full of life, full of energy, full of goodness and affection, and it is really good to know you. One thing I just want you to know is that God is a God of surprises, so don't predict your own life. There might be some suffering ahead of you, but don't think about that too much. In fact, there might be a lot more joy and peace than you yourself can imagine at this moment.

You are right when you say that I have gone through a lot myself, but I also want you to know that God has given me an immense amount of joy in my life, and He wants to give you the same. So really trust, trust, trust, and don't get entangled in the years to come. God really wants you to be alive and fully alive, and I certainly want that as well. You have a lot to give and you also have a lot of wonderful things to receive. I certainly want to be part of that and you can trust in my friendship and love, so be sure to stay in touch. It is good to be loved and it is good to love; that is what life is all about. Keep always listening to the words that Jesus heard and are also there for you: "You are my Beloved Son and on you my favour rests." I have a lot of hope for you especially because of your great love for Mary. She will hold you safe and close in the heart of Jesus.

Looking forward to your next letter,
Henri

---

* A Catholic community of laypeople as well as priests founded by Catherine de Hueck Doherty and based in Combermere, Ontario. This is the same community that Henri considered joining in the late 1970s.

Dan Wakefield, an American novelist, journalist and screenwriter, had written to Henri about his spiritual struggles following the collapse of a brief marriage.

OCTOBER 25, 1990

Dear Dan,*

Thanks so very much for your letter. It really means a lot to me that you took the time and energy to write and tell me about the painful crisis you lived through during the past year. Since receiving your letter, I have thought a lot about what you wrote and about how to strengthen your new-found faith during this very difficult time of your life. It seems really important to stay away from questions about why this happened to you and why people gave you the advice they did. The crucial question for me at this point is how can this wrenching and humiliating experience purify your faith and lead you to a closer communion with Jesus.

The situation in which you find yourself could well be described as the dark night of the soul. You have very little positive feelings, positive experiences, or obvious results to cling to. Your faith didn't "work." It didn't give you what you reasonably might have expected of it, and even the people to whom you entrusted yourself for spiritual direction were not able to give you the advice and direction that you needed at the time. So you really are left with your naked faith, and it is precisely in this darkness of faith that God is purifying your heart and calling you to be faithful, that is, to cling to nothing but Jesus himself, who died for you on the cross while living the experience that God had completely abandoned him.

---

* Letter to Dan Wakefield is printed with the kind courtesy of Lilly Library, Indiana University.

I vividly remember that I wrote you after I read your book, *Returning*, that you had embarked on a new journey of which you had only seen the very beginning.* I had a deep feeling that your conversion would only be permanent after you would be willing to go through many other conversions, and now, after reading this letter, I realize how you are faced again with a new choice and, in many ways, a harder choice than the one you had made before. I am very aware that the failure of your marriage can easily tempt you to become very bitter and even make you reject Jesus as useless or at least irrelevant for your day-to-day life. But this truly is a temptation because Jesus wants to lead you to the place where he himself becomes the only safe way to God. I have this vision of him taking away many of the support systems that you could rely on until now. It almost seems to me that he is saying to you, "Am I not enough for you?" People will criticize you; people will question your conversion; people will use your failure in your marriage as an argument against your faith, and in many ways you will be very alone. But, after your conversion, the aloneness can be seen as a second loneliness. It is not the loneliness of a person who needs emotional support, but it is the loneliness of the person who, after having discovered God as the only source of true life, is now asked to let go of everything but Him.

In your letter, you say that you cannot pray any more. I'd really like to encourage you to continue to pray, but to let your prayer be the prayer of a poor man, prayer which doesn't offer much satisfaction or insight, but is nothing but a simple being present to the One who came as we are, suffered like we do, and offers us his own poverty as a source of consolation and comfort. You really don't have to do anything more than say, "Lord Jesus Christ, have mercy on me, a sinner," or "Lord, make haste to help me," and with the eyes of your heart keep looking at Him who was stripped of

---

* Henri is referring to Wakefield's book *Returning: A Spiritual Journey* (Garden City, NY: Doubleday, 1988).

all human supports to offer you hope in the midst of despair and light in the midst of darkness.

I am deeply grateful to you for sharing with me your painful story. I feel a deep love for you and a deep desire to support you in your anguish. Although my own life story is very different from yours, I know intimately the places of the heart of which you speak, and I want to reassure you that God rewards the faithful friend. Maybe the most important thing I am saying in this letter is that you are called to a greater intimacy with God and that this intimacy is only possible through a greater communion with the heart of Jesus. Not too long ago when I experienced great anguish, I wrote three Prayers to the Heart of Jesus, and I thought you might like to have them.[*]

It is really good to be in touch with you again. You can be sure that I will definitely give you a special place in my prayers and will ask the people of our community, who are in so many ways weak and broken, to join me in that prayer.

Much love,
Henri

Henri writes to his friends Hans and Marinus in Holland about listening to God's will and taking risks in middle age.

NOVEMBER 23, 1990

Dear Hans and Marinus,

Thanks so much for your wonderful letter. It was really good to hear from you both again. I still have very good memories of my

---

[*] *Heart Speaks to Heart: Three Prayers to Jesus* (Notre Dame, IN: Ave Maria Press, 1989).

little visit to you, and you certainly have a special place in my heart and in my prayers. I will pray especially for you, Marinus, as you are having such a hard time. It might be that the situation in which you find yourself asks of you to take a drastic step; the time may have come for you to make a move and to look for another place to work. I am quite aware that it is hard to change work after so many years in the same job and that it often creates much anxiety and uncertainty, but it might be one way to be faithful to your vocation—"to live beyond the familiar and to follow Jesus more radically." I am quite sure that leaving your job would require some real risk-taking, and it might put you into a situation of uncertainty, but it seems to be always important to first of all pay attention to the voice of your heart and trust that God will reward you when you are faithful to that voice. The temptation to become bitter or angry or have some outsider dominate you in your inner life is always very great, and when you discover some "little boss" is taking away your inner peace and joy, you might have a sign that a move is asked for. Well, think about it. It is only a thought that came when I read Hans' letter.

My own brother made a very major shift for the same reason when he was fifty, and he has never regretted it, and I did the same when I left Harvard five years ago, and I also have never regretted it. So you are not alone in this situation. But be sure that I pray for you and I hope that, whatever decision you make, you will make it in prayer and in great trust for Jesus' love for you.

Dear Hans, thanks for your very encouraging words and your warm invitation to stay in touch and come to visit again. That really means a lot to me, I wish both of you a very blessed Advent season and a very joyful Christmas.

Yours,
Henri

John Dear, a young Jesuit priest and peace activist, questioned whether the comfortable Jesuit school in Berkeley would be a suitable setting in which to study theology.

DECEMBER 4, 1990

Dear John,*

Thanks so much for your very kind letter. I am really grateful that you took the time and energy to write me and to send me some of your recent articles. It means a lot to me that in this way you stay in touch and encourage me in my own thinking and writing.

I very well understand the doubts you express about studying scripture and theology in the Berkeley setting. I experienced some of the same doubts while I was at Yale and Harvard. Still, I do believe that when you keep living it a little bit like an exile, it can be very fruitful and very enriching. Just last week I gave a retreat for a group of ten people from very different parts of the United States who had come to our little Dayspring (Daybreak's house of prayer) to deepen their spiritual life. Some of them were Protestant ministers, one was a professor of pastoral theology, one an accountant, one the leader of the Canadian Breakfast Prayer Movement, one a Catholic priest and one an Anglican seminarian. They were joined by two handicapped members of our community and two assistants. During the day we offered much silence and some conferences [talks], and during the evening the retreatants were in the houses with the handicapped people. It was a very powerful experience for all of us, and we have discovered the great gift of the handicapped to bring people to conversion. Many of the ideas that we developed with them were received quite differently

---

* Letters to John Dear by kind courtesy of Swarthmore College Peace Collection, Swarthmore College.

because they were received in the context of a community of which the handicapped people form the center. So, in a way, the retreat was given more by our community than by those who gave presentations. I found this a very important experience, and, more than ever, I realize the importance of the context in which theological visions are being offered.

It was very good to hear that you had a chance to go to El Salvador and be close to the place of the martyrdom of the six Jesuits and Elba and Celina Ramos.* I wish I could have been there with you. I realize how profound this experience must have been for you.

Thanks again for your good letter and also for your warm words about *Beyond the Mirror*. That means a lot to me.

Wishing you a very blessed Advent season, and a very joy-filled Christmas.

Yours,
Henri

Henri replies to a letter from a man who is suffering from the aftermath of neglect and rejection in his early life.

DECEMBER 6, 1990

Dear Albin,

Thanks so much for your very good letter. I really do believe deeply that grieving over what you have missed will lead you to a deeper understanding of the unlimited love of God, to which your family could only give a limited expression. I still consider it as the greatest of all good news that we have been chosen by God from all

---

* See letter to Maurice Monette, November 22, 1989, for Henri's first reference to this incident in El Salvador.

eternity and belonged in His home before were touched by human hands, and will again belong to Him fully after our earthly journey. I have a deep trust in God's unlimited, eternal love, a trust that can be truly claimed in the center of our being, [a trust that] can give us the freedom to forgive those who could only give us a very imperfect love.

Prayer, indeed, is the way to that unlimited love and will open for us the place of gratitude for the ways that unlimited love has been refracted in our earthly life.

Be sure I keep you in my prayers and hold you close to the heart of God.

Yours,
Henri

Henri's friend Lawrence had received disappointing news about a job he wanted.

DECEMBER 11, 1990

Dear Lawrence and Joyce,

Many thanks for your warm Christmas letter. It was really good to hear from you and especially that, over all, things are well with you.

I can certainly understand what a great disappointment it must have been for you, Lawrence, not to get the job as librarian, but I trust that somehow this disappointment will not depress you, but lead you to a new and deeper claiming of your goodness and your blessedness. We obviously need affirmation from the world around us, and I hope and pray that you will receive a lot of that. But I also know that the value of your life and your person is deeply hidden in the palm of God's hand. I hope you have the inner strength and courage to keep returning to that knowledge of God's love and find in that knowledge a deep affirmation of who you are as a person.

It is wonderful to hear that you are going to travel to Europe. That will be very life-giving for you all. Be sure that I am with you in thought and prayer. I am doing well and busy, as always, but very happy to be in the L'Arche community.

With warm greetings,
Yours,
Henri

A letter to Henri's friend Frank Alton, who was in discernment about whether to move from his ministry in Mexico to the United States.

DECEMBER 21, 1990

Dear Frank,

Thanks so much for your very good letter. It was nice to hear from you again and to read how Judy, you and the family have been doing. I do want very much to stay in touch with you and to continue to deepen our friendship.

I can quite well understand that you have a sense that your time in Mexico will be ending in the near future, and I trust that, as you discern the question of future directions, there will be an increasing clarity about where you are being called. I do very much appreciate the thought that the time may have come to share what you have learned in Mexico with others in the United States, and I also wonder if it might be time to look for ways to deepen your spiritual life and to move a little from action to contemplation.

Here at Daybreak I have become increasingly aware of the enormous spiritual need of ministers and priests and the importance of coming into touch with the mystical life. Just recently we had a retreat for ten ministers from different parts of the United States and Canada which was called "Introduction to the Mystical Life." These ministers were joined by assistants and handicapped people from our community. While spending the days praying, listening to a few conferences [talks] and sharing their experiences, in the evenings all the retreatants lived in our homes and experienced very directly the life with people with a mental handicap. Thus, the retreat was an introduction to the mystical life guided by people who are very broken and very poor. It was amazing to see how deeply these ministers and priests were touched and how profound the changes were that took place.

I am really grateful that some of the things I hoped to do in Latin America I am now doing here. It is very rewarding and I very much hope that you and Judy can one day also spend some time with us, praying and sharing our life. Somehow, I sense that while psychotherapy is of great value, there is also a healing beyond psychotherapy. It is a healing that brings us in touch with the love of God that was there for us even before we were touched by human hands, whether the hands were those of our teachers, parents, church leaders or anyone else. Discovering this early love of God is one of the most healing experiences that can take place, and I am more and more convinced that people with a mental handicap often have the gift to lead us to that early love.

Meanwhile, I am doing well, busy in the community, busy giving talks here and there and busy trying to finish a manuscript on the Prodigal Son. It is really nice to be in touch with you again. Be sure of my love and prayers and my great desire that your Christmas season is filled with joy and peace.

Enclosed I am sending you a big print copy of two of my books.

With warm greetings,
Yours,
Henri

Henri writes to a man about aging and the choices facing people in their fifties about how to live their retirement.

JANUARY 10, 1991

Dear Colin,

Thanks so much for your very good card. I know very well what you are talking about when you say that many people in their fifties are losing their vitality and starting to think about retirement, but, as disciples of Jesus, I think our life becomes more and more the opportunity to love the older we become. I think we have to stay close to the words of Jesus, "When you were young you girded yourself and went where you wanted to go, but when you grow old someone else will gird you and lead you where you do not want to go." It is this openness to new and unknown directions that makes growing old a real spiritual challenge.

I, indeed, feel that we are faced with a choice when we are in our fifties. It is a choice between considering our life as practically over or looking at our life as reaching the place of total commitment and total surrender. In a way, life and death are always placed before us, and God keeps saying, "Choose life." I am deeply convinced that the most important spiritual gifts can be offered precisely by those who choose life again when others think they have "seen it all."

Be assured of my gratitude to you for your vitality and your love.

With warm greetings,
Yours,
Henri

Henri writes to a Dutch friend whose sister is dying.

JANUARY 22, 1991

Dear Antoinette,

Many thanks for your very kind letter. Thank you for writing me about your sister in Tasmania. I promise you that I will keep her in my prayers and also will ask our community to pray for her. I hope you will let her know that our people, many of whom are mentally handicapped, have a great gift of prayer and are surrounding your sister with their love.

It is important that we think about death as a gateway into the house of God and that our life, with all its pain, is to make us ready to live in lasting communion with the One who wants to fulfill the deepest desires of our hearts.

I trust that Gerard is already fully part of that special joy and peace that only God can offer and that, indeed, your sister will join him in that when she is called.

With warm greetings,
Yours,
Henri Nouwen

Henri writes to his anchoress friend Sister Marcia Hobart about the Persian Gulf War. A few weeks prior to writing this letter, Henri participated

---

* On August 2, 1990, a coalition of thirty-four nations led by the United States began the Persian Gulf War in response to Iraq's invasion and annexation of Kuwait. The war ended on February 28, 1991.

in a prayer vigil in Washington, DC, to pray for a peaceful solution to the conflict in the Gulf.

FEBRUARY 5, 1991

Dear Marcia,

Thanks so much for your kind note and for your continuing prayers for me. I am really grateful that I have a special place in our solitude and silence.   ·

The Gulf crisis also preoccupies me very much, and I am holding on to the words of Jesus: "Pray unceasingly to survive what is going to happen and to stand confidently with heads erect in the presence of the Son of Man, trusting that not a hair on your head will be lost." It is important for me to know that Jesus' primary concern was that we would not let the darkness overwhelm us and would continue to trust in his life-giving presence.

We in our community are trying to find ways to live peacefully in the midst of this very disturbing time, and thus be a sign of hope for others.

Much love,
Henri

As the war intensified, Henri wrote a prayer and meditation for his community. Afterward, in response to the many people requesting his counsel for how to respond to the war, he shared them more broadly. One of these people was Sheila Cassidy, an English doctor known for her work in the hospice movement and a survivor of torture under the Pinochet regime in Chile.

Prayer During the Gulf War

Dear God, with you everything is possible. Let this cup of war, killing and destruction, this cup of bloodshed, human anguish and desolation, this cup of torture, breakage in human relationships and abandonment. . . . Dear God, let this cup pass us by.

We are afraid. We are trembling in the depth of our being. We feel the sweat and tears of thousands of people all over the world, people who are afraid—afraid to fight, afraid to kill, afraid of being killed, afraid of an uncertain future.

Please, dear Lord, let this cup pass us by.

But, dear Lord—and we say this with the same trust as your son, Jesus—not our will, but your will be done. We look ahead and see only darkness. We look around and see only despair. We so much want our desire to be the same as your will, but when you call us to walk through this valley of tears and darkness, help us to be faithful, faithful to the end.

Protect our hearts from bitterness, resentment and the desire for revenge; keep our hearts close to the heart of Jesus, who was willing to die for us and so give us new life.

As we pray, speak to us in the depths of our being and remind us that, whatever happens in this dark world, we are and remain your blessed daughters and sons.

About Prayer in a Time of War

As our world becomes more and more entangled in the war raging in the Middle East, we are called to pray with more fervor and with more trust than ever. But how to pray when our hearts are so fearful, our attempts to stop this war so futile, and our hopes for a peaceful future so radically tested? How to pray when we feel so completely powerless?

In a time as desperate as ours, we have to dare to claim the truth that the power of the powerless is the power of prayer. As a community in which people with mental handicaps are the core members holding us together by their vulnerability, we know a secret. It is the secret that God reveals himself in a unique way through those who are powerless. The secret was revealed centuries ago, when God became a small, vulnerable child, lived for thirty years as a humble carpenter in an unpretentious village, preached for three years as a sometimes praised and sometimes ridiculed itinerant preacher, and died as a common criminal on a cross. Indeed, God revealed to us his divine glory in the humble and powerless Jesus. This powerless Jesus shows us how to pray in a time when the powers of our world make such frightening noises.

With what kind of heart, then, do we have to pray? We have to pray first of all with a repentant heart. A repentant heart is a heart that is willing to see the darkness of the world reflected in our innermost being. It is a heart that is willing to confess that the anger, jealousy, hatred and desire for revenge that lead to destructive wars are not foreign to the one who prays. It is a heart that does not shrink from the realization that it carries seeds of destruction within itself. It is a heart that is broken, contrite, humble and aware of its own part in the evil it wants to expel.

A heart that prays for peace is a poor heart. A poor heart knows that it cannot control the future, cannot set things straight, cannot fix the problems of the world. Jesus said, "Blessed are the poor," he did not say, "Blessed are those who care for the poor" but "Blessed are the poor." To pray for peace is to pray from that place where we are poor, where we do not know much, where we are confused about our feelings and where we are often lost about what to do. It is precisely in this poor place that the Spirit of Jesus chooses to dwell. It is from that poor place that the Spirit of Jesus calls out, "Abba, Father." When we touch this poor place in ourselves, we also touch the poverty of all the poor in the world. When we pray from the place of poverty, we pray in solidarity with millions of poor people who are the innocent victims of wars fought by the mighty and the powerful.

A heart that prays for peace is a child-like heart. It is a heart of a child who knows that it is the Beloved of God. When Jesus was baptized in the Jordan, he heard a voice that said, "You are my Beloved; on you my favor rests." It is this voice that each one who follows Jesus must hear. It is a voice that allows us to live in this world with great confidence, knowing that, whether we are liked or disliked, praised or despised, we always will remain the beloved children of God. When we truly believe in this voice of love, we can truly pray for peace because the peace we pray for is not something to satisfy our needs or give us a sense of respect, but it is a peace that freely flows from those who live as members of the family of God.

As members of the Daybreak community, we know something about repentance as we constantly have to face our own brokenness. As members of the Daybreak community, we know something about poverty because we live with those who are not successful or powerful and are constantly faced with their own poverty. As members of the Daybreak community, we know something about the voice that calls us the Beloved because those who are weakest among us are often the ones who carry within themselves the great gift of peace. No one praises them for their accomplishments; no one calls on them to perform; but each person who lives with them discovers that they are in a special way the Beloved of God and, therefore, unique carriers of His peace.

As we live in this period of war and are constantly faced with the images of destruction and violence, we know that, more than ever, we are called to be faithful to the powerless Jesus and to trust that He will continue to send his peace-making Spirit.

For his friend Jutta, who was preparing to enter the Catholic Church, Henri shared reflections on suffering.

PALM SUNDAY, MARCH 1991

For Jutta

Jesus was handed over to suffering. Judas became the instrument of God's handing Jesus over to his passion. The mystery of Jesus' life is that he fulfilled his mission not in action but in passion, not through what he did, but through what was done to him.

Our suffering is passion. We suffer most from what is said to us, done to us and thought about us. Our suffering makes us subject to the actions, words and feelings of others over whom we have no control. We share the passion of Jesus precisely when our life is out of our own hands. And the older we grow, the more we become aware that most of our life is passion. How then to live our passion? Jesus shows us the way.

Jesus lived his passion in total freedom. He embraced his suffering, he "befriended" it, he stood in it with trust. How can we do this? The great spiritual challenge is to not accuse, not condemn, not judge those who make us suffer but to embrace our pain, our loneliness, our sense of being rejected, our feelings of abandonment as the way to fulfill our deepest vocation. That is what Jesus means when he says: "Take up your cross and follow me." We cannot change others, we cannot force our surroundings to please us, but we can fully choose to live our pain and find there the gateway to Glory—

Jesus lived his passion as the Beloved Son of God. Even in the midst of his most severe suffering he never doubted that he was the Beloved of the Father. We too are the Beloved Daughters and Sons of God, and when we claim that truth for ourselves we can stand in our suffering with confidence and we can even let our suffering "prune" us, so that we can bear more fruit.

Love,
Henri

In a message addressed to pastoral workers gathered for an annual conference of the Free Methodist Church, Henri shares reflections on weakness and vulnerability in ministry—a concept that he explored in his 1972 classic The Wounded Healer *and that he later exemplified as a member of L'Arche Daybreak.*

MARCH 1991

Dear Friends,

As you are gathering at your April meeting, I want to express to you my great regret that I will not be able to be with you. I am spending the month of April in Germany to do some writing.

Brian asked me to send you a few words to encourage you in your work and to assure you of my great desire to be connected with you.

As I think of the words that are your theme for your gathering, I realize how much I identify with those words.* The longer I live in the ministry, the more I feel the call to become weak with the weak, vulnerable with the vulnerable, broken with the broken. My

---

* The words of the conference were: "To the weak I made myself weak. I accommodated myself to people in all kinds of different situations, so that by all possible means I might bring some to salvation. All this I do for the sake of the Gospel, that I may share its benefits with others" (Paul to the Corinthians, 9:22-23).

life with people who have a mental handicap has confronted me more and more with my own handicaps, my own weaknesses, and my own brokenness. But the more I was willing to be confronted in a gentle loving way, the more I discovered that God, indeed, chose to dwell where we can come together in a fellowship of the weak.

There was a time when I really wanted to help the poor, the sick and the broken, but to do it as one who was wealthy, healthy and strong. Now I see more and more how it is precisely through my weakness and brokenness that I minister to others. I am increasingly aware of the fact that Jesus does not say, "Blessed are those who help the poor" but "Blessed are the poor." For me, this means that I have to come in touch with my own poverty to discover there the blessings of God and to minister from that place to others. It is only as the "blessed ones" that we can be a blessing for others, and I pray that we all dare to claim the blessing that rests in our poverty, our weakness, our non-togetherness, and that we can proclaim to others that where they are broken and in great need, the voice of God's love can often be heard.

It is clear we need to heal. It is clear we need to protest against violence and injustice. It is clear we have to do anything possible to avoid oppression, exploitation and war. But this ministry of healing has to be a ministry in the name of the One who healed through his wounds and who revealed his healing presence as the crucified one, who took the marks of his crucifixion into his new life with God.

So I pray that you embrace your own weakness and your own suffering and your own pain with trust that, in this way, you can follow your Lord and make your own wounds a source of healing for others. Thus you can also become a true light for the world and a sign of hope and a prophetic voice that calls for peace and justice.

Your brother in Christ,
Henri Nouwen

To a woman facing a terminal illness, Henri answers her questions about the soul.

MAY 10, 1991

Dear Margaret,

Thanks for your kind letter. The way I think about the soul is simply as the place where God dwells. It is hard to distinguish it from ego, mind, self, DNA, simply because it is a spiritual concept. When I think about the soul, I think about myself as a child of God, infinitely loved and called to an eternal communion with God. My ego, mind, self and DNA are part of my mortal being, and I know that one day I have to let go of that. But my soul is eternal in me, that aspect of me where I am part of God's life. When I pray, I nurture my soul. When I care for the sick, dying and weak, I nurture my soul, and it is that soul in me that will be held eternally in God's embrace.

Thanks again for writing. I hope these few words give some hope and courage.

With warm greetings,
Yours,
Henri Nouwen

A letter to a friend who has lost his job.

MAY 29, 1991

Dear Hans and Marinus,

Many warm greetings from Toronto! Thanks for writing. It is really good to hear that you, Marinus, have found a new task. I know it is hard for you to let go of the work you had before, but I hope that you can live this pain and this feeling of rejection as a way to grow closer to the heart of Jesus and to enter into a deeper communion with the many people who suffer so much from a sense of abandonment. I know it is not easy to live that way, but, as I have lived through it myself, I dare to write it to you, trusting that you will receive it in a good way.

All is well in our community. We had a wonderful Easter season.

Please keep me in your prayers, and be sure that I will be in touch with you when I am back in Holland again.

Much love,
Henri

Richard Sipe is a mental health counselor and author who earlier had spent eighteen years as a Benedictine monk and priest. Henri met him while studying at the Menninger Foundation in Topeka, Kansas, in the mid-1960s. Sipe wrote about sexuality and priestly celibacy. (Later he would become a leading figure in helping the Church comprehend the dimensions of the clergy sex-abuse scandal.)

JULY 2, 1991

Dear Richard,

Thanks so much for sending me your talks of December 4th and of June 22nd.* I really appreciated hearing from you.

I wish we had more time to talk because I still have many ques-

---

* The talks referred to are: "Spirituality and Integrity," and "Remaining Credible Witnesses to Our Faith," Princeton Theological, December 4, 1990; "The Celibate/Sexual Agenda," CORPUS National Meeting, New York, June 22, 1991.

tions around your presentation on June 22nd. While many of the facts you mention are quite startling and really force us to think, I also feel there is a dimension to the issue of celibacy that is absent from your presentation and, by its absence, gives your presentation an overly strong "political" character. Somehow, I think that we really need to think more deeply about the mystery of communion and start talking in a new way about sexuality from there. I am certainly not yet able to do so, and I find myself quite wordless around this very sacred area. But I do feel that we have to move beyond pointing to the many weaknesses and failures in living a credible sexual ethic to a rediscovery of the deep meaning of the "vacare Deo" [Latin for "to be empty for God."]

I personally feel that you have a great vocation in this area especially since you are so articulate and well-informed about the many facts and figures of the issues involved. You have very important things to say, and I have the feeling that rediscovering or reliving the mystical dimension of the sexual life may help you and me and all of us to grow to a reclaiming of life's sacredness.

I very much enjoyed your "Spirituality and Integrity." I love the way that paper is put together, and I got a lot out of it.

Thanks so much for staying in touch. Both Sue [Mosteller] and I hope to see you again someday soon.

With warm greetings,
Yours,
Henri

Henri writes a letter of appreciation to Ari Goldman, a religion reporter for The New York Times, *whose book* The Search for God at Harvard *recounted his experiences during a sabbatical leave that he spent as a student at Harvard Divinity School.**

Dear Ari,

Thanks so much for writing *The Search for God at Harvard*. I read it with increasing appreciation and gratitude. What I would most like to say to you is how much I regret not having been at Harvard during the year you were there. It would have been such a joy for me to meet you and to talk with you about many of the concerns you express in your book. What you write about your own struggle to integrate your Sabbath observance with your life in the secular world speaks very deeply to me. Although my questions are different, my own struggle to create space for God in my life feels very much like yours.

While I was on the faculty at Harvard, I felt an increasing desire to have sacred space and time to be with my God, and I realize how hard it was for me to prevent the pulsating demands of the academic and social world around me from invading all empty space and time. The practice of "being empty for God" has been far from easy for me, but every time I was able to do it, I discovered that God spoke to me as concretely as he spoke to Jacob when he was sleeping with a rock for his pillow.

I am also very grateful for the many things you wrote about Harvard Divinity School and Weston School of Theology. I know all the people you mention, and I was very touched by the appreciation you express as well as the questions you raise. Both your appreciation and your critical questions reflect very much my own years at Harvard. You made me very aware again of the personal pain I felt when I realized that I couldn't stay there while still having a deep desire to continue to speak about the spiritual life and especially about the life of intimacy with God. Somehow, I knew

---

* Ari Goldman, *The Search for God at Harvard* (New York: Times Books, 1991).

that a long stay at Harvard would not allow me to deepen my own life of prayer and that, in the long run, I would have nothing to say unless I were able to strengthen that life of prayer day by day. So it is much more my own spiritual weakness that made me decide to leave than my criticisms of the Divinity School.

One paradox of my life at Harvard Divinity School is that, while I found it extremely difficult to live an integrated spiritual life there, I made many wonderful friends at Harvard. Many of the students I met at Harvard are still very present to me, and some of my deepest friendships were established during that time. Just a few days ago I became aware that the people I am still writing to and talking with on the phone and who still visit me are the people whom I met at the Divinity School. I also realized that these friendships were very much connected with the fact that they were developed in the context of a common life of prayer. During my last year at Harvard I lived at the Carriage House, which you will probably now remember as a classroom space. One of the rooms I had set aside as a room of prayer. Every morning quite a few Harvard Divinity School students from very different religious backgrounds came there just to pray silently and, at times, read some sacred texts together. It is mostly these encounters in silence and prayer that were the basis of relationships that are now still very much alive.

I was of course, sad to read that your time at Harvard wasn't a time in which you were able to come to an interior understanding of Jesus and his Gospel. I so much would have liked to share with you how I am trying to live a life in communion with Jesus and to hear from you where and how that connects with your own experience as an Orthodox Jew. Your book certainly helped me to see how your mitzvah-centered spirituality and my Jesus-centered mysticism are different, but your book also opens up for me many places where I can see how the differences can be made very fruitful.

Finally, I want to tell you a little bit about my close friendship with Fred Bratman. While I was teaching at Yale, Fred came to interview me for the Connecticut section of the *New York Times*. After the interview I asked him about his own life and work, and he expressed a great desire to find more time to write and read. Soon after that I was able to offer him a fellowship that allowed him to come for a year to the Yale Divinity School and be there as a scholar in residence. During that year we became very good friends, and that friendship has deepened and strengthened over the years. When I met Fred, he was not visiting a synagogue on any regular basis, but over the past years he has grown in appreciation of his own tradition and is now a very active member of a reformed synagogue close to Lincoln Center, in which area he also lives. Just a few months ago I attended his wedding and enjoyed very much being allowed to come so close to his family and his friends. I mention this to you because Fred has been a very important, loving but also critical, voice in my life and he continues to call me to a way of writing about the spiritual life that can speak to people like himself. Reading your book made me even more deeply aware of how much I had been influenced by Fred and how much I continue to feel strengthened by dialogue with my Jewish friends.

Well, this is just a way of saying how grateful to you I am for writing the book and how grateful I am that you are presently Religion correspondent for the *New York Times*.

With warm greetings and much gratitude,
Yours,
Henri Nouwen

Henri writes to his Dutch friend Antoinette, who is struggling with anxiety.

Dear Antoinette,

It was so good to hear from you again, and I am very happy that you felt comforted by my prayer and the prayer of the people in my community. Thanks also for keeping me in your prayers.

Meanwhile, I really wish you an ever deeper peace. I know that that peace quite often lives underneath the turmoils and anxieties of our heart and doesn't always mean inner harmony or emotional tranquillity. That peace that God gives us quite often is beyond our thoughts and feelings, and we have to really trust that that peace is there for us to claim even in the midst of our moments of despair. When, a few years ago, I had a car accident, I got a real glimpse of this peace that I certainly do not always experience directly, so I send you a copy of the book I wrote about it.* I hope it is of some help to you.

Thanks again for writing. May the peace and joy of Jesus continue to nurture you.

Yours,
Henri

Henri writes to his friend John Dear to congratulate him on his recent ordination to the diaconate.

Dear John,

Thanks so much for writing again. It was really good to hear from you. I appreciate very much your sending me a copy of your book

---

* *Beyond the Mirror: Reflections on Death and Life* (New York: Crossroad, 1990).

about Oscar Romero.* He certainly is a very important source of inspiration for me.

I am sorry we did not meet when I was in Oakland at the end of May. I came there to give a fund-raising lecture for the Bethany House for AIDS patients. Mike Harank, who is a good friend of mine, is in charge of the house and had asked me to help him a little bit. It was a brief but very wonderful visit, and I was really glad to see Mike's inspired work in Oakland.

The Gulf War has certainly been a horrible event. I was in Washington on the 14th of January at the National Cathedral to pray with many Church leaders in the hope the war could be prevented. Regretfully, the war started a few days later and we only lately know how much suffering it has brought. Reaction in Canada was probably a lot less nationalistic than in the United States, but the government decided to support the war militarily even against the desire of the majority of the people. But now it seems that people don't talk about it much anymore. It seems to be, in many ways, a forgotten event, horrible as it was. It certainly caused a lot of pain, and I have become more aware than ever of how hard it is to proclaim radically the peace of Jesus in a world that so quickly gravitates to violent solution of its problems.

Many congratulations on your Ordination to the Diaconate! As far as reflections about the priesthood are concerned, I am increasingly aware that the four words of the Eucharistic Prayer, "He took; he blessed; he broke; he gave," summarize not only the life and ministry of Jesus, but also the life and ministry of every priest. The priest is chosen by God to reveal the chosen-ness of God's people. The priest is blessed by God to reveal the blessedness of God's people. The priest is broken by God to help other people live their brokenness under the blessing, and the priest is given to the world to reveal to its people that they are given to bear fruit in this world.

_____

* John Dear, *Oscar Romero and the Nonviolent Struggle for Justice* (Erie, PA: Pax Christi USA, 1991).

One day I hope to write more about these words, but I thought I would give them to you as you prepare for the priesthood.* Be assured of my prayers, my love, and my support.

Yours,
Henri

To a reader who wrote about her mother's death, Henri addresses questions about eternity.

SEPTEMBER 3, 1991

Dear Marca,†

I am deeply grateful for the beautiful letter you wrote me about your mother's death and the way you have lived it. I am so grateful to read that my books and tapes could be of some support to you during this very difficult time. I admire your faith and your great love that is so beautifully expressed in your letter, and I am grateful that I have become such an intimate part of your life and the life of your family.

You are asking me if I have any thoughts about eternity and, more specifically, about what is going on in God's light. Enclosed I am sending you a little book I wrote for my father six months after my mother's death,‡ and also a little book that was the result of my own experience of death.§ I hope that both of these books can give you some sense of God's immense love for His people. My main

---

* These words would be explored in his book *Life of the Beloved: Spiritual Living in a Secular World* (New York: Crossroad, 1992).

† An excerpt from a letter by Marca to Henri about the impact of his counsel on how to live her mother's death is quoted in the preface.

‡ *In Memoriam* (Notre Dame, IN: Ave Maria Press, 1980).

§ *Beyond the Mirror: Reflections on Death and Life* (New York: Crossroad, 1990).

conviction is that God, who has loved us from all eternity, will hold us in that love through all eternity, and that love is stronger than death. That is the message of Jesus for us to say "yes" to the One who says to us, "You are my beloved; on you my favor rests." As I grow older, I experience more and more that the few years of my life are years in which I have the opportunity to give a great "YES" to the One who says to me, "I love you," and that our final death is a return to that sacred place of love from where we have come.

What goes on in the "light" is a continuation of the mutual love between God and his sons and daughters whom he calls to himself through his Beloved Son Jesus, and this mutuality of love is never-ending, always new, always joyful, always bringing new life and new beauty. The fact that we can't say much about it is only a sign of our human limitations, but God's love has no limitations and, as we enter more fully into that love, we will experience the fullness of life as we have not been able to experience it during our earthly existence.

Thanks so much for writing and for all the caring words you sent me. Give my special warm greetings to your father. I keep him very much in my thoughts and prayers.

With many blessings,
Yours,
Henri

Henri responds to his friend Walter, who has questions about the nature of life.

SEPTEMBER 13, 1991

Dear Walt,

So good to hear from you! I am realizing that I was only partially aware of all that you were living, and I am really grateful that you let me know more about what has happened to you in the past few years.

Maybe you should say that life as a constant attempt to survive in the competitiveness of our society is unfair, chaotic and brief, but that life as a gift of God, starting long before we were born and continuing after we have lived this brief sojourn, is not only fair, but very harmonious and long. The real struggle obviously is to somewhere integrate both realities with humor and with great hope.

I really hope and pray that you will find the kind of work that will give you life and energy and inspiration.

If you ever have time, it would be great to see you here for a few days. It has been so long and we have so much to catch up on. I really would love you to get to know our community and get a taste of what I am living here.

With warm greetings,
Yours,
Henri

Henri writes to Jean, a student from Bethany Theological Seminary, who has shared her essays about Henri's books.

SEPTEMBER 13, 1991

Dear Jean,

Many thanks for your very warm letter and for sharing with me the letters you wrote in response to my writing. I am really very impressed by the way you responded to what I have written, and I am deeply grateful that somewhere our lives have touched each other.

As you will have noticed from my writings, they came from a lot of struggle and pain, and I am very encouraged to realize that some of what I wrote connected with your own struggle and pain. In this way we could really form a fellowship of the weak where God can reveal his love to us. Lately I have been experiencing more and more how important it is that we claim our identity as the beloved sons and daughters of God. I know that at times, God seems so absent or so distant, but I trust that when you set aside a time and place to be alone with God, you will gradually be able to hear that soft, gentle voice that says "You are my beloved daughter; on you my favor rests." I very much hope that you will create for yourself the solitude in which that voice can be heard beneath the many noisy, often accusing and condemning voices of our world.

I am especially grateful that you found some strength in the prayers I wrote at the Abbey of the Genesee. They are still very real for me, but, over the years, I have moved from the intense anguish to a place of more inner rest. I am glad to tell you this because I really want you to know that we can truly grow into a deeper knowledge of being loved with an everlasting love and feel safe in that knowledge.

Meanwhile, I have just finished writing the text of [*The Return of*] *the Prodigal Son*, and I hope when the book comes out, which will not be before May, I will be able to send a copy to you.

Thanks again for sharing your letters with me. Be assured of my prayers and my care for you and your future.

With warm greetings,
Yours, Henri Nouwen

Henri writes to his friend Cathy, who was the primary caregiver for her gravely ill mother and was feeling inadequate to the task.

DECEMBER 2, 1991

Dear Cathy,

Thanks so much for your very kind letter. I have just returned from Europe and want you to know that I keep you close to my heart and to the heart of God.

It is so good to know you were touched during your visit here, and I hope that you will continue to have the strength to face without fear your mother's situation. Just keep giving her to God and trust that His love is stronger than death. Don't give in to your feelings of inadequacy, but keep thinking of yourself as the truly beloved daughter of God.

With warm greetings,
Yours,
Henri

Henri writes to a pastor of the United Church of Christ whom he met at the UCC Consultation XVII on Parish Ministry Conference in January 1992, in Orlando, Florida, where he was the keynote speaker. She had written about her feelings about being excluded from celebrating the Eucharist with a Catholic priest in a center for the World Community for Christian Meditation in Oakland, California.

JANUARY 31, 1992

Dear Judy,

Thanks so much for your kind letter. It was good to talk to you at Orlando, and I very much appreciate your writing and telling me about your experience at Holy Name College. I can very well understand your pain and suffering around what happened at the Eucharist, and I can identify with your feelings of being treated as an acolyte.

Having thought a little bit more about it, I feel that I have to write you that the situation you describe was a situation in which pain and conflict could hardly not come about whether on the side of the presiding priest or your own. I really think it was not very wise to invite you to be a con-celebrant in a Eucharist celebrated by a Catholic priest. At these moments in the Catholic Church, that creates tension whether we want it or not, and I think it is very important that we do not make the Eucharist a place where feelings are hurt and people are anxious. Although I very much wish that a greater unity in the Eucharist could be realized, the Catholic Church at this moment is not at that place, and I, therefore, feel that we should avoid celebrations that create pain either for the celebrant, the con-celebrant or the people who want to celebrate the Eucharist.

Personally, I feel it is important for us to explore areas of celebration that are conflict-free and that have a real sacramental quality. In Orlando, I told you how we often have a foot-washing ceremony at L'Arche, in which we do what Jesus asked us to do, and in which we can really experience deep unity and communion without conflict. I am really convinced that, within the larger context of sacramentality, there are other ways in which we can celebrate together that allow people from very different traditions to be together in a true spirit of unity and peace.

I very much hope that you can talk about these things with A. so that there can be a maximum of good feeling among the different members of the Hesed community.* I do not think it is wise for me to write to your community about our ecumenical experience in L'Arche, simply because I have to limit my own involvement with other communities, and I feel that our community has its own history and dynamics. I hope you understand my hesitation to become directly involved in the struggles, but I am deeply convinced that in conversations and sharing among you in the community, new life will emerge out of the painful situation you describe.

Be assured of my love and prayers.

With warm greetings,
Yours,
Henri Nouwen

Henri writes to his friend Steve, a bank branch manager, who is reevaluating his career as a result of a bank merger.

FEBRUARY 25, 1992

Dear Steve,

So good to hear from you! I think of you often, and I really appreciated very much talking to you on the phone and reading your letter.

As I think about your question of going or not going to Holden [Village, Chelan, Washington], my main question is how good it is for your spiritual journey. I am not too worried about it being an easy route or an escapist choice. Any period of time you can

---

* The Hesed Community was founded in 1981 in Oakland, California, and is part of the World Community for Christian Meditation, centered in London, England. The community is based upon Benedictine spirituality with a mission to teach and practice Christian meditation as taught by John Main, OSB.

claim for yourself to come to inner peace and to a deep inner sense of well-being in your relationship with God and God's people is worth all your time and attention.

On the other hand, I also want to say that, if you can find that kind of safety and spiritual nurture in Philadelphia, Holden seems to be less urgent or important.

Well, the main thing I want to tell you is to let your spiritual well-being be your main criterion and don't worry about the money, the job, your career or physical concerns. They will all be taken care of. "First the Kingdom, then the rest will fall into place." I still hope to have a chance to meet you in the future.

Much love,
Henri

Henri writes to encourage a friend, Ed Dufresne, a Protestant minister, whose long-term marriage is floundering.

MARCH 27, 1992

Dear Ed,

What a wonderful surprise it was to receive your loving and caring letter! It is so good to hear about the many developments in your life and of the new way in which you are living now. I really admire your openness to new directions and especially your willingness to be a "house husband" and live a more spirit-centered life. I certainly hope that you use this new situation to do more writing. You have a gift for that, and I trust that something very creative can come forth from your new solitude.

I obviously want to pray very specially for your relationship with Sandy and I do hope that you both can grow in friendship for one another and with a deep faith that God called you together to be a source of hope for each other, for your children, and for the many people connected with your lives. As you will know, the final ministry is not through what we say, but through what we live, and I realize more and more how hard it is to live a marriage well over a long period of time, but I really pray that you both will discover ever new ways of being together and letting the way you share your joy and pain be a sign of hope in this world.

Yours,
Henri

While at Daybreak, Henri was in charge of the spiritual life of the community. He directed all aspects of faith formation. Here, he writes on the meaning of the Eucharist to the parents of children preparing for their First Communion.

MARCH 30, 1992

Dear Kathy, Joe and Mary, Joan and Robin,

As you prepare Timmy, Patrick and Laura for their first Communion, I would like to send you a few thoughts, more for yourselves than for them. It might help you to put your instruction in a good context.

The Church becomes the Church in the Eucharist because there people come together in the name of Jesus and become one body by eating and drinking the same divine gifts. In a very profound sense, the Church means double fellowship. It is not simply that there is a Church that celebrates the Eucharist, but that, in celebrating the Eucharist, the Church becomes truly Church, i.e., the body of Christ.

St. Augustine said that Jesus is really present among those who come together in his name and form one body and, therefore, is also mystically present in the gifts of bread and wine they share. Later on, the terms have been reversed so that now we say Jesus is really present in the Eucharist and mystically present among those who come together in his name (the Church). This is just to explain that mystical and real are two words for the same truth and that we cannot claim the presence of Jesus in the Eucharist without claiming his presence among us as a people; and we cannot claim his presence among us as a people without claiming his presence in the Eucharist.

I also want to say to you that the Eucharist is the central Sacrament of the Church. It is the place through which God really enters into our lives. That is why you can look at the other six Sacraments as standing in a circle around the Eucharist. Baptism introduces us to the Eucharist; the Sacrament of Reconciliation restores us to the double fellowship of the Eucharist; ordination to the Priesthood is to set some people aside to preside over the Eucharist in the name of Jesus; Marriage is to bind husband and wife to each other in the same Faithfulness with which Jesus has bound himself to the Church; and Sacrament of the Sick is a Sacrament to heal people for an ongoing Eucharistic life and/or to prepare them to enter into the final, full communion with Jesus.

Thus the Eucharist is really the center of our spiritual life, and, if we live it that way, gradually all of our life can become Eucharistic, i.e., lived in deep communion with Jesus.

It also might be good to remember that the word Eucharist means Thanksgiving. By celebrating the Eucharist we give special thanks to God for our lives and dedicate ourselves to live our life in gratitude. The Eucharist is really meant to help us to become more intimately aware of life as a gift so that, whatever we do and with whoever we are in touch, we become ever more aware that all these moments are opportunities for a deeper communion with God's love.

These thoughts are not necessarily meant for the children, but simply to help you in your own spiritual growth as you prepare them. I hope they are of some help to you.

Much love,
Henri

Henri responds to a man who is trying to determine where God is calling him.

JUNE 9, 1992

Dear Ken,

Thanks so very much for your kind letter. It took me about five years to move out of the academic world and make the decision to join L'Arche. It was a slow, prayerful but very Spirit-led process. I hope this gives you some comfort when you are in a situation where you wonder where God is calling you. It is obviously terribly important that whatever you do will also find support and deep understanding from your wife. I am very much open to staying in touch with you in the months or year to come as you try to discern God's hand in your life. I know it is a hard and often painful journey, but I am deeply convinced that if you could keep saying the simple prayer of "Not my will, but Your will be done," you will gradually hear the gentle voice of God's love for you and come to know which direction he is leading you. It might be good in the year to come if you, and maybe your wife, could spend a few days in our community in Toronto. We could then have a chance to discuss in more depth your vocation. Be sure that I am keeping you in my prayers.

Warm greetings,
Yours,
Henri

After visiting Henri at Daybreak in February, his friend Lee Udell wrote to say that he was disappointed with the amount of time they had been able to spend together.

Dear Lee,

Thanks so much for your very good letter. I am really sorry I have been out of touch for such a long time. Many things have happened to me, and it has been very hard for me to be faithful to my friends.

The most important thing is that Connie, my secretary, had a brain tumor and was operated on Good Friday. The tumor proved to be malignant, and although she is home and well cared for, she is still very weak and obviously is no longer able to work with me. It has been a very hard setback for her and also for me, since she is such a beautiful person, a good friend and a faithful co-worker. I visit her regularly, and we have good conversations, but it is very clear that she tires quickly and that she needs a lot of emotional and physical support.

In the month of May I went for a few weeks to Germany and continued my travels with the group of German artists, with whom I have become good friends.* It was a very exciting time to go from town to town and to live close to these wonderful friends. My dream is to write a book about their life and their art. I was also able to spend a week with my publisher in Germany and a few days with my family in Holland.

Since I returned to Canada I have been very busy with lecturing

---

* Henri is referring to the Flying Rodleighs, the trapeze troupe he befriended after seeing them perform in Freiburg with the Simoneit-Barum Circus in April 1991.

in different places. Last Thursday I was in San Francisco to speak for a fund-raising lecture for two centers that help AIDS patients. It was a very moving and life-giving experience for me. On June 20, I went to Crystal Cathedral in Garden Grove, California, and on Father's Day I spoke at all the services there. Some day in the near future all of this will be televised, but I don't know when it will happen.*

Well, I am back home now until the first of August, trying to catch up with my work in the community and looking for someone to take Connie's place.

I was sorry to hear that you felt that we didn't have enough time together to process some of your personal issues. I really want to be as available as possible, and I am sad to realize that you have the feeling that I don't fully understand your special situation. I very much want to support your healing ministry, and I do believe in your great gift of healing through prayer.

I have a strong feeling that there is a real difference between your ability to heal others and your being healed from your own partial blindness. It seems to me important that you really continue to trust fully in your power to heal, while remaining free around the question of whether the Lord wants to heal you or not. I do have a sense that your concern about your own healing might get in the way of your ability to heal others, but Jesus was a wounded healer, and your own physical disability might in fact be a remarkable source of healing for others.

I do want to assure you that I will pray for you in a very special way in the coming days and weeks, and really ask God to give you a full insight into the meaning and fruitfulness of your illness.

Enclosed I am sending you a copy of The [Return of the] Prodigal

---

* Henri spoke on the Hour of Power television program on August 23 and 30, and September 6, 1992. Crystal Cathedral Ministries was a congregation of the Reformed Church in America, founded in 1955 by Robert H. Schuller.

Son, with much love and hope that you can find there some comfort and consolation in your own struggles. As you can see, I have not hidden my own.

Yours,
Henri

A letter of consolation to a young man who has lost his best friend to suicide.

JULY 24, 1992

Dear Ashok,

Yesterday your mother told me about the sudden death of your dear friend Nevin. Ever since she spoke to me about this, I have been thinking a lot about you and about the deep pain, confusion and inner anguish that you must be experiencing. I realize that you and Nevin were very close friends, and his sudden death must be really ripping you apart and making you feel very lost and filled with questions for which there are no answers.

I am really happy that I can write to you simply to let you know that I feel very deeply for you and I wish I could really be of support to you at this very hard moment in your life. I know you are asking yourself why did Nevin die, why did I lose my best friend, why is my life so coldly interrupted, why could we not prevent this from happening? I really do not have any answers for these questions. I don't know why, and I know that makes it so hard for you to live through this period of grief. Even though I do not have any answers to the many why's, I still want to write to you and tell you that I am convinced that your friendship with Nevin was certainly not in vain and the good things that existed between the two of you will not get lost, because real love and real friendship is stronger than death. Whenever two people love each other well, that love is eternal.

As a Christian I often think about the words of Jesus, who said just before he died, "It is good for you that I go, because unless I go I cannot send you my spirit." I hope that somehow you can hear that Nevin is saying something like this to you: although I am leaving you, Ashok, I am not leaving you alone, I am sending you my spirit of friendship and love. I hope you can really believe that although Nevin died, his spirit, his love, his joy, his peace will remain and will continue to nurture your heart.

You are in great pain now and feel great sadness, but I trust deeply that as you live this pain and feel tears coming to your eyes, you can trust that Nevin's love and friendship will enter your heart more deeply and that you will find the strength to live on with the knowledge that he will continue to guide you and support you. I am sure that Nevin wants you to be a hopeful and a very fruitful person, and I know that you will find the strength to live up to Nevin's deepest desire.

Dear Ashok, please do not feel that you could in any way have done anything to prevent his death. Maybe there are places in your heart where you feel that you have not done enough for him, or maybe there are places in your heart where you are angry that he left you alone. I very much understand these feelings because I have had them too when dear friends died, but I really want you to know that Nevin's death in no way is your fault, nor that he wanted to hurt you in any way by leaving you.

Trust that you are a very good person and that you are deeply loved by God and that your friendship was a gift given to you that will bear fruit in your life as you continue living it.

If you would ever like to get together with me and talk, I will be very happy to do that. Feel free to call me or visit me any time you like. Enclosed I am sending you my address.

With warm greetings and wishing you much hope, courage and confidence.

Yours,
Henri Nouwen

Henri writes to a reader about how to comfort her parish priest whose parents have recently been killed in a car accident. He emphasizes being willing to sit with feelings of powerlessness.

JULY 27, 1992

Dear Susan,

Many thanks for your very kind letter. I am very grateful for what you write about my *Letter of Consolation* and *Beyond the Mirror.* I really hope and pray that you can be of support to Josh in these days of his grief. As you know, it is not a question of particular words or ideas but just your willingness to be there for him and to be willing to have few words, to experience the feeling of being powerless in the face of death.

Enclosed I am sending you a little book that I wrote shortly after the death of my mother, *In Memoriam.* This might also give some comfort and love.

Warm regards,
Yours,
Henri Nouwen

Henri writes to a young friend who is struggling with intimacy and loneliness. He refers to a short hospitalization in June to receive care for a serious infection.

JULY 30, 1992

Dear Terry,

What a joy it was to receive your long and very lovely letter. It certainly was a pleasure that it was easy to read! As you know, in the past your handwritten letters asked for some real work! Thanks so much for telling me about what has happened to you during the last year.

I am so grateful that you shared that with me, and I can really sense in your letter a new openness, freedom and courage to be intimate and to let people know you more deeply.

Reading your letter, I was really moved by the warmth that you radiated and by the honesty and openness with which you shared your life with me. I know that many questions remain unanswered and the direction of your life is not yet fully clear to you, but I do believe that God is being very active in your heart, making you less fearful and more trusting. I know the experience of deep loneliness and you will most likely experience that again in the future, but I have a sense that you are embracing your loneliness more directly and allowing your friends to enter it with you. That gives me real confidence that your pain and your struggle will bear ample fruit.

On Friday I am leaving for a month's vacation. I am really happy to have this time to read and write. I am quite tired, especially as a result of a severe infection that got me into the hospital for a week, but I am fine now and getting my strength back quickly.

Thanks again for writing and be sure of my love and affection. Maybe we will talk on the phone before I leave.

Yours,

Henri

As mentioned in his letter to Lee Udell on June 25, in June of 1992, Henri was the keynote speaker at a conference held by Kairos and Bethany House, a Catholic Worker house of hospitality for people living with HIV/ AIDS, in San Francisco, California. Henri spoke on "Support and Recognition for Persons Dealing with HIV and Special Acknowledgement of Their Caregivers."

In this letter, Henri responds to a man who attended the lecture and is upset that some of the talk went against his understanding of Catholic teaching.

SEPTEMBER 1, 1992

Dear Mark,

Many thanks for your very good letter. I am very sorry that my lecture in San Francisco created some questions in you about my faithfulness to the teaching of the Catholic Church. That is the last thing that I would want to have happened.

I did not want to make any statement about homosexual unions, nor did I want to deny the uniqueness of Jesus Christ. What I did want to say was that those who are facing death are invited by Jesus to make their death a way to greater fruitfulness, just as the fruits of Jesus' life only became visible long after he had died and the fruits of our lives will only become visible long after we have died. It is very important that we prepare ourselves well for our deaths so that our dying can become the beginning of a new fecundity.

I also want to say that it is important that we realize the presence of God's Spirit "who blows where he wants" in Judaism, Buddhism, Hinduism and the faith of the Moslems.

I am deeply convinced that Jesus is completely unique in the world as the full revelation of God's life, but I also believe that many people can come to Christ even when they have never formally known Christ or had the opportunity to accept him. The final judgment, as Jesus says, is not based on whether or not they have known Jesus but whether or not the people have cared for those who are hungry, naked, prisoners; all the people in need.

Thanks so much for asking these questions. I hope that I have put your heart at peace. Warm regards.

Yours,
Henri

Henri writes to Nathan from Freiburg, Germany, where he is on a writing retreat, working on a book about death and dying, later published as Our Greatest Gift: A Meditation on Dying and Caring *(San Francisco: HarperSanFrancisco, 1994).*

Seven years after the breakdown of their friendship, the two men have reconciled and now enjoy visiting, working together and exchanging letters of support and encouragement. Henri is nine days away from his sixty-first birthday.

JANUARY 15, 1993

Dear Nathan,

After much outer and inner movement I am back in Freiburg. Thanks so much for welcoming me back in Toronto and bringing me back to the airport. That gave me a true sense of belonging and made all these movements more livable. Your friendship and support are very life-giving for me. Without it I would feel very lost. Interiorly I am often very needy and lonely, and knowing that you are there, in a very concrete tangible way, gives me a sense of rootedness. Thanks so very much. Your Christmas letter was also a real gift and offered me much inner safety.

I am very glad to be in Freiburg again. The weeks before Christmas had been much too full and intense for me, and the return to Toronto and all the events around Maurice's death,* as well as the trip to Holland with all the events around my father's birthday,† squeezed most energy out of me. Since I returned here I have been sleeping most of the time. At the moment every new encounter seems too much. But my body and mind are finding gradually some new balance and all the aches are vanishing little by little.

In Holland I spoke for L'Arche and had a very interesting meeting with the directors of eight large organizations who oversee many homes and institutions for people with mental handicaps. I was deeply impressed with their openness to L'Arche and to me personally but also with their great sophistication and progressive attitudes in the field of mental retardation. We have a lot to learn from them. They offered me a tour of all their institutions. Maybe one day we should do this together. On the spiritual level they were very open and eager to learn, but also open and eager to teach.

I am more and more convinced of the importance to keep a large vision on life. Daybreak can easily become so all absorbing that we lose perspective and become over anxious. When I see the enormous upheavals in Europe, the radical spiritual changes, the economic struggles in the world and the unbelievable human

---

* Maurice "Moe" Gould was a core member at L'Arche Daybreak who lived with Henri in the Green House before developing Alzheimer's disease and needing more intensive care.

† Henri's father, Laurent J. M. Nouwen, turned ninety on January 3, 1993. Henri and the Nouwen family gathered for the special occasion at his home in Geijsteren, Netherlands. Henri conducted Mass for the family at the local church, Sint Willibrorduskerk, Geijsteren.

sufferings all over the planet, I am able to think about our life together in L'Arche in a freer and more grateful way. I felt that freedom and gratitude also in you when we were together in Swissotel. Somehow a deep knowledge of our world, its history and present condition can help us a lot to live our small lives with joy and peace, even when much of that knowledge is a knowledge of human pain.

Meanwhile, I hope that the last two weeks have been good for you and that you feel confident in your work and daily life. I was very glad with the new confidence you have in your own leadership. It is so important for you to trust in your own gifts as shepherd of our community, especially when you experience resistance or criticism. I frankly feel that Daybreak is one of the most exciting communities in the church, and your leadership has a lot to do with that.

I hope to be able to write soon. It always takes me long to find the inner silence I need to write. But now even more than ever since I am so "wound up" by all that took place during the last few months. Writing requires such a completely different mind-set than flying around and giving talks and asking people's attention. I need to go from the most out-going to the most in-going attitude. That takes time and patience, but I trust that it will happen.

But I did some "small" work. I finished editing the circus diary for the *New Oxford Review** and wrote five responses to manuscripts by others (Jean Vanier, Gary Smith, friend of David Rothrock, Fred Bratman, Joe Basini and Richard White). It's good to read and reflect on other people's work, but I better start on my own now.

Be sure of my love and affection.

Henri

---

* This article was published in two parts: "Finding the Trapeze Artist in the Priest," *New Oxford Review* 60, no. 5 (June 1993): 8–14, and "Finding a New Way to Get a Glimpse of God," *New Oxford Review* 60, no. 6 (July–August 1993): 6–8, 10–13.

FEBRUARY 4, 1993

Dear Nathan,

Just a little note on a beautiful Rembrandt card.* Rembrandt painted this portrait of his son in a time full of unrest, with the black plague going on around him and much political upheaval. We have forgotten most of the misery of the 17th century but this portrait is still there to lift up our spirits.

I keep thinking about this as I wonder what to *do* when all around me there is so much human suffering. Rembrandt seems to say that it is important to do well the few things we can do and remain faithful to our vocation, limited as it may seem.

Niebelschütz,† a German novelist, wrote once: "during a time when people can't see the abyss, it is important to show the abyss. But during a time when everyone sees the abyss, showing the abyss brings Owls to Athens. It is not the task of art to carry owls but to be Athens."

Well, all of this to defend my decision not to go anywhere for a while and to trust in the fruitfulness of being and staying in my hermitage.

Love,
Henri

---

* Rembrandt van Rijn, *Portrait of the Artist's Son, Titus*, 1653.
† Wolf Friedrich Magnus von Niebelschütz.

Henri writes to a gathering of youth for a social justice weekend. He declined an invitation to be the keynote speaker but writes to the participants of the event with some reflections on the subject of fruitfulness.

FEBRUARY 5, 1993

Dear Friends,

Many warm greetings from Germany. I am spending here a few weeks to pray, read and write and live a little solitude after much action here and there!

I pray for you as you meet for your Social Justice weekend, and I very much hope that your time together will be fruitful.

Fruitfulness is what Jesus calls us to. Not successfulness. Successes come from strength and power. Fruits are born in weakness. Jesus was born in weakness and died in weakness. His life was a failure but very fruitful.

Your fruitfulness starts in community. When you come together as a fellowship of the weak always willing to forgive and be forgiven, then you start experiencing the fruits of the Spirit among you: peace, joy, gentleness, perseverance and, most of all, love. These are the fruits that the world is waiting for. These fruits will not be brought by individual heroes or great stars who know what everybody should do, but by small communities of faith who are like lights in the midst of our darkness. Such communities always need to focus on the poor, the physically poor, the mentally poor, the emotionally poor, the spiritually poor. We need to focus on the poor, not primarily because the poor need us, but because we need the poor. Jesus says: "Blessed are the poor." He does not say: "Blessed are those who care for the poor." The poor are holding a blessing for us that we need to receive. As receivers of the blessing of the poor, we can bring justice to the world. All injustice somehow comes from looking down on the poor and not expect-ing anything from them. We first of all have to discover Jesus in those who come to us in their poverty. Then we won't burn out caring for them and walking with them.

All of this requires that you yourselves are also in touch with your own poverty. You too carry a blessing precisely there where you feel weak. But trust that in your weakness you have a gift for others, a gift you should not hide.

Here in Europe enormous upheavals are taking place. There is much violence, much hatred, much displacement of people, much homelessness and hunger. Much, very much, injustice. We have to do any possible thing to heal these wounds of injustice, whether in Europe, North America or Africa, Asia and Australia. But we have to do this not in a spirit of fear, panic or alarm. We need to work for justice in the deep knowledge that Jesus has already overcome the world and that all our actions flow forth from this spiritual knowledge. This spiritual knowledge will grow deeper in us when we remain faithful to a life in community always dedicated to care for the poor. There you will find true joy and peace and this joy and peace will help you to discern where and how to make your life a life for justice in this world.

Be sure to pray much, that is, to keep your inner eye focused on Jesus. When you will discover Jesus within you, you will also be able to recognize him around you and have the energy to care for him. Also be very good to each other. You need good friendship and a lot of affection. You deserve it as God's beloved daughters and sons, sisters and brothers of Jesus.

I think of you and pray for you and wish you a wonderful joy-and peace-filled weekend.

Henri Nouwen

✦

Henri writes to his friend Walter, who is going through a painful separation from his wife and is struggling with self-rejection and feelings of worthlessness.

APRIL 12, 1993

Dear Walt,

Many thanks for your letter. Although you feel so low after trying to deal with so many inner struggles, I am really grateful that you write me about it and keep in touch. I really wish I could fly over and be with you for a few days, but regretfully this is not possible in the near future, but if it is at all possible for you to fly over here, I would love to pay your ticket and have you spend some time with us again.* I really feel you need support in this difficult time of your life, and I would love to offer it in any way I can.

The great temptation that you struggle with is self-rejection and feeling so low about yourself that you can hardly remember how much you have to offer. You are a beautiful person and a very gifted man, and it is important that you do not let Jet make you believe otherwise. In the separation between you and Jet it is really important that you are not loading all the guilt and blame on yourself, and certainly do not allow Jet's rejection to make you feel worthless. So please try to hold on to your own goodness and really stay in touch with me as much as you can. I would love to hear from you soon. Please call me in my room collect.

Much love,
Yours,
Henri

---

* Walter had visited Henri at Daybreak on February 29, 1992.

*Henri writes to an academic, Grace Adolphsen Brame, who has started
writing about spirituality for the Lutheran Church. She has received some
negative comments about earlier publications—"Lutherans aren't ready for
this"—and is discouraged.*

APRIL 19, 1993

Dear Grace,

Many thanks for your very kind letter. I very much hope that you
and Ed [Dufresne]* can work well together to call members in the
Lutheran church to a deeper and more intimate prayer life. Do
not be too surprised by the kind of response you are receiving. I
encounter that response all over, but on the other hand there will
always be people, even though a small group, who will respond
very deeply and very receptively to what you have to say. In the area
of spirituality, statistics do not count. Two or three people who
hear you well, may be able to do miracles. Thank you so much for
your letter.

Warm regards,
Yours,
Henri

*Henri was frequently asked for blessing and prayers, even by people who
didn't know him personally—in this case, at the request of a daughter for
her parents' twenty-fifth wedding anniversary.*

---

* Henri has connected these two Lutherans who are interested in spirituality and
the Lutheran church.

Dear Rick and Bonnie,

May the Lord bless you and fill you with joy and peace as you celebrate the 25th anniversary of your marriage.

May the Lord give you the deep trust that He will bring to fulfilment the work that He has begun in you. May He give you confidence that as you grow older and maybe weaker, His strength and His grace will manifest themselves more and more in you.

May he give you hope in His promise that whatever happens in your lives and the lives of your family, He is always with you and walks with you to guide your mind and your heart.

And most of all, may the Lord give you a deep gratitude not only for all the beautiful moments of your lives, but also for the times of struggle and pain that have purified your hearts and made you more aware of your great dependence on His love.

On this very special day I also pray for all those who are dear to you—your family and your friends—that they may celebrate in a very special way the great gift that you have been in their lives.

Sincerely,
Henri Nouwen

Henri writes to his friend Peggy, whose Jewish and Catholic roots have raised questions as to how to live her faith identity.

Dear Peggy,

Thanks so much for your good letter. Don't worry about bothering me or overwhelming me with your problems. I trust in our friendship, and it is very good for me to know what you are living and what you are thinking.

I really appreciate what you say about the conflict between your Jewish roots and the Catholic faith. I think it is very important to claim your Judaism, but knowing you and knowing all that you have lived, I also feel that Jesus has called you in a very special way and that He wants you to live your Judaism with Him and be supported by Him. It is so tragic that the Judaic tradition and the Catholic tradition have become so separate, and you might really be called to live the close connection of the two. The Catholic faith cannot exist unless it keeps rooting itself in the Judaic tradition, and I therefore don't think that your deep love for Jesus and your praying to him are really in conflict with your Judaic heritage.

Please don't think of yourself as a hypocrite. It is good for you to keep reading religious poetry at the nursing home even when at times you might not be fully able to live yet what you are reading. This is what I experience myself every day and God is asking me to be humble but not to give up my call to be a spiritual leader for others.

Be sure to stay close to your Catholic friends in Newton [Massachusetts]. God is such a great gift.

Much love,
Henri

Henri responds to a reader who has written both to encourage him in his writing and to reflect on his own struggles with faith.

Dear Bill,

Many thanks for your very beautiful, caring and strongly encouraging letter. It really means a lot to me that you consider my voice
of such importance. I think you are right that I am not too aware
of it. Although I am quite aware that many people do appreciate
my writings very much, I have never given them the value that you
are giving to them, and I am grateful that you ask me to be more
fully aware of my responsibility and my call within the contemporary world because that is what I am hearing when I claim my
importance. I should also claim my great responsibility.

Thank you for the personal story you tell me. I just recently
have been reflecting in a new way on the story of the disciples
who went to Emmaus, and I wonder if your "loss of faith" is not
in some way similar to theirs. We often have to rediscover Jesus
Christ in a whole new way, a more interior and a more spiritual
way. I have been struck by the fact that when they recognized Jesus
in the "breaking of the bread" he disappeared before their eyes, so
there is a deep connection between recognizing and disappearing,
between presence and absence, between knowing and not knowing. I often wonder if for those who really leave the spiritual life
there is not a real crisis to be faced that comes about in the later
years. It is a crisis of a second loneliness, a loneliness we should not
try to get rid of, which is the place where we can rediscover Jesus.
Not the Jesus who we knew in the past but the spirit of Jesus who
can really fill our hearts and senses and help us to live in the midst
of our mad world.

Enclosed I am sending you a book that I recently wrote and in
which I share some of my own journey.* I hope it speaks to you.
Please keep me in your prayers. I really need it, and pray especially

---

* He likely sent *The Return of the Prodigal Son: A Meditation on Fathers, Brothers, and
Sons* (New York: Doubleday, 1992).

for me as you say the rosary. I feel really cared for by you, and I will be grateful with the special place in your prayers. Thanks so much for your wonderful and loving letter.

Yours,
Henri

This is a letter to a reader who wonders how to live with loneliness.

JANUARY 20, 1994

Dear Olga,

Many thanks for your very beautiful letter. I am deeply moved by what you write about your search for intimacy and your discovery that a new sense of freedom might indeed be an alternative to inter-personal addiction. I personally believe deeply that our loneliness can be a gateway to the special knowledge of a real presence which goes beyond intellectual understanding or emotional experience, and as you already indicated in your letter, we can choose to live our loneliness as a way to discover this presence, a presence that liberates us from a search for intimacy that frustrates us by its ongoing unfulfilment. I really do believe that God is giving you a glimpse of the mystery that goes beyond all understanding and feeling.

Thanks again for your kind letter.

Warm regards,
Yours,
Henri

Henri writes to his friend Alan Johnson, a Protestant minister who has just suffered a stroke.

JANUARY 21, 1994

Dear Alan,

Many thanks for your wonderful letter. I really appreciate that you took the time and energy to write me such a lovely letter, and I am especially grateful that your stroke affirmed your conviction that God is intimate and personal. Do not worry about not feeling a strong pull from Jesus. What the people around you do with you and for you, that is Jesus coming to you. When you want to deepen your more direct relationship with Jesus, you might say the Jesus Prayer, "Lord Jesus Christ, have mercy on me" in a simple way, repeating it gently and lovingly.

Thank you also for sending me a copy of your message to the UCC [United Church of Christ] Consultation on Parish Ministry. I was very moved by it. I hope you keep trusting that beyond the self there is always the spirit of Jesus who prays in you and dwells in you even when your mind cannot make all the connections.

Meanwhile I and our community really pray for you and Martie [Johnson's wife], and we really hope that maximum healing will take place. We all love you a lot and want to assure you of our affection and friendship and many, many prayers.

Yours,
Henri

Writing to Geraldine, a Sunday school teacher in Minnesota, Henri shares his thoughts about Mary.

FEBRUARY 2, 1994

Dear Geri,

Many thanks for your kind letter. I really appreciate your kind words, and I am happy that *The Return of the Prodigal Son* and *In the Name of Jesus* spoke to your pastor and to you. Regarding your concern about Mary, I really do think about Mary as the mother of God, the human person who brought God into the world. Thus we can say that Mary is the one through whom God entered the human race. As the mother of God, she has been closest to Jesus, and because of that intimacy we can see the fullness of redemption and the fruits of God's work through Jesus, which is most visible through her, and since she is the one who is closest to Jesus, praying to her simply means asking Mary to lead us to a closer intimacy with her son. Of all human beings she is the one who understands Jesus best. Who would be a better guide than Mary to let Jesus be born into us.

Enclosed I am sending a small book that I wrote about Mary, and maybe that might help you to understand a little better the role of Mary in the mystery of salvation.* Feel free to write again. I would be glad to respond to any questions you might have.

Warm regards,
Yours,
Henri

---

* *Jesus and Mary: Finding Our Sacred Center* (Cincinnati: St. Anthony Messenger Press, 1993).

Henri writes to a Dutch friend who is being ordained as a Catholic priest.

MARCH 29, 1994

Dear Norbert,

During the days of your ordination to the priesthood and the celebration of your first Eucharist, I want to be very present to you. I want to be present to you as a friend who loves you a lot, as a fellow priest who wants to offer you encouragement and support and as a "little prophet" who wants to challenge you to live your vocation faithfully, joyfully and with great hope. What I most want to say to you is that living a deep and intimate relationship with your Lord Jesus will allow you to be a source of healing for many people as you walk through life full of contradictions, conflicts and violence. I also want to say to you how important it is to be surrounded by good, caring friends who will hold you close to Christ by their affection, their care and their encouragement. Finally, I want you to fully trust that when you stay close to Jesus and to those who in the name of Jesus will embrace you with their love, you cannot be other than a source of life to others.

You know that Jesus spent the night in prayer on the mountain top, he formed community with his apostles in the morning and spent the afternoon ministering to others. Everybody who touched him was helped. I really pray that you also will be spending your "nights" in prayer, spending a significant amount of time to form community around you and will move out into the world with the conviction that those who will touch you will experience healing.

I am so glad that you are committing yourself to Jesus in this unique way, and I just want you to know that I surround you with my love and prayers.

Yours,

Henri

The Jesuit Father John Dear was serving a prison sentence in Edenton, North Carolina, as a result of his participation in a Plowshares protest against nuclear weapons. While offering friendship and support, Henri describes his own busy life.

MAY 17, 1994

Dear John,

It is so good to hear from you, and I am grateful for all that you are sharing with me. There was a time in which I thought about prison as a place where I could be quiet, pray and write, but your story makes it very clear that all of this is pure fantasy. I am deeply aware of the suffering that the noise and the restlessness around you creates. For me that too would be the greatest source of pain. Hopefully you can gradually find some inner silence and inner space in the midst of all the clamor and shouts. It certainly must ask for a generous discipline.

As far as my life is concerned, I have been extremely busy. I went to Edmonton, Vancouver and Mobile, Alabama, to give retreats to L'Arche communities there and to help them in their fund-raising. There were always large groups of people who came to the talks, and mostly I did not have much time for myself. After most of the presentations there were two hours of signing books and talking with individual people about their struggles and pains. I really want to be very attentive to people's suffering, but after a long time of listening I often feel very exhausted and sometimes a little depleted and am in need for a more intimate space, and my desire for personal friendship always grows in these situations. I also went to Houston, [to] Fort Worth and to Manhattan and to Rye, New York, with two members of my community to speak about L'Arche and to offer some reflections on solitude, community and care. Although these retreats were very intense and demanding spiritually as well as emotionally, at the same time I felt that many good things happened and people felt called to a deeper relationship with God and a deeper knowledge of their call to live in community. Now I am back in my community for a few days, trying to keep up with the mail and with all the community events. Next week I will give a seven-day covenant retreat in Toronto. On the 2nd of June I will receive an honorary degree from the Chicago Theological Society and then I fly on to Brussels to give two L'Arche retreats in Belgium and Holland.

In between I hope to have a few days vacation and during that time I plan to visit my trapeze friends in a German circus. I have been close to them for the last four years, and I have a great dream to write a small book about the life of these trapeze artists. In July I am planning to go back to Chicago for the Catholic AIDS Ministry Conference at Loyola University. I hope to go with three other members of my community. Rodney DeMartini, the organizer of the conference, has asked me to give the final meditation at the end of the conference. I also hope to have a week of retreat myself with the Camaldolese monks at Big Sur, together with a friend of mine. In August I am going with three members of my community to Ukraine for two weeks to offer a retreat there for several youth organizations.

Well, this just gives you a little idea about my life. As you can see, it has been quite intense, busy and often quite tiring and emotionally quite draining, but I am also very grateful for the opportunity to do all of this and to announce good news to people and give them some new hope, courage and confidence.

A few weeks ago I, together with Sr. Sue Mosteller of my

community, took part in the "Street Level Conference" in Toronto. It is a conference where all those who work with street people in Canada came together. Most of them were Evangelicals. It was a very inspiring time, and I was deeply impressed with the great dedication and the great love of Jesus that many of these street level workers have. I continue to be impressed by so much goodness that exists between so much darkness and so much evil, and in this sense I am constantly surprised by joy. One of my main problems remains to find time to write. Hopefully the future will be less busy. Next year L'Arche Daybreak celebrates its 25th Anniversary, and I am planning to stay most of that year, September–July, 1995, in Toronto. After that I plan to take a sabbatical and focus more on my writing. I hope it will work out that way. Meanwhile, I think about you with much love and affection, and I want to do any possible thing to give you support. Never hesitate to ask me anything that you think I can do for you. I have never spent time in prison, but I realize that prison is one of the places where the poor are and where Jesus is very present. Thank you for your great love for God, for your great love for all those who suffer and especially for your friendship with me.

Much love,
Yours,
Henri

Earlier in the year, Henri had answered his friend Geraldine's questions about Mary. In this letter he responds to a question about the doctrine of Purgatory.

Dear Geraldine,

May thanks for your kind letter. I really appreciate hearing from you. The question about purgatory is not easy to answer, since it is a question that has to with what happens to us after death. After our death, when we are no longer in the mortal body, there is no time and no space. I do believe that purgation is necessary to face God, but how it happens is hard to say since it has nothing to do with a physical time or space. The doctrine of purgatory is a doctrine to assure us that God will fulfil our deepest desire to be united with him even when our heart is not totally pure yet. God will then offer us this purification. So it has very little to do with punishment. It is an expression of God's infinite desire to unite himself with us, and in that sense, as a doctrine, purgatory offers consolation and help.
   Warm regards.

Yours,
Henri

Henri responds to a reader about inclusivity and the Eucharist.

Dear Phyllis,

Many thanks for your wonderful letter. What a gift it is to hear from you and to read about your very warm response to my witting. It means so much that you have come to God in such a beautiful way. I also am really moved by the way you have rediscovered the Eucharist. I very much understand your deep pain around the fact that often the church excludes non-Catholics from the

Eucharist. I personally find it extremely painful, and I have found myself often in a situation where the pastoral and spiritual reality of the moment lead me to a much more inclusive ministry. The only thing that I can say to you is that I have felt the pain in my own heart that you have felt, and I keep hoping and praying that the church will be more and more able to offer the Eucharistic hospitality to all people around the table who realize that Jesus is very present. Personally I am deeply convinced that Jesus' ministry is inclusive as well as compassionate, and I keep hoping and praying that the church will find ways to live that on a daily basis.

Thank you so much also for your beautiful prayer.

Enclosed I am sending you a little book on the Eucharist that was just published.*

Warm regards,
Yours,
Henri

Henri writes to a Canadian woman working in South Africa for an agency documenting human rights abuses, particularly violence against women. She met Henri during a visit to Daybreak in 1994 and has written him for direction about how to respond to a "brutalized society." The letter is written four days before his sixty-third birthday.

JANUARY 20, 1995

Dear Karen:

Many thanks for your very kind letter that you wrote on December 5th. I very vividly remember your time at Daybreak and your

---

* *With Burning Hearts: A Meditation on the Eucharistic Life* (Maryknoll, NY: Orbis, 1994).

feelings about returning to South Africa. We prayed for you at that time and hoped that God would protect you as you entered this violent and dangerous situation. I am very glad to hear what you have lived since you were last here, and I very much appreciate hearing about the joys as well as the great pain of your ministry. Reflecting on your letter, I really feel that the voice within that calls you to a more contemplative kind of peaceful ministry is a voice you have to take very seriously. Your fatigue, exhaustion and depression suggest to me that the time has come for you to move in a new direction. Just as I finally realized that I would not be able to live out my ministry in the complexity of Latin America, so I also feel that you are now discovering that God might call you to something more communal, more nurturing, more prayerful and more life-giving.

Sometimes we have to go through a period of exhaustion and depression to find our true call. I deeply sympathize with what you are living, especially since I have lived it myself. My question for you is not what it takes to be really compassionate in a brutalized society but what is God's unique call for you in this time of your life. You might discover that a life that is life-giving to you in a very real way also is the life that can be real witness in our brutalized society. I am also very aware that you were deeply touched by L'Arche, and it might be good to stay in touch with some of the L'Arche communities, to listen there with the people with mental handicaps to God's call for you.

Maybe it would be wonderful if you could spend a few weeks at Trosly at "La Ferme," the retreat center,* and listen to God in solitude but surrounded by gentle people. Thanks so much for writing me, and please feel free to write again so that we can continue to be in dialogue with one another.

Much love,
Yours,
Henri

---

* This is a retreat center for L'Arche located in Trosly-Breuil, France.

Henri writes to a good friend and benefactor who is nearing retirement and struggling with health, work and family issues.

FEBRUARY 20, 1995

Dear Ron,

The last few weeks have been quite full for me with travelling and lectures and Daybreak things, but I have constantly felt a desire to write to you and express to you my friendship and my gratitude. I wish you could have been here with Julie [Ron's wife] for the Gala.* It was such a high moment for our community, and many things happened during that weekend that were much more than just a successful performance. Our community really came together in a new way and experienced a lot of new energy to move toward the next phase of our life together, but it was certainly good that Julie could come and witness that event.

My talks with Julie have made it clear to me that life has not been terribly easy for you, the struggle with your eyes, the struggle with Francis [their son] and also the struggles at your work. I often think of you and pray for you as I realize that you are living something difficult at this juncture, and I wanted to offer you my friendship and support especially as you live these many pressures.

Maybe it is important to live all of this as a transition. A transition to a new way of being, a new way of handling life, a new way of praying to God. It is a transition from successfulness to fruitfulness, from competition to compassion, from doing to being, from

---

* Henri is referring to the "One Heart at a Time" twenty-fifth anniversary gala of L'Arche Daybreak, held February 3 and 4, 1995, at the Winter Garden Theatre (Toronto, Ontario). The gala consisted of skits performed by Daybreak's dance troupe, the Spirit Movers, and by other members of the L'Arche Daybreak community, including Henri.

asking to praising. It is probably one of the hardest transitions in our life since it calls us to let go of many old ways of living and to trust that something radically new is being born. Personally I believe that being an elder can be a real grace. After having seen so much of life and having made it in so many ways, there is still that possibility of growing into a second childhood, a second naiveté. I think that is quite an exciting possibility, and I pray that God will allow you to be reborn in such a new way of being.

I am deeply grateful for the many ways that you have supported my community and myself. It means a lot to me that you are not only interested in the Dayspring project* but also in my own writing. I am looking forward very much to my sabbatical that starts in September, and I hope that during that time I can write things I have not been able to write so far, things about the spirit, things about love and about hope. It is really wonderful to know that you are there to encourage me and to give me strength, so be sure of my deep gratitude. I very much look forward to seeing you when I am in New York at the end of March. Be sure of my prayers and love.

Yours,
Henri

Henri responds to a reader who has written previously about loneliness (see letter of January 20, 1994), and is now making an inquiry about mantras.

---

* A fund-raising campaign to build a new spiritual center at L'Arche Daybreak.

Dear Olga,

It is pretty hard for me to suggest a mantra for you. It has to really come from your own heart and fit your own deepest needs. As you know, the most used Christian mantra is "Lord Jesus Christ, have mercy on me." Other Christian mantras, "Come, Lord Jesus, come." Another example, "The Lord is my shepherd, there is nothing I shall want," and some people say "Make me an instrument of your peace," but your mantra is beautiful too, and "You are my beloved, on you my favor rests," may be the most appropriate for you even when you use only the first part, and then there is always the name of Jesus, his name is a beautiful mantra to carry in your heart. Thanks so much for your beautiful note and for your loving attention.

Warm regards,

Yours,

Henri

Ginny, a reader, first wrote in 1994 to express appreciation for Henri's writing. As he did with many people, he began to send her copies of his books. For Easter 1995 he sent her Life of the Beloved: Spiritual Living in a Secular World *with an inscription about Jesus' teachings on money.*

EASTER 1995

Dear Ginny,

Many thanks for your kind and very gracious letter and the beautiful poem.

Yes, I do think that Jesus, who loved the rich young man, asked him to let go of everything that prevented him from returning that love.

His wealth prevented him to be "empty" enough to welcome Jesus in the center of his heart. Both did love each other, but their love couldn't come to full fruition—

Wishing you joy and peace.

Henri Nouwen

P.S. I hope you like this little book!

Henri responds to a Dutch reader who, after thanking him for his writing, has criticized his books for being overly simplistic and repetitive.

MAY 15, 1995

Dear Piet,

Many thanks for your very wonderful letter. I really appreciate that you took the time and energy to write me about the influence that my writing has on your spirituality. It meant a lot to me that you expressed the different ways in which I had affected your life. I also am grateful for your critical comments. I think you touched a true side of me when you say that I often seem to have found "it," and that there is a kind of enthusiasm that seems a little bit too easy. Still I can tell you that when I write I am unusually fully there and put down what I experience in the moment without realizing that in other books I have expressed similar enthusiasm about other things. But maybe that is a little bit of my naiveté shining through. It is not always easy to know the difference between being a child and being childlike, but I feel that I am more and more called to become a child, as Jesus says.

Thanks again for your generous response to my writing. It gives me much courage and stimulates me to keep writing.

Warm regards,
Yours,
Henri

Henri responds to a query about finding a spiritual director.

JUNE 1, 1995

Dear Bonnie,

Many thanks for your very kind letter and for *The Roots of Christian Mysticism* by Olivier Clément.*

I am deeply grateful for this rich gift, and I also am sure that many people in our community will enjoy it when they see it in our library. As far as a spiritual director is concerned, I am really not sure what to say. I do not know any spiritual directors in New York City. The only suggestion that I have is that you give a call to my friend Wendy Greer and discuss this with her.† She is in close touch with a contemplative order of Anglican Sisters (the Order of the Holy Spirit), and I wonder if a member of that order might be of help to you.

Meanwhile, I want to write you that you should not expect too much from any spiritual director. The most important spiritual direction comes from living the liturgical life in the church through reading and the mystics and from living a simple but

---

* Olivier Clément, *Roots of Christian Mysticism: Texts from the Patristic Era and Commentary* (New York: New City Press, 1993).

† Wendy Greer was a good friend of Henri. Greer founded the Henri Nouwen Society in the United States and published an anthology of his writings on prayer entitled *The Only Necessary Thing: Living a Prayerful Life* (New York: Crossroad, 1999).

quite regular prayer life. Once these things are in place, it might be helpful to once in a while share with a wise spiritual person your relationship with God, but when you expect too much of a spiritual director you might be quickly disappointed. Well, feel free to talk to Wendy.

Warm regards,
Yours,
Henri

This is a letter to a Canadian nun who has experienced rejection in her ministry in Rwanda.

AUGUST 30, 1995

Dear Catherine,

Many thanks for your very kind letter. I appreciate your thinking of me. It is so nice to know that the poster of the "Prodigal Son" found a place in your bedroom. I understand the great pain that you must have suffered from what happened to you in Rwanda. It must really feel like a rejection, and from my own experience I know how deeply that can hurt. I pray for you that you will live through this pain faithfully and be able to unite yourself with the broken heart of Jesus. It will be a real struggle for you not to become bitter or resentful and to choose gratitude instead, but I also know when you are able to choose gratitude, your prayer life will move to a deeper place and you will experience great new inner freedom.

Thanks so much for writing. Be sure of my love and prayers.

Yours,
Henri

At the outset of his one-year sabbatical, Henri writes to a Dutch woman who has written for help with a number of questions about prayer and the spiritual life.

SEPTEMBER 6, 1995

Dear Dineke,

Many thanks for your very direct, open and personal and challenging letter. I hope you don't mind my writing in English. That allows my secretary to type it for you.

First of all my thanks for trusting me and letting me become part of your struggles. You probably realize that I have no answer for all your questions, but I receive your questions more as an invitation for a relationship between two searching Christians than as a request to be taught.

In this letter I simply want to encourage you to develop an intimate relationship with Jesus. "God" who seems far away is somewhat of a problem! God is called all powerful, almighty, etc. Jesus, however, is "God with us," vulnerable, weak, broken, dependent and very approachable. Jesus is the God who needs us and asks us for our love: "Do you love me? Do you love me? Do you love me?" When you pray, look at Jesus, who says: "Come to me, all you who labor and are overburdened, and I will give you rest—for I am gentle and humble in heart."

The most important thing you are called to do is to connect your burden with God's burden as seen in Jesus and to gradually come to experience the "new" burden as a light burden. Thus your heart and the heart of Jesus will become united. In that intimacy you can ask whatever you want and you will receive a real answer giving you more than you even could ask for.

My own prayer life is quite simple. I simply look at Jesus and say: "Lord Jesus Christ, have mercy on me." The word mercy is a tender word, it is not asking for pity, but for a consoling and encouraging embrace. When you say that simple prayer often and from your heart, many graces will come to you.

Another good way to pray is to read the Gospel passage of the day (a lectionary may help you) and simply look with your inner eye at what the story presents. Thus Jesus can become your companion on your journey.

Finally I want to say that as you connect your suffering with the suffering of Jesus, you also connect your suffering with the suffering of the whole world. Because Jesus carries the pain of all the humanity in his heart. Thus our life becomes more and more a life for others, not only for your husband and daughter but for all people. Thus you participate in the saving work of God.

Just a word about myself. After nine years at the Daybreak Community I have been given a sabbatical year that I will mostly live in Boston.* If you want to write, keep writing to Toronto (Richmond Hill) and your letter will reach me.

I think of you with much love and affection and with many prayers. Let's stay in touch.

Yours,
Henri J. M. Nouwen

Henri was a spiritual director for many people, including a number of high-profile American and Canadian politicians, businesspeople, and other celebrities. Joan Kroc, the wife of the founder of the McDonald's hamburger

---

* Henri would spend the first few months of his sabbatical with Robert Jonas and his family in Boston.

chain, began meeting regularly to discuss the spiritual life with Henri after being introduced by their mutual friend Fred Rogers. In 1995, after one of their meetings, Henri wrote her this reflection on unconditional love.

A Reflection on Unconditional Love
For Joan Kroc

Unconditional love is love without conditions, without strings attached, without prerequisites, without demands. It is giving without expecting anything in return. It is inviting without wanting to be invited. It is forgiving without waiting to be forgiven. It is offering help without hoping to be helped.

This unconditional love is the love that Jesus calls us to, "If you love those who love you, what credit can you expect? . . . If you do good to those who do good to you, what credit can you expect? . . . If you lend to those from whom you hope to get money back, what credit can you expect? . . . Instead, love your enemies and do good to them and lend without any hope of return. You will have a great reward and you will be children of the Most High, for he himself is kind to the ungrateful and the wicked" (Luke 6:32–35).

Is this a human possibility? It sounds completely unrealistic. Don't we need to be loved? Don't we have our own need for affection, attention and care? Isn't giving without receiving a set-up for burnout? Isn't this kind of love making us into a doormat that everyone can walk over and use at will?

The answer is quite simple. No, it is not impossible to love unconditionally because we are loved unconditionally! God loved us before we were born, and God will still love us after we have died. We belong to God from eternity to eternity. We are held by God in an everlasting embrace.

God molded us in the depth of the earth. God knitted us together in our mother's womb. God has written us in the palm of his hand. We are God's beloved children. Every hair on our head has been counted by God. Yes, we are unconditionally loved. Before we could do anything, prove anything or give anything, God loved us, and God will still love us even when we have done nothing, proved nothing or given anything to deserve God's love. It is fatherly and motherly love. It is a love that holds us safe wherever we go and whatever we do.

Our first and most important spiritual task is to claim that unconditional love of God for ourselves. We have to dare to say: "Whether I feel it or not, whether I comprehend it or not, I know with a spiritual knowledge that I am God's beloved child, and nobody can take that divine childhood away from me." This is not easy to say because the society in which we live keeps suggesting to us that we need to be successful, popular or powerful to deserve being loved. But God does not need our success, popularity or power in order to love us.

God has given us a heart that wants to be loved unconditionally. If we can accept God's unconditional love for us, we can live in a world in which people often put all sorts of conditions on us. If we can accept God's unconditional love for us, we can forgive those who hurt us or disappoint us and we can prevent bitterness, jealousy and resentment to enter into our hearts. Many people in our lives who love us also hurt us because their own needs and unresolved conflicts prevent them from loving us in the way we want to be loved. But when we radically claim God's unconditional love for us, we can forgive those who have wounded us and set them free by our forgiveness. If we do not claim that divine love, we will waste much of our time and energy in trying to change people and make them fit our needs. That only increases tension and conflict.

The most beautiful fruit of accepting God's unconditional love for us is that it allows us to share that unconditional love with others. Indeed, strange as it may sound, we can become like God for others. It becomes possible to love without demanding love in return. That is the marvelous possibility of the children of God. They are free to love. It is a strong, energetic, vital and very active love. It is not a sentimental, all approving and always agreeing love. It even can be a confronting love. But it is unconditional!

Unconditional love, therefore, does not include approval of everything the person we love does. The father of the prodigal son did not approve the behavior of his younger son, who swallowed his property in an alien country. Nor did he approve the behavior of the elder son, who stayed home but was stingy and angry. But he loved them both unconditionally and was always willing to welcome them home when they wanted to come home. His disapproval did not diminish his love. His approval would have diminished his own integrity as a father.

It is not always easy to believe that we are unconditionally loved even when those who love us disagree with us or disapprove of us. But this is the love with which God loves us and wants us to love each other. It is a love that includes even those who treat us as enemies, who reject us or are angry with us. Because once we know in the depth of our hearts that we are forgiven children of God, we will always be able to forgive those who cannot respond to our love.

What are the implications of all of this for our daily life? Here are a few.

1. Keep in touch with your own belovedness. Prayer, good friends and nature can help you a lot with this.
2. Never react impulsively to those who hurt you. Respond from the heart where you know that you are loved. Al-

ways take time and ask yourself, "What is the best and most honest response I can make?'

3. Do not compromise your own integrity. Simply trying to please the person who hurts you is a way of compromising yourself. Always stand straight!

4. Be consistent in your relationships. Sudden outbursts of anger or sudden gestures of intimacy make you lose solid ground and only make real healing and reconciliation more difficult.

5. Always be kind, open to listen, willing to talk and generous in forgiving, but never at the cost of losing your freedom as a child of God.

6. Be very patient. What seems impossible one year might be quite possible the next!

7. In everything keep a sense of humor and deep gratitude for the gifts of life and love.

8. Always trust, trust and trust.

Henri J. M. Nouwen

Carolyn (Carrie) and Geoff Whitney-Brown (along with their children, Janet and Monica) joined the L'Arche Daybreak community shortly after Henri; the family developed a close friendship with him.

Here he writes to welcome their third child, David Friend, to their family and to Daybreak.

NOVEMBER 28, 1995

Dear Carrie and Geoff,

Many, many joyful wishes at the birth of David Friend. May he bring peace, joy, hope, love, care and goodness to our world. May he bring you both many blessings and an always new knowledge of

God's immense love. May he be a fun brother for Janet and Monica. May he be a source of great pleasure to your parents and all the people of Daybreak. And may he always delight in the truth that Jesus, who became a baby like him, is his loving companion.

I send this special van Gogh card for this occasion. So I wish that one day David will enjoy beauty, music, art and literature and be an artist himself in whatever he will do.

Henri

Dear Janet and Monica,

Many hugs and kisses to you for having a little brother. Give him an extra kiss from me.

Love,
Henri

Henri writes a loving letter to his friend Everet, who is struggling with loneliness.

DECEMBER 26, 1995

Dear Everet,

Your letter was a real gift to me. Thank you so much for the expression of your desire and hope.

You know already that the young, attractive, affectionate, caring, intelligent, spiritual and socially conscious gay man has only one name: God!

I know your pain and your yearning. I understand deeply your loneliness. But please trust that Jesus loves you so much that he will send to you the man you are waiting for. Be patient, love deeply and allow your loneliness to purify your heart. Don't be jealous of

Phil! He has enough struggles you wouldn't want to have! We all have our unique crosses to bear.

But keep trusting that your sexuality is your gift and that you are called to love deeply and generously.

I feel very close to you and keep you close to my heart and the heart of God. All will be well!

My father (93 years old) and I are spending ten days in Germany and enjoying it immensely.

Don't forget that our deep loneliness is our gateway to the love that our world hungers for.

Trust that there is someone waiting to embrace you in the Name of Jesus and empower you to fulfill your unique mission.

Let the Eucharist give you hope and strength to wait patiently in expectation.

Love, much love,
Henri

From Peapack, New Jersey, where he is in the sixth month of his sabbatical year, Henri writes to his friend Chris and Chris's partner, Mark.

He writes of the death of his friend Adam, who died on February 16, 1996. Adam's death and the impact of his life were the subjects of one of his last books, Adam: God's Beloved *(Maryknoll, NY: Orbis, 1997), completed only a few weeks before his own death.*

FEBRUARY 26, 1996

Dear Chris and Mark,

Your letter was a great joy to me! Thanks for telling me about your busy lives. Please slow down a little so that you can be more creative! I discover myself during Sabbatical that I am doing more by doing less. You both are writers and need time to think, play with ideas, sentences and words and have a long time to "dance." I am reading Thomas Mann's *American Journal*. His commitment to his writing is astonishing. Even in the midst of the most emotional events he keeps faithful to his writing.

The many projects you both are involved with are all good and useful, but in the long run they leave you dissatisfied and a little empty. It is as if the past dies away behind you and there is little to hold on to. A life of contemplation, creative writing and great attentiveness to each other's needs gives you three ways of catching the eternal already now. What comes from the center of your heart stays because it belongs to God.

Well, these are some wise thoughts of a usually over-busy old guy! Oscar Wilde's book is great! For Thomas Moore's book I wrote a "blurb" for the first edition in hardback. Now they don't need my recommendation anymore! A great book.

Did you read Alan Helms's book *A Young Man from the Provinces?*[*] Very revealing and raising important questions about living a spiritual life as a gay man. I am amazed he stayed alive amidst all his risk-taking. I am glad he did and can speak a word of hope and encouragement.

My friend Adam died. He was 34 years old. We celebrated his life and death in our community with many tears and many smiles. I am thinking about writing a small book about him.

I'd love to visit you both. Maybe in May. Is that a good month for you? Let me know. March and April are quite full for me.

Be sure of my prayers, love and desire to see you soon both healthy, wealthy and wise.

Love,
Henri

---

[*] Alan Helms, *A Young Man from the Provinces: A Gay Life Before Stonewall* (Boston: Faber and Faber, 1995).

This is a prayer Henri wrote for a friend, a military chaplain who was being promoted. He emphasizes that just as we are called to be in the world without being of it, some of us are called to minister in the military without being of it.*

APRIL 30, 1996

Dear Lord,

As I come to the half-way point of my life, I want to enter into your presence and recommit myself to you. During the last four decades you have guided me and gradually brought me to a mature faith, to a new confidence in my gifts and to a new spiritual adulthood. Along the way I have struggled with many things, trying to find my place in life, trying to find my place among my family, trying to find my place among my colleagues, trying to find my place as your minister. It has been a long journey with many joys and many pains, with many doubts and many hopes with many moments of loneliness and with moments of beautiful friendship. Now, as I receive the affirmation of my colleagues in being promoted to the rank of Major in the U.S. Air Force, I come again to ask you to lead me always closer to your heart, and to the hearts of those who are entrusted to me. Precisely because I find myself in a secure place with good health and good friends, I am free to choose you again as my shepherd and my guide. Help me to be humble in the midst of a world that is so full of ambition, help me to be vulnerable in a world so concerned with power, help me to be simple in a surrounding that is so complicated, help me to be forgiving in a society where revenge and retaliation create so much pain, help me to be poor of spirit in a milieu that desires so many

---

* Henri wrote about this prayer in his book *Sabbatical Journey: The Diary of his Final Year* (New York: Crossroad, 1998), 158.

riches and aspires to so much success. As I enter the second half of my life, I come to you with an open heart, asking you that I may trust in the gifts that you have given me and may have the courage to take risks of service.

I do not know where you will lead me, I do not know where I will be two, five or ten years from now. I do not know the road ahead of me, but I know now that you are with me to guide me and that wherever you lead me, even there where I would rather not go, you will bring me closer to my true home. Thank you, Lord, for my life, for my vocation and for the hope that you have planted in my heart.

Amen

Henri Nouwen died on September 21, 1996. His death was sudden and unexpected. He continued to write up until his final days. This letter, addressed to a reader who has expressed appreciation for The Return of the Prodigal Son, *is one of his last. He shares his continuing struggle to claim his role as father and elder.*

AUGUST 4, 1996

Dear Mr. Chisholm,

Many, many thanks for your very warm letter in response to my book *The Return of the Prodigal Son.* I am truly grateful that you took the time and energy to let me know what the book meant to you.

As you will have noticed, this book could never have been written if I had not been part of a community of mentally handicapped people. Although life in that community is not always easy, it continues to be for me a great source of energy and vision.

I deeply appreciate your sharing with me the story about the young David and your very strong and beautiful response to his pulling away from you.* Meanwhile I am still struggling to become the father as Jesus portrays him in the parable. I frankly think that we will never be the perfect fathers we would like to be, but simply knowing that we are called to not only a new childhood but a new fatherhood can give us a way to live our life gratefully.

What you write about your son and girlfriend not giving you their address or telephone number makes me feel quite close to you in your pain, but I want to encourage you to not focus on their "rejection" but on your own belovedness so that when they will return home they will find you with a forgiving, peaceful and rejoicing heart.

Many thanks again for your lovely letter and be assured of my prayers for you.

Warm greetings,
Henri Nouwen

---

* Mr. Chisholm and David were partners in an architectural firm. David, though not a biological son, had become like a son, and the two men had come into conflict over some of David's choices.

EPILOGUE

BY SUE MOSTELLER

his volume of Henri's letters, revealing his true and deep care for friends, graced me with memories of the last ten years of his life at L'Arche Daybreak and of our friendship during that time. They also reminded me of a time he was present to me in crisis.

A disagreement with leadership that precipitated the departure of two of my beloved assistant-friends at Daybreak had literally broken my spirit. I carried this grief in silent rage, preparing to boldly accuse and challenge our leader at the next meeting of our community council. But of course in the meanwhile, my inner seething "leaked out" into my relationships and functions. Henri became aware mainly because we lived in the same house, prayed together in the mornings, and usually had breakfast together.

I didn't want to talk about it. And I didn't seek help to process my dilemma. I shunned relationships but found it hard to hide the fact that I was miserable and angry. One morning Henri ventured to say, "If you're not already getting help with whatever is bothering you, I'd be glad to listen if you like." But I refused his offer. Henri, however, persisted, and a day or two later he cautiously reminded me of his offer to listen. Again I refused, but plunged deeper into pain when the meeting of the council was postponed for a week. Being "shut down," furious, and incapable of normal relationships wasn't my usual stance. Thus, my frame of mind became more and more stressful so that midweek I broke down and accepted Henri's offer. I warned him not to say anything to me until I finished what I wanted to say, so he sat for over an hour listening to my self-righteous tirade about a perceived injustice I was unable to tolerate, and about how the perpetrator should and would be held responsible. Henri was silent, his only gesture the offer of his handkerchief to stay the flood of my tears. Then we sat in silence as he pondered, as though praying. I remember my rage and my inner thoughts, "Hah! Just try to give me advice if you think you can!"

After a few minutes he spoke hesitantly and quietly. "We've known each other for quite a few years now, and I've witnessed you in your life and your ministry. I love working with you and listening to your talks, because you tell stories and you speak from experience. The only thing I can say to you today, in front of your obvious and real pain is this. Your talks are almost always about your experience of faithful love in family and community, revealing love's precious wonders and desperate challenges. I've heard you say that we need to be careful not to attempt to play God in any situation. You've been living and working with our leader for many years now, and I think you know that your response to him in this crisis is critical for you and for all the people in our community. So, perhaps today you have reached the point where the rubber hits the road. Today, it seems to me, you have to honestly ask yourself if you really believe what you announce to others about faithful love and forgiving of enemies. Your judgments about our leader may very well be right. But it's also possible that you don't know the whole truth. It might be good for you to consider that before openly displaying your unhappiness in the community council. That's all I can say to you."

As he spoke, I was struck by his obvious respect for me, and his courage to speak the truth to me with so much kindness and care.

His words were brutally honest, piercing my heart and draining the wound of my indignation. I *did* believe what I had tried to announce, and I clearly knew that love *had* to govern my response. I looked at Henri and humbly asked, "What should I do?"

He answered, "Maybe you need to sit down with our leader and ask his help to understand what happened. After all, he deserves to be understood by you before he is judged. Try not to go to him in anger, but try to tell him you need his help to understand his rationale. Listen deeply. Then, let your loving heart tell you how to respond."

I left Henri and walked directly to the office of my most criticized "brother." To this day, I'm humbled by how wrong I had been. I'm also grateful for Henri's persistent, tough and tender love.

Most of Henri's friends knew that relationships energized his spirit, and nowhere is this more evident than in his vast and faithful correspondence. But beneath this stimulant, another chosen layer of motivation is found, about which Henri was scrupulous: his passion to liberate and be liberated from any burden of pain-causing guilt or shame.

Only six weeks after writing the final letter selected here he quite suddenly went home to eternity, and his dying reveals a final, deeper, level of his passionate affection for others. He had deliberately chosen to ensure that his dying would be good, not harmful, for friends and readers.

Earlier when he was near death from being hit by a car in 1989, he said:

> I knew that my dying could be good or bad for others, depending on the choice I made in the face of it. I said again to Sue,
>
> "In case I die, tell everyone that I feel an immense love for all the people I have come to know, also toward those with whom I live in conflict. Tell them not to feel anxious or guilty but to let me go into the house of my Father and to

trust that there my communion with them will grow deeper and stronger. Tell them to celebrate with me and be grateful for all that God has given me."*

Seven years later, suffering from a heart attack in a hospital in Hilversum, The Netherlands, Henri bid his friend, Nathan, "Goodnight," and added:

"I think I'm going to be OK, but you never know. So if I die, just tell everybody that I'm grateful, that I'm enormously grateful. Make sure you tell everybody that!"†

Those proved to be his last known words because early the next morning, this profoundly passionate, struggling man entered through the portal of death into the infinite hospitality of his God. Home at last! It was September 21, 1996.

My first read of this collection of letters was rapid and motivated by curiosity. To whom did he write? And what did he reveal? But I knew this book deserved another read from the perspective of my personal, inner, journey of life. I knew his caring support was present for me in my life-questions: "What did he do with every person's real, human questions about undeserved suffering, unwanted loss of control, physical and emotional vulnerability, inevitable broken-heartedness, and fear of death?" His wisdom connects with my life questions today.

I love this collection. It is for me, a spiritual autobiography. Henri's letters reveal the ever-evolving, ever-deepening, ever-struggling heart of my strong yet vulnerable friend.

So, from his generous and vulnerable heart, I offer Henri the

---

* *Beyond the Mirror: Reflections on Death and Life* (New York: Crossroad, 1990), 41, 42, 43.

† Nathan Ball in *Journey to the Heart: The Life of Henri Nouwen,* a documentary by Windborne Productions, 2004.

final summary of his inner passion to liberate and bless in free and forgiving love.

When, four years ago, I went to St. Petersburg to see Rembrandt's Return of the Prodigal Son, I had little idea how much I would have to live what I then saw. I stand with awe at the place where Rembrandt brought me. He led me from the kneeling disheveled young son to the standing, bent-over father, from the place of being blessed to the place of blessing. As I look at my own aging hands, I know that they have been given to me to stretch out towards all who suffer, to rest upon the shoulders of all who come, and to offer the blessing that emerges from the immensity of God's love.*

* *The Return of the Prodigal Son: A Meditation on Fathers, Brothers, and Sons* (New York: Doubleday, 1996), 139.

ACKNOWLEDGMENTS

I t is only fitting that my first words of gratitude go to Henri Nouwen himself. Although I never met him, his example of a life lived with an open and fearless heart has changed the way I live. He has helped me to believe in the possibility of inner freedom that comes from intimacy with a compassionate and loving God. It is not a freedom that allows us to escape the difficulties of life but one that frees us for generative, creative living. It is a privilege to be part of efforts to extend his legacy to others.

My gratitude also goes out to the multitudes who donated their letters to the Henri Nouwen Archives, especially to those who actively supported this book project. There were some for whom sharing your letters was hard—I want to extend my special thanks to you—your generosity of spirit and depth of courage is deeply appreciated. Like Henri, I believe that your gift of vulnerability will bear much fruit.

This project would not have been possible without Brynn Lawrence, coordinator of the Henri Nouwen Letter Project from 2009 to 2015. Brynn worked tirelessly to contact as many letter-holders as possible and then asked the hard question: "Are you ready to share them?" Her recent efforts as permissions assistant for this volume have ensured that we reached out to everyone whose letters were selected for inclusion. She helped address privacy concerns and ensured anonymity for those we weren't able to reach.

My thanks goes to Judith Leckie and my mother, Marlene Gordon, for transcribing the letters. Both Marlene and Judith transcribed, with care and precision, more than one hundred letters each, while meeting a very tight deadline.

Judith must also be thanked for the other myriad of tasks, large and small, that she undertook with characteristic straightforward efficiency. These included checking citations, providing feedback on early drafts, helping with the pre-selection of letters, listening carefully to questions, suggesting good responses and accompanying me on good, long walks.

I also would like to thank Karen Pascal, Sally Keefe Cohen, Hume Martin, Kevin Burns, Michael Higgins, Sarah Nouwen, Danielle Robichaud, Noel McFerran, Michael Bramah, Ruth Bastedo, Catherine Smith, Moira Callahan, Y.P., Catherine Manning, Heidi Earnshaw, Christine Earnshaw, Bridget Ring, Lindsey Yeskoo and Brad Ratzlaff, for their support and encouragement at various stages of this project.

Special thanks to Mirabai Starr who provided an English translation of an excerpt by Teresa of Ávila and Patricia A. Burton who verified a Merton quote in the nick of time.

Gary Jansen, my editor at Convergent, has provided insightful editorial assistance and excellent management of this project; it has been a pleasure working with him, along with copy editor Lynn Anderson, cover designer Jessie Bright, production editor Cathy Hennessy, interior designer Andrea Lau and all the Convergent staff.

Special gratitude goes to Robert Ellsberg. Robert provided steadfast guidance and mentorship through precise editing of early drafts. Intervention at critical junctures helped me hone the craft of letting the letters speak for themselves. It was an honor to work with such a talented editor, deep thinker, and elegant writer. It is truly a gift to call him friend.

A big thank-you to my husband, Don Willms, who served as my first reader. It is essential to have a first reader whom you can trust, but who at the same time pushes you to your full potential. Don was this for me, and more—cheerleader, copy editor and big-picture thinker. His sharp eye for the redundant adjective proved invaluable.

My final acknowledgment must go to Sue Mosteller. I thank Sue for the trust she placed in me by coaxing me out from behind my archivist's desk and into the editor's seat. She supported me with a critical eye, sound advice, spiritual wisdom and faithful friendship.

Sue was Henri's trusted friend, intellectual equal and confidant. Her insightful epilogue for this book provides the perfect bridge from Henri's life to his fruitful legacy.

As Henri's literary executrix, Sue initiated the collection of Henri's letters from his legion of friends, family, colleagues and readers. This volume would not exist if it weren't for her vision and determination to ensure the preservation of these priceless documents. It is to her that this book is dedicated.

ALSO AVAILABLE FROM HENRI NOUWEN

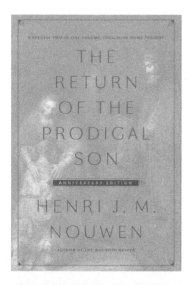

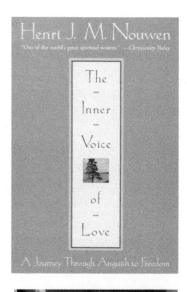

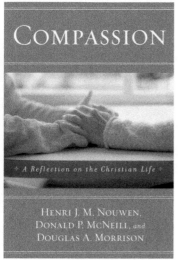

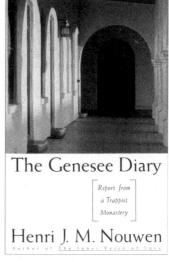

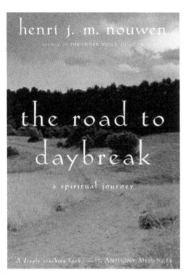

henri j. m. nouwen

AUTHOR OF THE INNER VOICE OF LOVE

the road to daybreak

a spiritual journey

"A deeply touching book." —ST. ANTHONY MESSENGER

A CRY FOR MERCY

PRAYERS FROM THE GENESEE

HENRI J. M. NOUWEN

AUTHOR OF THE INNER VOICE OF LOVE

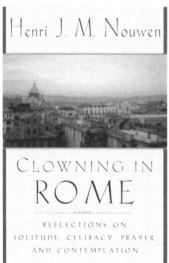

Henri J. M. Nouwen

CLOWNING IN ROME

REFLECTIONS ON
SOLITUDE, CELIBACY, PRAYER,
AND CONTEMPLATION

The
WOUNDED HEALER

Ministry in Contemporary Society

In our own woundedness, we can become a source of life for others

HENRI J. M. NOUWEN